Secrets to Editing Success

The Creative Story Editing Method

by K. Stanley and L. Cooke

Published by Fictionary Press
Library of Congress Cataloging-in-Publication
Data is in file with the publisher.
Trade Paperback ISBN: 978-1-9992762-6-3
e-Book ISBN: 978-1-9992762-3-2
Cover Design by K. Stanley and L. Cooke
Formatted in Affinity Publisher by K. Stanley and L. Cooke

Praise for Secrets to Editing Success

"One of the most frequent questions a novelist asks is "Does my draft contain a story?" Stanley and Cooke have written a practical guide that shows you how to answer that question. Secrets to Editing Success gives you actionable advice and a process to edit and revise your novel so that you can take your novel draft and turn it into a publishable book."

Grant Faulkner, Executive Director of National Novel Writing Month

"Secrets to Editing Success is every editor's dream. Whether you're a new author reviewing your first book or professional editor, this is without doubt, the most comprehensive and detailed guide to editing I've ever had the pleasure of reading. This book will hold your hand, explain, clarify and give you step by step instructions for editing your novel. Paired best when using the incomparable developmental editing software Fictionary, this guide will change your editing life. Read it. Immediately."

Sacha Black, Rebel Author Podcast

Kristina Stanley Dedication

To Mathew, who is my life.

Lucy Cooke Dedication

Andrew, Edward, William, you fill my life with joy.

We Wrote This Book for You

We spent a year writing this book, and years researching it,

and we hope you love it as much as we do. Our hearts and minds

went into creating this book, so you can be one of

the world's best creative story editors.

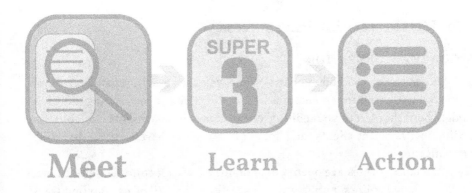

Meet Learn Action

Chapter One:
Meet the Secrets

"Editors can be great only when they understand what makes a powerful story AND have the knowledge and tools to give advice that is comprehensive, objective, and actionable."—Kristina Stanley, CEO of Fictionary

Editors have superpowers. They give actionable advice that turns rough drafts into structurally sound stories readers love.

To gain these superpowers, editors don't need to be bitten by a radioactive spider or be part of some military experiment.

Instead, they need only to embrace a super editing process.

Editors need knowledge. And those with story-editing knowledge control stories.

We believe story-editing knowledge shouldn't be a secret.

And so, we wrote this book…

The First Secret of Editing Success

YOU ARE A STORY EDITOR

The moment you edit your first scene, you are an editor. Just as the first time you write your first scene, you are a writer. Some of you reading this book might be at the start of your editing journey, some of you might be established editors with repeat clients, and some of you might have structural-editing qualifications.

The editing gates are open. Come on in. We are all editors—self-editors, self-employed editors, publishing-house editors, and all of us who find ways to improve a draft. That's editing. And we are all creative story editors.

A creative story editor focuses on the structure, characters, plot, and settings of a story. The creative story editor's goal is to give comprehensive, objective, and actionable advice that makes the story better.

"I am an editor." Try saying it when you are at the dentist, or when you are at the hockey game or the hairdressers. People respond well when you tell them you are an editor.

Why?

Because people are in awe of stories. Quite right, too, as even the tamest of stories is full of wild monsters, magic, and wonder, and a wonderful editor is a magic wild-monster tamer.

We're going to help you join some of the world's best story editors: Fictionary Story Editors.

And all editors of merit, no matter our experience, have similar burning questions when we hold a new draft.

QUESTIONS FOR A DRAFT:

Q1: Is there a great story in this manuscript?

Q2: When is the draft finished?

Q3: Are we holding the next award-winning, best-selling

book?

ANSWER: NOT YET.

These two words—not yet—answer all three questions. These two words match the potential that is in the manuscript. They match our potential as editors. Editing, when done well, is one of the most powerful jobs in the world. We are saving a story's life.

And there are secrets to performing an edit well. Secrets that—once you know them—will make you wonder why every editor hasn't read this book and why every editor does not use this "believe in yourself" superpower.

The Second Secret of Editing Success

STORY EDITORS NEED A STORY-EDITING PROCESS

Story editing means evaluating a draft and making an editing plan. It is not revising the manuscript, and it is not copyediting. Revising without story editing won't work. Copyediting before story editing won't create a great story.

> **Creative story editing: structural editing that mixes artistry with craft knowledge to create a powerful story.**

In this book, you will find out how to structurally edit a manuscript. You will stand back and admire the story structure, then look closer and examine the scene level with a magnifying glass. Once you have edited the scenes, you will go back and review the story level, resulting in actionable edits for the draft. Don't worry. We'll explain how to create actionable edits. It is all part of the creative story editing process.

This process is so versatile, you can use it repeatedly. This process will make the next book easier to edit because you will know what makes a good story.

Self-editors and professional editors alike need editing plans. These plans are the blueprints, the building plans to turn the rough draft into a book of built-in beauty.

In this book, you will learn a structured process that helps you give advice that is comprehensive, objective, and actionable.

The Third Secret of Editing Success

STORY EDITORS CREATE ACTIONABLE STORY EDITS

After you finish an edit, you should have a list of actions that the writer needs to perform for thorough revisions. We will look at these in detail later, but the good news is there are only five types of actions a creative story editor will recommend. And the edit will inform the writer which of the five actions are necessary at each place. We cannot wait to introduce these to you, but first, let's explain why this book on structural editing is unique.

Unique to This Book

In this book, we'll use examples from professional editors.

"What's so unique about that?" you ask.

A few years ago, thirteen editors edited the same novel using Fictionary software to prove that Fictionary software works. Some of the editors were already story editors and some were copy editors making the transition to story editing. One story editor was early in the learning to edit process.

We have included advice from both the experienced and inexperienced editors to give you a view of what actionable and unactionable advice looks like.

Throughout this book, we'll show examples of these real-life edits. You'll see what the thirteen different editors said about the draft novel Evolution, which Kristina wrote one fall in National Novel Writing Month (NaNoWriMo). Evolution was written with intentional story errors with characters, plot, and settings to give a flawed story for the thirteen editors to edit.

We're going to give you actionable advice you can apply to a story. The theory is important, but only if you know how to use it. We'll use theory as a backdrop to our main event—a process that you can use again and again.

It is rare to see how a group of editors edited the same novel. This is what makes this book unique.

What This Book Is

Story editing is a process. This book gives you a process to follow and the insights behind why you should follow some—or all—of the process.

This book is your tool to hone your story editing skills.

What This Book Is Not

Writing is a craft, a great, exhilarating craft. This book is not a how-to-write book. It is a book about creative story editing using a process that generates comprehensive, objective, and actionable advice.

The art of beautiful prose comes after story editing. Beautiful prose contains the artist's voice plus the style that fits the genre of the story. This book is not a book about copyediting. It's a book about creative story editing.

Making sure all the words gleam with the letters in the right place on the page, and that all the punctuation points are placed perfectly, is a proofreader's passion. This is not a book about proofreading. It's a book about creative story editing.

Editing a story is about having a structured process that allows you to see a story. There is no point in perfecting prose, copyediting, or proofreading until the deep story structure is set.

A clear process will make you efficient.

Editing, especially for the novice editor, is time consuming as it is, so no one wants to waste time revising prose that might not make it into the final story.

> TEA with Kristina
>
> **Throughout this book, I, Kristina Stanley, will be giving my Top Editing Advice. I will spill the TEA, and I have lots of Top Editing Advice to spill with all my editing experience.**

Story Editors Are Artists

The most important aspect to remember is that you are the artist. Story editors edit the structure of a story. They make artistic choices throughout the process. We will demonstrate the process, but you're in control and get to decide the direction of the edit.

Let's Edit Your Future into a Success

Reading this book, learning from this book, and using the advice from this book ensures your future as an editor will be a success story.

Let's get started.

How to Use This Book

You have a manuscript ready to edit! You are a story editor, and you are going to make an editing plan with actionable advice. The writer will use this advice to revise the story.

Fantastic.

Or maybe you have a draft, and you're not sure if it's ready for a story edit.

Also, fantastic.

Together, we're going to help you figure out if there is a story in the manuscript. We'll figure out if the story is ready to edit.

And then we're going to make it the best story it can be.

> **You can use this book on its own. Or you can use the Fictionary software if you want to make the story editing process faster and the learning easier.**
>
> **Fictionary gives you a structured method to keep track of the vast amount of information involved in a story edit. It saves time with visual insights that show you where a story is or isn't working. And we're going to show you how to apply this brilliance to your story.**

Follow a Structured Editing Process

Why have you opened this book? You want to edit a draft and create a story every reader loves. Everything else—the fame, the fortune—all come from the book's connection with the reader. And that connection can be found in this book.

To become a creative story editor, you need to know what a great story is. Then you will need to learn how to edit on a scene-by-scene basis. In editing, there is a process to follow, and in reading this book, there is a process, too.

The creative story edit is based on editing a story structure and then editing each scene using the 38 Fictionary Story Elements. We cover each of the 38 Fictionary Story Elements later in this book.

Once you understand the process, you will understand the 38 Fictionary Story Elements intuitively, and then you will also know how to use them.

Difference between Editing and Revising

EDITING

The editor reads the story and does the following:

> **Editors edit the story, making notes that are comprehensive, objective, and actionable.**

Did you notice we didn't say make changes to the text?

These notes range from larger recommendations such as splitting scenes or even cutting whole sections to smaller recommendations such as pointing out that the scene must be anchored. A full structural edit, a creative story edit, addresses the protagonist, the story goal, and the stakes in every scene. Editing looks at the story to see if the key scenes are present and in the best place for the story.

REVISING

The writer takes the editing suggestions, and uses them to improve the draft.

> **Only the writer should revise. An editor who is not self-editing would not revise a draft.**

Editing and revising are two distinct tasks and should be kept apart. Edit the whole manuscript first, then revise the whole manuscript second. If one scene is edited and revisions are performed on that scene, these revisions might not make sense after the full manuscript edit is complete. This can also waste time if a scene ends up being cut.

The major reason to separate revision from editing is efficiency. If there is an investment of time on a revision, then when the recommendation to cut comes, there might be more resistance to that edit.

> **Edit first. Revise second. Keep them separate.**

Start by Becoming a Creative Story Editor

USE THIS BOOK TO LEARN AN EDITOR'S PROCESS.

One key to great story editing is to give actionable advice with every suggestion. Editors don't judge. They seek out weaknesses and find ways to support the story. A creative story editor wants to strengthen the stories and the writer's skills.

The process is:

1. Passing the story test

2. Scene-by-scene editing

3. Actionable advice

1. Passing the Story Test

A story synopsis is a tool you can use to determine if there is a story in the draft manuscript. We're going to use it to test for a story. Once you've read this book, you'll be able to look at a manuscript and determine whether a full story exists. This is the most important check you will make.

This book shows you in clear steps how this is possible: Chapter 3: Meet the Story Promise, Chapter 4: Meet the Fictionary Story Test, Chapter 5: Meet the Story Arc and Chapter 6: Meet the Working Synopsis, show you how to perform a story test.

PART A OF THE STORY TEST: CREATE A SKELETON BLURB.

The blurb is critical to editing success. Please don't be tempted to skip this step. The blurb keeps the edit focused and on track. You'll use it with every step on the path to an edited story.

We're going to show you a quick, easy way to write a skeleton blurb.

PART B OF THE STORY TEST: IDENTIFY THE STORY ARC SCENES.

We'll show you how to do this, too. It's not as hard as it seems.

The five story arc scenes are proof that the story exists and is strong.

Let us state that again, as it's the basis for this entire book.

The most important step in story editing is to make sure a story exists.

If not, rewriting to create a story must happen before the next step in the editing journey.

PART C OF THE STORY TEST: IDENTIFY THE ENDING.

A synopsis is not complete without the ending told.

When you add them together you have your skeleton synopsis:

Skeleton Synopsis = Skeleton Blurb + 5 Story Arc Scenes + Resolution

Story test passed. Now what?

2. Scene-by-Scene Editing

Once you're confident the draft contains a story, it's time to roll up your editing sleeves and start editing every scene. Chapters 7 through 12, all the "Learn" chapters, explain how that is done.

38 Fictionary Story Elements: the fun begins. How to edit with the 38 Fictionary Story Elements is all explained here. You will either edit the whole book one el-

ement at a time, making thirty-eight passes, or you will edit scene by scene with all thirty-eight story elements. Or you'll end up somewhere in between. No matter which way you edit, the results will be the same.

After the story test is done, we'll show you how to edit the scenes and structure of the story to create actionable advice.

3. Actionable Advice

Actionable advice entails specific recommendations to revise the draft after the edit is over.

An insight is a visual drawing of the structure of a novel. This can be the story arc, word count per scene, or scenes per chapter. We're going to show you how to examine visual insights to determine whether the story structure is strong. Chapter 13, Action the Visual Insights, shows you how to use insights to edit a story.

The actionable advice will be directed at the story level and then at the scene level, and then back to the scene level again.

The list of actionable advice for the draft is your editing plan, and that editing plan is the how to for revisions.

Revision will take less time for the author, as the editing advice will be actionable and specific.

Conclusion

When you apply the process covered in this book, you will have a fully edited draft, where every part of the structure will have passed through the creative story editor's rigorous evaluation process.

You'll have edited every scene and will have a wealth of revision advice for the writer, who may be yourself, and the draft will be ready to be revised.

This is what we mean by a creative story edit.

Only Three Steps to a Full Story Edit?

Yes, and when you take the steps with us, you will see the thoroughness of each step, and you will thoroughly enjoy each step, because this method is helping you create the strongest possible story.

A story that readers will love! A story that could be a bestseller!

Creativity is a huge factor in story editing, and great art comes from knowing how to harness your creativity. Turn the page, and we'll look at the art of creative story editing.

> **"Editing advice that is specific, and therefore actionable, means a writer will know how to revise any scene." — Kristina Stanley, CEO of Fictionary**

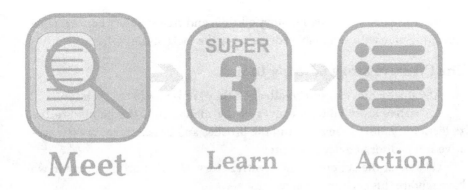

Meet   Learn   Action

Chapter Two:
Meet the Process

**"If a scene does not impact the protago-
nist or their main story goal, it might not
be needed in the story." —Kristina Stanley, CEO of Fictionary**

Creative Story Editing: The Path To Great Books

We believe every story editor should learn the tools that they can use to edit creatively.

Creative editing is form not formula.

Creative story editing is an equal mix of artistry and craft knowledge. Take a painter: the tools of their trade are the canvas, the brushes, and the paint. A painter's decision for each will affect the end masterpiece.

When a painter squeezes their paints onto their palette, they don't stick to the primary colors in each tub. They combine the colors, a little from one color and a little from another. Their knowledge and understanding of which colors combine to make the color they are looking for comes from experience, as does the placement of the colors with their subtleties on the canvas and the effect of different brushes and brushstrokes.

It is the same with creative story editing, and creative story editors make an editing plan with actionable advice using the tools of the craft.

The Creative Story Editor's Tools

Any story editor can edit creatively if they know how to use their tools.

A creative story editor's canvas is the manuscript, the paints are the 38 Fictionary Story Elements, and the brushes and brushstrokes are the creative story editor's advice to a writer.

Let's meet the actions in the creative story editor's portfolio. Should we have fanfare this early in the book?

Always!

Cue the trumpets.

THE ACTIONABLE MARCS:

Move or Add or Revise or Cut or Split a scene

Actionable editing advice is full of action! This means we should be looking to move, add, revise, cut, or split. It is as easy as that.

Each time something in the edit is not smooth, ask, "Does this need Moving, Adding, Revising, Cutting, or Splitting when considering the whole manuscript or to make a scene more powerful?"

MARCS turn your edit into actionable advice.

What Is a Great Story?

It's a story readers love. And don't we all want that for every story we edit? And we can all create a story readers love—if we edit creatively.

Does a love of stories resonate with you? Read on.

What Is the Point of a Great Story?

Storytelling is old. Storytelling makes us human. The human instinct to tell stories has existed since humans learned to communicate with each other. We all love a good story. Stories for children, stories for adults—all stories can make your heart quicken and your tears fall, make you laugh and draw a smile. A great story reminds you of your humanity.

Here's a bold statement: the form of story humans love to experience has not changed since The Epic of Gilgamesh was told somewhere between the eighteenth and twelfth century BC. It's so long ago, the exact date isn't known.

Our point is humans have been fighting monsters, falling in love, growing up, and figuring out mysteries since the beginning of time.

Stories honor human experiences.

The irony is that stories are about change and yet the story-structure building blocks have not changed since Gilgamesh, and this is not lost on us.

Story structure is the story's DNA. And DNA building blocks don't change; rather, the way those DNA building blocks combine is what makes life unique. Story structure is the same: the combinations in a story's deep structure are what story editors are looking at, working with, and figuring out.

This Book's Promise

By the time you finish this book, we'll have proven this story-structure form, and you'll know how to edit any story you have written or are asked to edit. How amazing is that promise?

This book takes the mystery out of story editing and shares the secrets of experienced story editors.

This book helps you perform a story edit on any story, be it a novel, novella, or narrative non-fiction story.

This book helps all story editors know how to quickly apply form to help a story work for a wide audience.

Readers read for great stories, and only stories with solid structures are great.

Some artists suspect that form leads to formulaic stories. We don't believe that. Writers all create their own stories in a unique way. Just look at all the different ways Romeo and Juliet has been told. Or compare the monster from a lake in Beowulf with the shark that terrorizes a town in Jaws over a thousand years later.

Story editors help make each unique story strong

We will be using creative story editing techniques together with a process and tools that make story editing comprehensive, objective, and actionable. By the time you finish this book, both the modern self-editor and professional editor will know the secrets to editing stories.

Beautiful prose is part of a story. Yet, without a sound structure, the most beautiful prose in the world won't matter. Because people won't read the story.

> **People connect first with the story's structure; then they fall in love with the prose.**

An Organized Process Works in Creative Story Editing

A creative story editor is organized and has a process. But that does not mean that every edit results in the same cookie-cutter story.

Far from it. Having an organized process in the editing world means having a method to discover every last territory of the story world.

We'll show you the fastest, most comprehensive route to a robust creative story edit.

Where to Next?

Perhaps you need more convincing on the whys and the hows; perhaps you are convinced already; perhaps you want to learn more about us. Let's look at why learning this process is so important.

Meet the authors

We are Kristina Stanley, the creator and CEO of Fictionary, who needed an app to help edit her award-winning books, and Lucy Cooke, who is a Fictionary Certified StoryCoach Editor, and a Business Development manager at Fictionary.

To build Fictionary, Kristina used all the secrets to editing that she had discovered over her years of writing and editing. And this book is packed full of these secrets.

And it is not just the two of us guiding you. There are also those thirteen editors whose edits we will be researching further in the book.

Thirteen Creative Story Editors Reveal How They Edit

That means there will be fifteen creative story editors teaching you. Kristina and Lucy will talk you through the process and review the edits completed by the thirteen editors.

> **TEA with Kristina**
>
> In 2020, I had the amazing experience of working with thirteen professional editors from around the world. They all performed a story edit on the same novel, and they did this individually but at the same time. The novel was Evolution, which I wrote one fall in NaNoWriMo for the purpose of training editors interested in story structure.

Throughout this book, we use examples taken from the creative story editors who worked on that draft. You will see how, with the training laid out in this book, an editor can be comprehensive, objective, and actionable in their advice. We are committed to writing the best book on creative story editing.

It's your turn to commit to becoming the best creative story editor and to following the process that we will lay out.

But why learn to creative story edit the Fictionary way?

The modern world and modern technological advances have leveled the publishing industry. Anyone can publish anything. When a book is published, the competition is fierce. Only the great stories are going to push through.

Self-publishing has been fabulous for both writers and editors, but it has also increased the competition for a reader's attention.

Authors need to publish more frequently and therefore write—and edit—faster, all while producing a great story every time. By learning the creative story-editing process, you can move one step ahead of the competition. Not only will your editing process be faster, more comprehensive, and actionable, but you will also have published stories that readers will flock to.

Remember, we wrote this book because the knowledge of how to story edit should not be a secret.

Let's Get Started with the Basics

You already know creative story editors make an editing plan with actionable advice. The editor does not revise the story, the writer does. You also know actionable advice means advice that enables MARCS. An editor gives actionable advice, so the writer can Move or Add or Revise or Cut or Split a scene.

Before an edit can begin, there must be a blurb. We're going to show you how to create a skeleton blurb. You'll use that blurb as a reference during the story edit. We guarantee the blurb will help you perform a better edit.

> **"Editing a story is a journey that is made more enjoyable when you are using a map and you have signposts along the way." —Kristina Stanley, CEO of Fictionary**

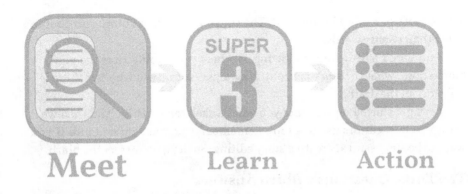

Chapter Three:
Meet the Story Promise

"There's no story to tell if it is not affecting the POV character." —Brigitte Lavoie, Fictionary Certified StoryCoach Editor

Promises, Promises, Promises!

At the start of a story, in fact, even before the start of the story, the writer makes a promise to the reader. This promise has a name in the publishing world: a blurb.

The blurb is the first promise to the reader. When reading the blurb, the reader knows what the story is about. It is the author's intent. The author's promise.

A blurb is an important tool, and all creative story editors must have a blurb before they start editing.

The Creative Story Edit Starts Here

You are going to love creating blurbs just as much as we do.

We know that's not the normal emotion when people talk about blurb creation. When you understand what a blurb is and follow the three steps, then creating a blurb is easy.

But even when it's easy, don't underestimate the power of the blurb. The full blurb will show you in under two hundred and fifty words whether there is a possibility of a story in the draft. The super-fast skeleton blurb can do it in fewer than twenty words.

And here's a little foreshadowing of where we're going after the blurb. A blurb shows what the story is about. A synopsis shows you whether there is a full story in the draft.

Let's get started on teaching you what a skeleton blurb is. And then we'll show you how editors use this tool. Remember, you must have a blurb if you want to be successful at creative story editing. So next, we dissect the blurb.

The Three Questions a Blurb Answers

A blurb answers three simple questions. And after you know these three questions, then we will show you an even easier way for getting a twenty-word skeleton blurb.

So how do you build a blurb? It is beyond easy, but first, we'll cover the three questions a blurb must answer. These are:

1. Who is the protagonist?

2. What is the story goal?

3. What is at stake?

The answers to these questions are found in every story. If you cannot answer them from the draft, then we can tell you the story promised is not there yet. And the draft is not ready to be edited.

What Does a Blurb Do?

Before starting a story edit, an editor needs to know there is the potential for the draft to contain a story. An episodic group of scenes is not a story. A manuscript not related to the blurb is not the right story. The blurb is the first test we use to see if there is a story.

> **Whether you're editing your work or someone else's, the blurb keeps the edit on point. While you read every scene, you'll have this blurb handy.**

A draft can be a beautiful collection of sentences without a story. A blurb shows there could be a story worth editing. Because without a story, what's the point of performing a story edit?

A Super-Fast Skeleton Blurb Method

If there is no blurb written yet, this can be addressed in under ten minutes. First things first, talk to the writer. If you are self-editing, this is easy: find a mirror. If you are editing someone else's work, then get them to write out this blurb statement.

Protagonist _____

(protagonist name)

must _____

(story goal)

otherwise _____

(what's at stake).

In the next few pages, we will look in depth at what a protagonist is, what a story goal is, and what the stakes are.

This is vital.

Without a clear protagonist, it's hard to get a reader engaged in a story, because they don't know whom to follow. Without a story goal, the protagonist has nothing to do, so there is no story. Without something at stake, the reader won't care what the protagonist does. All three elements of the blurb are critical to the success of a story.

The First Promise in the Blurb

The story will be about one protagonist. That protagonist will have a story goal, and there will be stakes involved.

You'll learn in this chapter how to create a skeleton blurb. The first step in writing a blurb is to decide who the protagonist is. Brace yourself. This may be more difficult than you think.

Know Your Protagonist

A common question we get is, "I have more than one protagonist. How do I handle that?"

"There can be only one protagonist," we answer.

Not all writers and not all editors like this answer, so the answer deserves an in-depth discussion.

What Is a Protagonist?

The protagonist is the main character of a story.

But, of course, it's not as simple as that. Remember Highlander? "There can be only one!" We are sure that the Kurgan was talking about story when he said his immortal line . . . anyway, get outside and shout at the top of your lungs: There can be only one—one protagonist, that is.

Identifying the Protagonist

It can be hard to identify who the protagonist is in a story. When we ask a writer who the protagonist is, the answer varies. Sometimes the answer is that there are two protagonists. Sometimes it's more than two.

The difficulty with these answers is that most commercially successful novels have one protagonist. The reader must connect with a protagonist and know whom to cheer for in the story. If they don't, there is a good chance they won't finish reading the book.

So how is it possible to have one protagonist in stories like A Game of Thrones: A Song of Ice and Fire or in a movie such as Thelma & Louise?

Although Thelma & Louise is a movie, it's a great example of when there are two lead characters but one protagonist, so we couldn't resist using it. We'll get into these stories later.

> **TEA with Kristina**
>
> By the time I perform a story edit for a writer, their draft is written, and I'll edit the story by analyzing the following:
>
> Was the best character chosen as the protagonist?
>
> Does the protagonist have enough page time?
>
> Does every scene impact the protagonist (even if they are not in the scene)?

What Is a Protagonist Beyond the Main Character?

The protagonist is the main character who pursues the story goal and has the most to win or lose.

The next sentence is super important:

The first step in finding the protagonist is to think of the protagonist as an entity that can be made up of one or more characters.

This is slightly different from how we usually look at a protagonist: an entity versus a character. We're doing this, so the reader knows whom to cheer for.

Types of Protagonists

Sometimes it's hard to determine who the protagonist is, so we've categorized a protagonist into three types:

- Single
- Combined
- Group

SINGLE PROTAGONIST

A single protagonist means there is one main character in the story. They will have a main goal for the story, and they either succeed or fail at achieving that goal.

This is the easiest to write, so if you're a first-time novelist, we recommend trying this before going on to more complex styles.

For an editor, this is also the easiest type of story to perform a story edit on.

COMBINED PROTAGONIST

This means there are two main characters, and both characters want the same thing, meaning their goal for the story is the same.

In their struggle to achieve the goal, they will both suffer or benefit from the same events. This doesn't mean there won't be conflict between the two. There should be. The two characters should also have different personalities.

This is more difficult to write than a single protagonist because the writer must ensure the characters are different enough to be interesting and cause conflict but also similar enough to want the same goal.

With the single goal, they can be considered two characters combined into a single protagonist.

A creative story editor has the extra work of making sure the two characters are balanced in page time, the conflict between the two doesn't feel forced, the conflict drives the story forward, and each scene impacts the characters in the same way.

GROUP PROTAGONIST

This is most likely a story with multiple points of view (POVs). It could also be an omniscient story. The POV characters will suffer and benefit separately. One event may cause one character to suffer and the other to benefit. In this case, the author will be telling multiple stories that are related; hence the protagonist becomes a group, the world, or the society the characters live in.

The group protagonist is one entity, hence a single protagonist.

This is the most difficult type of protagonist to write. It will involve multiple POV characters, so the writer must make sure the readers are connected with each character. They must ensure the story doesn't feel episodic. And they must ensure the reader doesn't lose track of who each character is and how they are contributing to or against the main story goal.

This is also the hardest type of story to edit, because it takes strong story knowledge and analytical skills to ensure the story works.

REASON FOR ONE PROTAGONIST

Readers are human, and stories unite people. We all are searching for answers to our lives, and readers are a little nosier than non-readers of stories. Readers live vicariously through a story's protagonist.

The reason for only one protagonist is that the reader is only one person. While they read, the reader becomes the protagonist. And if you have more than one character as the protagonist, you are asking the reader to be more than one person. Multiple POVs are fine, but the reader wants to follow one protagonist, as they are just one person.

For any of the protagonist types, the story can have multiple POVs. Who doesn't like to know what others are thinking of them and see the disconnect between others' words and actions.

Now that you know what the three types of protagonists are, we challenge you to define one protagonist no matter the genre of the story.

If you can't define the protagonist yet, state the story goal and story stakes, then come back and look again at who the protagonist is. The next section of this chapter gives you a process to find the protagonist.

Let's get to know the protagonist better.

Did You Have Trouble Finding One Protagonist?

We've given you the first step to having only one protagonist, so now let's look in more depth at a way to figure out who that protagonist really is.

Remember, the first step is to think of the protagonist as an entity that can be made up of one or more characters.

Think of a protagonist as an entity more than a character. The reader must always have someone to cheer for.

SINGLE PROTAGONIST

As stated above, a single protagonist means there is one main character in the story. They will have a main goal for the story, and they either succeed or fail at achieving that goal.

The single protagonist is the easiest to find.

If you're using Fictionary, you have awesome resources to help you figure out who the protagonist is.

Which character is in the greatest number of scenes?

The Fictionary Scenes per Character insight shows you the answer in a second.

Which character is the POV character for the greatest number of scenes?

The Fictionary POV Character insight gives you the answer to both questions in a second.

Use the answers to these questions to find the character who does the following:

- Who drives the external story goal?
- Who has the most to lose if the goal fails?
- Who is in the greatest number of scenes?
- Who is the POV character with the greatest number of scenes?

This is a sure-fire way to find a single protagonist.

COMBINED PROTAGONIST

A combined protagonist entails two main characters who both want the same thing, this means their goal for the story is the same. In their struggle to achieve the goal, they will both suffer or benefit from the same events.

The combined protagonist is harder to find than a single protagonist. You have the tools listed for the single protagonist, but there's more to it. Let's add in the internal story goal.

INTERNAL STORY GOAL

The protagonist will have an internal story goal as well as an external story goal stated in the blurb.

Later in this book, we will cover the POV character's external and internal goals for every scene. What we're talking about here is the protagonist's overall external and internal story goals.

Let's look at Thelma & Louise by Joe Escobar as an example.

The external story goal is to escape from the police. Their freedom is at stake. But which one is the protagonist?

> **The characters Thelma and Louise are a combined protagonist. They have the same external story goal AND the same internal story goal.**

The internal story goal is to form an intimate relationship with another human being. They fail at the external goal of escaping the police, but they succeed at the internal goal of forming an intimate relationship with another human. It's not the human they expect; that's part of what makes the ending powerful.

CRITERIA FOR A COMBINED PROTAGONIST

The two characters must do the following:

- Have the same external story goal.
- Have the same internal story goal.
- Both fail or succeed at obtaining the external story goal.
- Both fail or succeed at obtaining the internal story goal.

Romance novels are where we get the most resistance to this theory. Writers and editors argue that a romance has two main characters; therefore there are two protagonists.

The way to figure out whether your protagonist in a romance novel is single or combined is to look at whether the inner goal is the same or different for both characters.

If it's different, then one of the characters is the protagonist. Go back to the single protagonist section and use the questions to help you decide which one is the protagonist.

Group Protagonist

The group protagonist entails multiple characters treated as one entity. This group of characters has the same external story goal.

The group protagonist differs from the combined protagonist in that each character has a different inner goal even though they have the same external goal.

Our favorite example of a group protagonist is Game of Thrones, by George R.R. Martin.

CRITERIA FOR A GROUP PROTAGONIST

The characters do the following:

- Have the same external story goal.
- Have a different internal story goal.
- Fail or succeed as a group at obtaining the external story goal.
- Fail or succeed individually at obtaining their internal story goal.

The group protagonist is the human society: the society in the kingdoms.

A GAME OF THRONES: SONG OF ICE AND FIRE

Let's take a deeper look at a group protagonist and analyze A Game of Thrones. This book has eight POV characters.

The external story goal: humans must beat the White Walkers.

The internal goals of the eight POV characters are:

- Eddard Stark: reconcile family safety with the success of the realm.
- Catelyn Stark: protect her children at all costs.
- Tyrion Lannister: be accepted for who he is.
- Jon Snow: make Eddard Stark proud.
- Bran Stark: be as strong as his brothers.
- Sansa Stark: please those around her.
- Arya Stark: be independent.
- Will: live.

The protagonist entity achieves the external goal because the White Walkers die.

Some characters who belong to the protagonist entity succeed, and some fail at achieving their internal goal.

- Eddard Stark: fails.
- Catelyn Stark: fails because most of her children die (Robb dies in front of her).
- Tyrion Lannister: succeeds as he becomes a leader in winning the war against the White Walkers.

- Jon Snow: succeeds, joining the Night Watch and becoming a leader there. Jon also discovers his inner goal to make his father proud was the wrong goal. It was to make himself proud.
- Bran Stark: succeeds as he becomes more powerful.
- Sansa Stark: succeeds because she discovers her need is to be strong and lead, and the goal to please others was the wrong goal.
- Arya Stark: succeeds as she becomes a warrior in her own right.
- Will: fails as he is beheaded by Eddard Stark (this was a great bit of foreshadowing that Eddard was going to lose his head, too).

Where to Next?

Now that we are confident with the one protagonist (or one entity), let's look at the story goal. The blurb should have one strong external story goal that the readers can connect with.

The Second Promise in the Blurb

By now you've determined who the protagonist is. That was the first step in creating a blurb. Now we'll make sure we understand the story goal before moving on to the story stakes.

The story goal, the second promise, will be achieved or not by the protagonist by the end of the story.

If the reader doesn't discover if the story goal was achieved or not, the story is not over.

KNOW THE STORY GOAL

The story goal is what the protagonist "must" do in the story. The word "must" is nonnegotiable in a story goal, because it adds a level to the conflict.

The story goal is the purpose of the story. And as a creative story editor, this knowledge is profound. A story must have a protagonist, and there must be a clear story goal. A reason for the reader to read.

Readers read with the purpose of being immersed in a story. The reader expects the protagonist to have a purpose, too, and that purpose is to achieve the story goal.

The story goal propels the protagonist through the story from chapter to chapter just as a POV character's scene goal propels the reader from scene to scene. If the protagonist "must" do something, it sets off questions inside the reader's head. Will they achieve their goal? Oh, I better keep reading to find out.

And that's why the story goal should be clear from the start. The story goal is about keeping the reader glued to the story. They need to find out if that story goal will be achieved.

What Is a Story Goal?

From the last section, you know if the protagonist is a story-worthy protagonist. The draft must have a worthy story goal, and that story goal must be in the blurb.

A worthy story goal must be about something, and something physical is better. Yes, the internal goals are important, but the main external story goal gets the protagonist to move. And that movement drives the story from the first page to the last. The main external story goal is the fuel that the reader uses to keep their reading engines fired up.

The story goal must be powerful, and the reader must wonder how the character can possibly achieve the story goal.

There are some questions you can ask to test the strength of the story goal.

1.   Can the reader visualize the story goal?

2.   Will the reader care about the story goal?

3.   Can reader see that there is a possibility of success or of failure?

We cannot emphasize enough that the story goal's possibilities are reasons for the reader to read the story. And as the story goal is the fuel that propels the reader through the story, the story goal has to matter. The story goal has to be understandable. And the story goal must be achieved or not at the end of the story.

The story goal sets up the climax scene.

The climax scene answers the story goal.

If you're editing the story, and you need to find the story goal quickly, read the climax scene.

In Fictionary this is easy enough to do. Pull up the Story Arc visual insight, click on the climax scene, and read.

If you're working on pen and paper or a spreadsheet, then chapter 4 ("The Fictionary Story Test") explains how to find the climax scene. The climax scene must show if the protagonist achieves the story goal. How it answers it is not important, not yet.

If the climax scene doesn't show the protagonist achieving or failing to achieve the story goal, you have found an issue that must be fixed. Without fixing this issue, there is no story yet.

How quick was that! An important check, all by learning what a story goal is! Aren't you glad you didn't skip this section?

Searching for Story Goals

Story goals create forward momentum in the story. A story goal gets the protagonist in motion as they move toward or get pushed away from their goal.

TYPES OF STORY GOALS

This list is not comprehensive. It's a place to get you looking at the story goal in the blurb, and then in the story itself. Universal goals can be survival, justice, power, pleasure, or security.

- Finding object: quest-type stories
- Finding safety: escape/chase-type stories
- Finding another's weakness: combat/end battle stories
- Finding understanding: coming-of-age stories, personal-growth stories
- Finding justice: mysteries, thrillers
- Finding love: romance
- Finding new normal: dystopian stories, disaster stories

Where to Next?

You have the protagonist and the story goal. We now need to know the story stakes. We need to care, and we need the readers to care.

The Third Promise in the Blurb

We know who the protagonist is and what their story goal is. But that's not enough. We now need to know what the stakes are.

The story stakes must be big enough to make the reader care. If the protagonist does not achieve their story goal, then the consequences must be huge.

Know the Story Stakes

Story stakes explain the consequences of failure. If the protagonist doesn't achieve the story goal, the story stakes spell out the protagonist's downfall. The blurb's third promise ratchets up the tension for the reader.

A reader knowing these risks is part of the story's power. And as a creative story editor, we want to make all stories as powerful as they can be.

Story power is what lifts the story off the page and turns the reader into a lifelong superfan.

Let's look at story stakes in action. In The Bourne Identity by Robert Ludlum, Jason Bourne must find out who he is; otherwise he will die. Those are pretty big stakes, and that's one of the reasons the story is such a success.

This story stake is why this story has such story power.

The story stakes tell the reader how much they have to worry about the protagonist. The story stakes tell the reader how important the story goal is. The story stakes are the reason the reader should care.

Because without the consequences—without story stakes—the reader Does. Not. Care.

Story Stakes Must Be Big

The common editing advice is that story stakes must be big. That statement looks like two-thirds of a skeleton blurb. There is an unsaid part of that statement, which is the last third of the reason a story must have big stakes. Let's finish off the statement with what will happen to the story if there are no big stakes. Let's add an otherwise.

Let's take the common advice that story stakes must be big and transform it into a skeleton blurb to include the story stakes:

Story stakes must be big; otherwise the reader does not care and won't read on.

Oh, okay, understanding story stakes is critical for the creative story editor. Readers who don't care don't read on.

A creative story editor must understand story stakes; otherwise, the story edit will fail.

Yikes, before we use too many more skeleton blurbs to prove our point, let's look at what makes a big story stake.

> ## TEA with Kristina
>
> **Remember, a skeleton blurb is the following statement.**
> **The protagonist** _____
> **(protagonist name)**
> **must** _____
> **(story goal)**
> **otherwise** _____
> **(what's at stake).**

What Are Big Story Stakes?

Do you know one of the worst criticisms of a book?

"Didn't care for it."

Professional critics don't have a drop of power compared to those four soul-destroying words from the perfect reader. The criticism means the story is weak and has no power.

The blurb is a measure of the story power.

Before you start editing on a scene-be-scene basis, you must now if there is a story. There is a huge indication about the story power in the skeleton blurb, and that's this question: Are the stakes big enough?

The big story stakes always have a finality about them. And the biggest finality is death. If you can see death or the end of something in the story stakes, you know the stakes are big.

In romance books, the protagonist risks their love life. In thrillers, the protagonist risks their life. In sci-fi, the risks can be more than one life; they can be the fates of whole planets. In coming-of-age stories, the protagonist risks not being able to grow up, and they risk their adult life.

Big story stakes are life and death to the protagonist. And as a creative story editor, we have to read the book and wonder whose fate is at risk. Would this make the reader invest their money, their time, and their emotions in the story?

Smaller story stakes are fine, but as a creative story editor, our mission is to make each draft into a great story. Smaller story stakes have the potential to turn into weak story stakes.

Read the Blurb Out Loud

We like to have fun when we perform a creative story edit, so we read the blurb dramatically, with a Hollywood narrator voice, and we sometimes have been known to add a verbal dun dun dunnn.

When you read the skeleton blurb out loud, and when you get to the word otherwise, ham it up. Go big. You can hear with the speed of sound whether there is enough power in the story stakes.

> **Have you read the blurb out loud? Did you feel the urge to add a dun dun dunnn?**

When you get that urge to add the dun dun dunnn, you know the story stakes are going to make the reader care.

A Published Blurb

Let's look at this blurb for a book that has been edited in Fictionary using the Fictionary story-editing process. Lisa Stringfellow edited her debut novel in Fictionary StoryTeller. A Comb of Wishes won the inaugural Kweli Color of Children's Literature Manuscript Award in 2019.

> **Blurb:**
>
> **Ever since her mother's death, Kela feels every bit as broken as the shards of glass, known as "mermaid's tears," that sparkle on the Caribbean beaches of St. Rita. So when Kela and her friend Lissy stumble across an ancient-looking comb in a coral cave, with all she's already lost, Kela can't help but bring home her very own found treasure.**

Far away, deep in the cold ocean, the mermaid Ophidia can feel that her comb has been taken. And despite her hatred of all humans, her magic requires that she make a bargain: the comb in exchange for a wish.

But what Kela wants most is for her mother to be alive. And a wish that big will exact an even bigger price...

Let's take it back down to a skeleton blurb.

Protagonist: Kela

Must: give the comb back to the mermaid

Otherwise: her mother will remain dead.

In this story, the story stakes are that the protagonist will never see her mother again. Now doesn't this story make you want to read it? And please do!

A Comb of Wishes by Lisa Stringfellow is a super Fictionary-edited book.

There is a promise of a story, so where to next?

We have found out that when using the power of a blurb, there is a promise of a story that a creative story editor can edit. But in the title of this book, we promised to spill the TEA on all the secrets that is the creative Fictionary story-editing process, which edits drafts into great stories.

But first . . .

Remember in the "Why Learn How to Story Edit?" section when we mentioned having thirteen other editors who are going to teach you? Here is your first chance to learn from those editors.

Two of our thirteen experts are going to show you how they used the blurb to gain insight into whether the blurb promise held up.

A blurb promise shows the reader what they are signing up for. It's the reason to spend hours with a book. This section was about making the complex simple, and the next is using this simple blurb tool to test the strength of the story.

Suggestions from an Editor

In Chapter 1, Meet the Secrets, we talked about having thirteen creative story editors who will show you how they edited Evolution, a book Kristina wrote for the team of editors to edit.

She also wrote a blurb for the purpose of having a book edited.

This is not a polished blurb ready for publication; rather it is a draft blurb for the editors to edit from. We are showing you actual expert editors who used the blurb during their edits. This enables you to see behind the scenes and understand the process an editor must go through.

The original blurb for Evolution was as follows:

Blurb:

After her husband and dog die, Jaz Cooper, a woman with a debilitating fear of crowds, discovers she has a special connection with dogs and draws further away from human interaction. But when she discovers her husband was murdered, she must fight her need to hide and use her newfound skill with dogs to search for the killer, only to learn the new ability might get her killed.

What does this blurb promise?

Protagonist: Jaz Cooper
Must: find out who killed her husband
Otherwise: her life is in danger

The following is an extract from Evolution:

My vision blurred, and my head felt foggy. Confusion swept through me. I bent forward and rested my head on Daisy's neck. The fog thickened, and I moved away from Daisy.

"What's wrong?" Katie asked.

It took me a moment to clear my head. "Why didn't you tell me earlier? What did the doctor say you should do?" I asked.

"Doctor?"

Daisy pressed her nose harder into my leg. My stomach lurched, and I tasted bile. "About the tumor."

"What tumor?"

"The one in your breast."

Katie held a knife in the air and stared at me. "What are you talking about?"

Below are two of the expert Fictionary StoryCoach Editors' comments referring to the extract above:

EDITOR 1:

Hmmm . . . I may have mistaken the genre of the book. I may have more comments as the book progresses and I see where the plot is going.

EDITOR 2:

Oh wow. A vision. And it's about a tumor. There are consequences. This is an interesting turn for the book. Visions are an intriguing element but for sure make it a particular kind of book (a bit of supernatural?).

TEA with Kristina

Without a blurb, the editors would not have been able to make these comments. They would not be able to tell if this scene has a purpose in the story. The skeleton blurb is about keeping sight of the story, which can get lost when you are deep in the scenes.

Updated Blurb:
After her husband and dog die, Jaz Cooper, a woman with a debilitating fear of crowds, discovers she has a special connection with dogs.

> **Touch one, and she can see into their minds. She uses this talent as an excuse to draw further away from human interaction.**
>
> **But when she discovers her husband was murdered, she must fight her need to hide and use her newfound skill with dogs to search for the killer, only to learn the new ability might get her killed.**

What does this promise?

Protagonist: Jaz Cooper
Must: use her newfound dog visions to find out who killed her husband
Otherwise: she could be killed
The blurb now shows there is a paranormal aspect to the story.

> **This example highlights the importance of writing a blurb. In this case, the blurb did not reflect the core aspect of the story.**

TEA with Kristina

Phew. Glad that was caught. Every aspect of the creative story editor's job is to find any story issue that readers will not like and take note of them, so the author can revise the story and make it better.

Imagine being a reader and buying the book because the first blurb intrigued them. They would feel the blurb promise had not been kept. And the blurb would have broken the trust of the reader. Ultimately, they would put the book down.

Not only does the blurb show the reader what the story is about, but it can also check to see if the promises made in the blurb themselves are met. And there can be one of two options. Revise the story or rewrite the blurb.

Note that the above is still a draft blurb.

Where to Next?

Now you can see how important a skeleton blurb really is. We believe understanding the concepts means you're ready to use the editing tools. We are not going to tell you what to do. That's up to you as the artist. We'll explain the importance of each part of a creative story edit in detail, and you get to choose how you use it.

Before continuing, make sure you have a blurb that shows the protagonist, the story goal, and the story stakes. Then you're ready to determine whether a story exists in the manuscript.

Turn the page, and meet the Fictionary Story Test.

"All stories make promises; a successful story keeps them." —Kristina Stanley, CEO of Fictionary

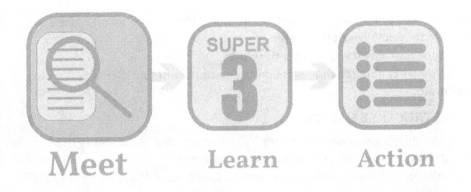

Meet   Learn   Action

Chapter Four:
Meet the Fictionary Story Test

"Stories with one protagonist allow the reader unique intimacy with character, creating a bond through that singular lens that can transcend the page." — **Heather Wood, Fictionary Certified StoryCoach Editor**

The Fictionary Story Test: Is There a Story?

You know as a creative story editor that you're creating an actionable editing plan the writer will use to revise their story. This enables a writer to Move or Add or Revise or Cut or Split a scene as they perform revisions. You have the skeleton blurb in hand, and now you're going to answer an important question: Is there a story?

Once you know that, you'll perform a story edit and help turn that story into a great story.

WHAT IS A GREAT STORY?

What do we mean by a great story? We mean a story that lives, a story that has superfans, a story that wins awards, a story that becomes immortal.

The method is a cinch. The results are not.

The questions you will ask of the draft are clear, and the answers you get are profound. And each time you ask a question based on the story elements, the answer's profundity will increase, until you have a revision plan that can be used to turn the draft into a great story.

Look how easy it was to write the blurb.

Now we're going to show you how to determine whether there is a story in the draft.

DOES THE GENRE MATTER?

The story's genre doesn't matter. What matters first is the ability to tell a good story, because the story is the core of the novel.

All genres have five scenes in common. Don't worry. We're going to share what those five scenes are. They are the five Fictionary Story Arc scenes.

But first let's define a scene:

A scene is a section of a story that has a POV character, with a POV scene goal, and this scene goal is addressed in the scene climax.

The Powerful Fictionary Story Test

This test checks if there is a story within the draft. This involves a full read-through of the draft.

We'll use the skeleton synopsis to test if there is a story. Here is a sneak peek, before you meet it more formally in Chapter 6: Meet the Skeleton Synopsis.

Skeleton Synopsis = Skeleton Blurb + 5 Story Arc Scenes + Resolution

Find the five Fictionary Story Arc scenes and see if they are in the right order, in the right place, and doing the right things. Use this information to create the skeleton synopsis.

That's it?

Yep.

Seriously?

Yep.

What's the Catch?

The Fictionary story edit is about making the edit comprehensive, objective, and actionable. And when an expert teaches you, learning to be comprehensive, objective, and actionable should be powerfully simple to achieve.

Simple should not be confused with no value.

Einstein was able to take his complex theory of relativity and make up an equation that a seven-year-old can repeat. Energy is mass multiplied by the speed of light squared. Fortunately, this is a book on creative story editing and not physics. Don't forget: that equation revolutionized the world of physics.

Just as creative story editing is revolutionizing the world of editing.

The catch is that you will change. And that's why you are here. Creative story editing revolutionizes not only the edits but also the editors who use the process.

The Fictionary Story Test

The Fictionary Story Test is a fill-in-the-blanks test. Once you have read the draft, pop on your creative story editor hat, refer to the skeleton blurb, and create the skeleton synopsis.

When a draft has the right makeup, it has the potential to be a great story.

Now write the following:

The protagonist _____ finds out the story goal _____ (Inciting Incident).

Then _____ happens, and the protagonist must go forward toward the story goal, (Plot Point 1).

In the new "world," _____ happens, and the protagonist becomes proactive to the Story Goal (Middle Plot Point).

But _____ happens, and the protagonist's hope is destroyed, they realize they must change to achieve the story goal (Plot Point 2).

But the protagonist _____ ,and the world changes, they finally address the story goal (Climax).

With your skeleton blurb, you found the protagonist, the story goal, and the story stakes. With your skeleton synopsis, you found the story.

To fill in the blanks, read the draft and find the inciting incident, plot point 1, the middle plot point, plot point 2, and the climax. Use the action in each of these scenes to fill in the blanks. The next chapter, Chapter 5: Meet the Story Arc, explains each of the plot points and where in the story you should be looking to find the plot point scenes. Don't worry. The next several sections explain each of the five story arc scenes in detail.

To save more time, let Fictionary do the work for you. Fictionary draws the story arc and shows the location of each Fictionary Story Arc scene.

Name each scene and use those names to fill in the blanks.

LISTING THE STORY ARC SCENES SHOWS YOU WHETHER THERE IS A STORY.

- Does the protagonist find out the story goal,
- then something happens that propels the protagonist onto chasing the story goal,
- so that they can learn to be proactive,
- change themselves after all hope is lost,
- and use what they have learned on their journey to answer the story goal that they found at the start of their journey?

What you just read is the most basic form of a story. And all great stories are structurally similar. But all great stories don't show their structure to the world.

Where to Next?

We're not asking you to write the synopsis yet. There's more to learn before that can be done with ease.

It's time for the big reveal. Let's get on to the details of the Fictionary Story Arc scenes. After that, we'll show you how to find each of the story arc scenes. You're moving toward answering the most important question: Is there a story in the manuscript?

What Is in the Story Test?

What do we mean when we talk about having proof that there is a story? We are asking if you can write a synopsis.

We define a synopsis as a blurb plus the five story arc scenes plus the ending. A synopsis is a cinch when you know that's all it boils down to.

When people find it tough to write a synopsis, it's normally because either they don't have an understanding of what goes into the synopsis or there isn't a full story yet. After reading this section, you will know how to write a synopsis and understand why writing one is so important.

A synopsis is proof that there is a story in the draft.

We have the blurb, so let's find the plot points needed to write the skeleton synopsis.

The Fictionary Story Arc

The story arc acts as undeniable proof that there is a story. If a draft has the five Fictionary Story Arc scenes, then the story arc can be drawn.

If the five story arc scenes are nowhere to be found, then the story arc can't be created, and you, as the creative story editor, have found the draft is not finished. And if that draft is not finished, there is no story yet. See how easy the Fictionary Story Test is!

When you've checked for a story and found it missing, this must be fixed in the draft. And it is an important fix. Without fixing the story, the book can't be successfully published.

If the five story arc scenes are not in the draft, then there is just a collection of scenes. The story arc also shows the creative story editor how to make the draft into a book readers will love, but more on that later. First let's look at why this story arc works.

All great stories have an underlying structure. The structure is neither a restrictive structure nor a formula. Rather, the story arc is the defining feature. The human skeleton defines a human's shape. Our skeletal structure holds our bodies together.

So let's get reminded of those five story arc scenes.

THE FIVE STORY ARC SCENES

A story is made up of scenes. Nobody disputes that: scenes are a defining feature of a story. And to the untrained eye, these scenes might all look the same, but creative story editors know differently. We know in every story there will be the five key plot points (the five story arc scenes). Because if they are not there, then there is no story.

Where to Next?

Read on to learn about each of the five story arc scenes, what they must accomplish, and where they should be in the story.

"A Fictionary Story Editor points out how a reader will react to the story." — **Kristina Stanley, CEO of Fictionary**

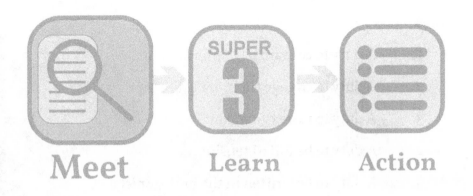

Meet   Learn   Action

Chapter Five:
Meet the Story Arc

"The story arc plots your story to greatness." —Kristina Stanley, CEO of Fictionary

You're about to get the most valuable knowledge when it comes to creative story editing. Without this knowledge, a story can't be edited.

In this chapter, we'll be looking at each of these scenes in greater depth:

- Inciting incident
- Plot point 1
- Middle plot point
- Plot point 2
- Climax

The Five Story Arc Scenes' Five Duties

These five story arc scenes are also called plot point scenes. These five scenes are multitaskers. They must work harder than other scenes, but that's okay. They love it, just as you will love these scenes.

These scenes are dutiful scenes. They have:

1.   A duty to contain new information

2.   A duty to change the story's direction

3.   A duty to raise the stakes

4.   A duty to be full of tension

5.   A duty to be written in the protagonist's POV

Other scenes can have some of the same attributes, but when you are reading the draft and looking for the story arc scenes, this list of the five duties is a super aid.

Become an Expert in the Five Story Arc Scenes

Becoming an expert in the five story arc scenes might seem like a monster task. It isn't. We promise. We will debunk that idea by using monsters to show you that the story arc scenes are all pretty tame once you become a story arc scene expert.

The five story arc scenes must be written from the protagonist's POV, because the protagonist drives these scenes.

The underlying message here is that the protagonist must be in the five story arc scenes.

We rarely talk about rules, but this is one of them: a story arc scene without the protagonist is disappointing to the reader.

Whether or not vampires are your thing, it's hard to ignore the fact that Twilight by Stephanie Meyer was a huge commercial success. People around the world loved reading it. In part, it's because Twilight follows the story arc beautifully.

We reveal the ending of the story below.

THE FIVE STORY ARC SCENES IN TWILIGHT

The inciting incident occurs at approximately 10 percent into Twilight: Bella is nearly killed, but Edward saves her.

Plot point 1 occurs approximately 25 percent into Twilight: Bella learns that Edward is a vampire.

The middle plot point occurs approximately 50 percent into Twilight: Bella sees Edward's vampiric power.

Plot point 2 occurs approximately 75 percent into Twilight: Bella must leave home to escape Edward's vampire enemy.

The climax occurs approximately 85 percent into Twilight: an evil vampire lures Bella into a trap. She faces him and wins the fight.

Visualizing the Story Arc

One way or another you must have sight of the story arc, either in your mind's eye or have it drawn for you, you can then get a handle of the story. Seeing it will help you answer the question: Is there a story?

Fictionary draws the story arc in real time, so any edit, reduction in scenes, or addition in word counts can be taken into account swiftly.

Fictionary will save you hours by plotting the story arc for you.

The Five Duties of a Story Arc Scene

The five story arc scenes have the following duties in common:

1. Contain new information about the story goal.

2. Change the story direction.

3. Raise the stakes.

4. Be full of tension (even in the quieter scenes).

5. Be written in the protagonist's POV.

They also have individual duties specific to the plot point. You'll have to read on to discover these.

Where to Next?

In the following pages, we will cover each of the five story arc scenes and what they need to accomplish. Every creative story editor must be an expert in the story arc.

Fictionary's Inciting Incident

To prove there is a story, the first scene a creative story editor should search out is the inciting incident.

If the draft is in Fictionary, the story arc is drawn for you. If you are using the pen or spreadsheet method, let's look at what inciting incidents are and where to find them. Even if you use Fictionary, it is good practice to understand what an inciting incident is, as sometimes a draft has the wrong scene written as the inciting incident, and you might need to mark that as a needed revision.

Why the Inciting Incident?

The inciting incident contains the action that changes or disrupts the protagonist's ordinary life. In addition to the five duties listed in the section titled "The Fictionary Story Arc," this scene must do the following:

1. Cause the protagonist to react to the action. The reaction is the start of the protagonist's journey.

2. Be early in the story

3. Be related to the story goal stated in the blurb.

The reader will want to experience the inciting incident along with the protagonist. At the beginning of the book, if the story doesn't show the inciting incident play out, this tells the reader the story won't show them everything. The reader may lose faith in the storyteller and put the book down.

The inciting incident gets the reader to ask, "What will happen to the protagonist's future?"

That question is one of the secrets to all good storytelling and all pageturners. Make sure the reader's interest is kept by getting them to say, "Ooh, I will read on just to find out what that event meant."

Check the question raised in the inciting incident scene is not answered until the climax.

If the question asked in the inciting incident is answered too soon, it is like telling the punch line of a joke too early. The buildup is lost, and the meaning and the power of the story are dashed.

When the climax scene addresses the inciting incident's question, the results are stories with the most satisfying endings. And that's what you are aiming to edit into the draft. A satisfying ending.

Inciting incidents get the story started, but they shape the ending too.

The inciting incident is the end of the setup phase of the story and occurs before 15 percent. The protagonist has moved out of their ordinary world and is moving toward plot point 1.

At the Start of a Story

The scenes before the inciting incident—the setup scenes—are to show the reader the protagonist's ordinary world, set the tone for the story, and show what's at stake when the changes come.

The setup scenes before are vital.

If the reader doesn't know what the consequences are for the protagonist, then the story power is lost. And from reading the section titled "Know the Story Stakes," you know that the consequences are the story power—the ability for a story to stay with a reader after they put the book down.

Ideally, the protagonist should be in the first scene of the story. The later the protagonist enters the story, the higher the risk the story won't work. If the protagonist is not introduced by the inciting incident, there is definitely a problem.

The reason a story structure issue occurs when a protagonist is not introduced before the inciting incident is that it's impossible for a character's life to be changed if they haven't been introduced yet.

The only solutions are to choose a different protagonist or figure out how to introduce the protagonist earlier. A scene cannot be considered the inciting incident scene if the reader doesn't already know who the protagonist is. The creative story editor will recommend the protagonist is introduced much earlier than the inciting incident for the setup stage of the story to work.

Finding the Inciting Incident

Read the story up to about the 15 percent mark. The inciting incident should be somewhere in there.

When you read the story, you should know when the inciting incident occurs, because the inciting incident is not a shrinking violet. It's no wallflower. No, if we keep on the flower theme, an inciting incident is like a red, red rose. You cannot miss it. Your senses notice this flower, just as your senses should notice an inciting incident.

Perfecting the Inciting Incident

The following are three things that can go wrong with an inciting incident.

THERE IS NO INCITING INCIDENT.

If there is no inciting incident or it occurs too late, the reader will get bored and wonder when the story is going to start, because the pacing of the story is wrong. No one wants this.

Editing Advice: Remind the writer of the story goal and suggest rewriting an existing scene or writing a new scene, so the scene meets the requirements of the inciting incident. The protagonist shouldn't be accepting the goal yet. It's enough at this point to show the shake-up in their life.

THE INCITING INCIDENT IS WEAK.

If the inciting incident is weak, the reader will wonder if the whole the story is weak. No one wants this.

Editing Advice: Use the story elements to edit why it is weak. Make suggestions based on what the story elements show you. You learn scene-by-scene editing starting in chapter 7. We'll get there, but it's important to look at the story structure first.

THE INCITING INCIDENT IS NOT RELEVANT TO THE STORY.

If the inciting incident is not relevant to the story, the reader will wonder if the whole the story lacks focus. No one wants this.

Editing Advice: If the question the inciting incident asks is not related to the story goal, suggest the writer rewrite the scene, so the main event in the scene is related to the story goal. Review the blurb if you need a reminder of what the story goal is. The protagonist shouldn't be accepting the goal yet. It's enough for now to show the shake-up in their life.

Remember:

The inciting incident is the moment the protagonist's world changes dramatically, causing them to react to the action. The protagonist's journey starts with the inciting incident.

Have you found an issue in the inciting incident? That means it's time to make suggestions on how to fix it.

Where to Next?

And now on to plot point 1. The protagonist knows what the story goal is, but they are not enamored with the idea of chasing that goal, so now what? Let's find out how to edit plot point 1 and get the protagonist hurtling toward the middle plot point.

Fictionary's Plot Point 1

At plot point 1, the protagonist must start doing things they were not doing throughout the setup of the story. The story transitions from the setup to the confrontation phase. In the first part of the confrontation phase, the protagonist will be in a reactionary mode.

Act 1 contains everything from the first word to plot point 1. Every scene in act 1 is part of the setup. Now the story moves from setup to a reactionary phase.

Plot point I is the point of no return for the protagonist. This is where they accept the story goal.

> **Plot point I is a big moment in a story. Do not underestimate its power.**

With great power comes great responsibilities. This scene connects two acts. And the best thing to remember is that this plot point is the death of act I, and there is no other option for the protagonist but to go into act 2.

This death of act I must somehow be in the scene. The possibility of returning home and putting the duvet over their head is no longer an option for the protagonist. This death can be a metaphorical death or a real death. For the metaphorical death, it could be the end of a relationship or the end of a job, and for a real death, it could be the threat of death if the protagonist does not go forward.

Plot Point I Moves the Story into Act 2

No matter how begrudgingly the protagonist moves into act 2. The protagonist will be running from the problem caused by the inciting incident.

Plot point I must be strongly related to the blurb. Now the protagonist accepts the story goal as something they must do. The option to turn around and call it a day no longer exists.

Finding Plot Point I

Plot point I differs from the inciting incident because the protagonist is now going after the main story goal and is motivated to do so. In the inciting incident, the protagonist just learns about the story goal. If you recall, the inciting incident occurred in the setup phase of the story, before fifteen percent. The setup showed what the protagonist has to lose.

> **By the time plot point I arrives, the story shows what's at stake for the protagonist. The greater the stakes, the greater the tension.**

Plot point I occurs at around the twenty-five percent mark. To be a plot point, this scene should be located between twenty and thirty percent into the story, and it must cause a shift in the story.

Plot Point 1 Must-Haves

All plot point scenes must be written from the protagonist's POV.

Generally, all major characters are introduced or mentioned before plot point 1.

Plot point 1 must do the following:

1. Contain new information about the story goal.

2. Change the story direction.

3. Raise the stakes.

4. Be full of tension.

5. Be written in the protagonist's POV.

Perfecting Plot Point 1

If you're not sure which scene in the story is plot point 1, read the scenes between twenty and thirty percent to see whether you can find one that meets some of the criteria.

Don't be lulled into thinking a plot twist is a plot point. A plot twist is a change in the story's direction. A plot point must perform all the duties listed above. Think big. This must be a rhino-in-the-room-type scene. If there was a rhino in the room, you would notice it, and you would move out of the room—into somewhere else, anywhere else. It's the same with plot point 1: the protagonist moves out of act 1 and into act 2.

After you read the scene, keep turning the page to see if the protagonist moves forward.

And if there is no scene between the twenty and thirty percent mark that fulfills all the duties, the creative story editor will recommend revising the story to fulfill the plot point scene duties.

Let's get into specifics with actionable advice.

NO PLOT POINT 1

Get out the blurb and remind yourself what the story goal is. If there isn't a scene performing the five duties of the plot point 1 scene, then there isn't a plot point 1.

Editing Advice: Write a scene in which the story goal forces the protagonist to move forward and the option to ignore the story goal is taken away.

WEAK PLOT POINT 1

You found a plot point 1 scene, but it doesn't meet all the requirements. Use the story elements to analyze why it's weak.

Editing Advice: Revise the scene, amping up the missing story elements.

IRRELEVANT PLOT POINT 1

This happens when the protagonist's reaction is not related to the story goal.

Editing Advice: Revise the scene so the protagonist reacts to the story goal.

REMEMBER:

Plot point 1 is when the protagonist can't back out of the central conflict. The character's desire to engage and pursue the story goal overrules all else.

Where to Next?

The next plot point is what happens at the middle of the story. It's the next plot point scene that must be in every story, regardless of genre. Often the middle of the story lags, and we're going to share how editors can help the writer create a great middle plot point scene.

Fictionary's Middle Plot Point

In the middle of a story, readers expect the protagonist's journey to go from reactionary to proactive. A reactive protagonist only ever reacts to things happening. They never make forward plans or think ahead, and they feel that there is not enough time or that there are not enough resources. But when they reach the middle plot point, the protagonist learns the rules of the game. And they can now plan. And that is what proactive means. They go after their story goal. They make the switch from accepting their fate to fighting for a new future and making plans to regroup.

The middle plot point scene should have something terrible or life-changing happen to the protagonist.

The protagonist must then find the strength to deal with whatever horrible thing you've made happen. This is where Dorothy realizes that the great and powerful Wizard of Oz is just some man behind a screen and that she must take matters into her own hands. This should be a balloon-popping moment of realization; the protagonist's worldview changes. Think of the proposal from Darcy in Pride and Prejudice. Her eyes are opened by the letter from him with the apology, and her worldview changes.

Types of Middle Plot Points

The middle plot point can be subtle or strong. The middle plot point is when the plot causes the protagonist's psychology to change. In The Princess Bride, Buttercup gives up her freedom in exchange for Westley's freedom. She actively tries to protect her true love. Until this point, she has been passive, and at this moment the reader understands she is worthy of true love.

The middle plot point must not only affect the protagonist but also have an effect on the reader. Whether the protagonist is successful or not in the end, the middle plot point should show the protagonist has gumption. Because at the middle plot point, the protagonist asks themselves who they really are, and that is the moment within the scene that they turn from reactive to proactive.

Middle Plot Point Foreshadowing

The middle plot point is a busy scene or scenes. It must have the plot collide with the protagonist's worldview and change the protagonist's psychology. That's how to get the protagonist from reactive to proactive. But it also must get the reader to believe in the ending. The middle plot point must foreshadow the ending. If the story has a happy-ever-after, then the midpoint scene must have the potential foreshadowing of the final scenes. The middle plot point must subtly get the reader ready for the end.

Therefore, the middle plot point must do the following:

1. Have action that collides with the protagonist's worldview.

2. Change the protagonist's psychology.

3. Get the protagonist from reactive to proactive.

4. Foreshadow the ending addressing of the story goal.

In Romeo and Juliet, Romeo kills Juliet's cousin in revenge for his cousin being killed. Both houses lose a young life because of a misunderstanding. SPOILER ALERT: At the end of Romeo and Juliet both houses lose a young life because of a misunderstanding.

We're not all Shakespeare! we can hear you shout. That's good news on two fronts. First, you are you, your edit will be shaped by who you are, your edit will be brilliant because you are doing it, and you are open to learning how to become a creative story editor. The second reason is that he is dead. And we would much rather you were alive. You make a better editor that way.

Where to Find the Middle Plot Point

The middle plot point should be in the middle of the story. Should we end there? No! But it really is as simple as that.

A story should have two halves. The first half is where the protagonist is reacting like a novice, and then, in the second half, even if they are making choices that are not always right, they are still making choices. So as the story editor, you are looking for the scene that is working harder than any other scene in this middle section.

Remember:

If finding the middle plot point is a chore, it probably is not there or is not fulfilling all its duties.

Perfecting the Middle Plot Point

Let's look at middle plot point issues.

NO MIDDLE PLOT POINT

If you can't find the middle plot point scene, search for a scene that mirrors the climax, figuratively or actually, and figure out how to edit the protagonist's worldview so the protagonist feels they can go after the story goal (this worldview will be changed by the plot).

Editing Advice: Revise or write a new scene so the protagonist and the reader understand what needs to change for the protagonist to achieve the story goal.

WEAK MIDDLE PLOT POINT

Not all of the requirements of the middle plot point exist.

Editing Advice: Use the 38 Fictionary Story Elements explained in chapters 9 through 12, where you learn all about each story element, and analyze why the scene is weak. Then give the writer actionable advice based on what you found.

IRRELEVANT MIDDLE PLOT POINT

This happens when neither the protagonist nor the reader believes the protagonist can succeed at achieving the story goal.

Editing Advice: Revise the scene so the protagonist believes they know how to change in order to achieve the story goal.

Remember:

The middle plot point is when the protagonist moves from reactive to proactive.

Make something terrible or life-changing happen to your protagonist. Your protagonist must then find the strength to deal with whatever horrible thing you've made happen.

Have you found an issue in your middle plot point? Yay. We truly believe this is good news. When you know you have an issue, you can easily edit that issue and give actionable advice.

Where to Next?

And now on to plot point 2. The protagonist has a new outlook on life, so now what? Let's find out how to write the plot point 2 scene that will grab readers and make them stay up late at night to finish the story.

Fictionary's Plot Point 2

It's the end of act 2, and the outlook for the protagonist is grim. The story goal was set at the inciting incident; then at plot point 1 they were propelled into act 2, and there was a middle plot point that made them understand and become proactive. Now the protagonist must work hard to get what they want or lose everything. Maybe even their life.

> The protagonist is also about to step into act 3.

This is the final place where new story information can be added. Sometimes the entirety of act 3 is referred to as the resolution, because this is where the protagonist does everything possible to reach their goal. The protagonist either achieves or doesn't achieve the main story goal in act 3.

This transition into act 3, the plot point 2 scene, is also about the protagonist not achieving the story goal in the right way. They try to fudge it, and they choose an option that is not the lesson that they need to learn. By choosing the easy option, the attempt fails and makes the whole situation worse.

In plot point 2, the protagonist thinks they have a shortcut idea to answer the story goal. They think they don't have to change (or not that much), and they will be able to win. Plot point 2 proves to them there are no shortcuts, and they will have to dig deep and really change.

Like plot point 1, the story changes direction here. The protagonist will face new challenges and risks.

In plot point 2, the protagonist is proactive, but they are misguided. It is like someone making soufflé and thinking that they didn't have to crack any eggs. The attempt at plot point 2 will be as successful as putting two uncracked raw chicken eggs into a soufflé dish and then into a hot oven and expecting a Michelin-starred soufflé to come out. Cracked thinking.

Plot Point 2 must:

1.   Mirror plot point 1.

2.   Be a low point for the protagonist.

3.   Be the death of act 2

4.   Make the protagonist realize they must change internally to address the story goal.

5.   Be written in the protagonist's POV.

End of Act 2

Plot point 2 is similar again to plot point 1. This is the death of act 2, so there must be an end of something. Again, it can be the end of someone or the end of something.

> **The protagonist realizes they must change their way of thinking to find a way to answer the story goal.**

Plot point 2 will be a low point for the protagonist. The actions they've taken since the middle plot point have caused disaster, and they don't know if they can recover. Some writers call this "hitting rock bottom" or the "dark night of the soul," and it marks a turning point in the story. After this, it's a rush to the climax.

There should not be any revelations, flashbacks, or backstory this late in the story. Everything must move the story forward. The momentum needs to hurtle forward from this point on. You can only know when to stop using revelations, flashbacks, or backstory if you know what scene plot point 2 is and that the story has reached that point.

Where to Find Plot Point 2

Plot point 2 occurs between seventy and eighty percent of the story. This is the first place to look for the key scene if you're not sure which scene it is.

If plot point 2 comes too late in the story, act 3 will lack depth and feel rushed. The reader may be let down. If it comes too early in the story, act 3 may drag, and the reader doesn't bother finishing the story.

Perfecting Plot Point 2

Let's look at issues with a plot point 2 scene.

NO PLOT POINT 2

If you can't find a plot point 2 scene, use the blurb, and remind yourself what the story goal is.

Editing Advice: Advise the writer to figure out the easiest answer to the story goal, but one that does not include a mindset change, and show how that will not work—the protagonist must fail. Then suggest they write or revise a scene that fulfills the plot point 2 requirements.

WEAK PLOT POINT 2

You found plot point 2, and not all the plot point 2 requirements are fulfilled.

Editing Advice: Rewrite the scene, amping up the missing story elements. See chapters 9 through 12 on editing a scene using the 38 Fictionary Story Elements.

IRRELEVANT PLOT POINT 2

You found plot point 2, but the protagonist tries to answer the story goal without having to change at all.

Editing Advice: Revise the scene so that the protagonist realizes they have to change in order to achieve the story goal. The reader must still doubt that the protagonist can reach the story goal.

Remember:

Plot point 2 is a low point for your protagonist. The actions they've taken since the middle plot point have caused a disaster, and they don't know if they can recover. More importantly, the readers worry the protagonist won't recover. It marks a turning point in the story.

Have you found an issue with the plot point 2 scene? When you find an issue, you can easily edit that issue.

Where to Next?

The protagonist is at the lowest of the low, so now what? Let's find out how to write a climax scene that grabs the readers and makes their pulses race.

Fictionary's Climax

The climax scene (or scenes) is where the protagonist either achieves or doesn't achieve the story goal. This is the most important tip we can give you about the climax of a novel. It's a nonnegotiable tip if you want to give readers a satisfying ending.

We have been accused of being blurb enthusiasts, and we hold our hands up. That's us. The skeleton blurb is a strong tool in the creative story editor's toolbox, and we'll come back to it again and again.

The blurb is the first promise you make to a reader. It's the main reason they decided to read the book.

The climax delivers on that promise.

If the climax does not deliver, the reader will believe the book broke its promise. The famous advice is that the first chapters sell the book, and the last chapters sell the next books. It comes back to the writer's delivery of the promise, so the readers trust the writer.

Climax Must-Haves

I. The protagonist must be in the climactic scene, or else the book will confuse and alienate your reader. The reader has followed the protagonist through the story journey, and if at the biggest, most emotional scene of the book, they are missing, the reader will feel annoyed.

2.   The climax must be written from the protagonist's POV.

3.   The protagonist should face the biggest obstacle in the story and determine their own fate.

4.   The climax must have the highest level of conflict, the greatest tension, or the most devastating emotional upheaval. The scene will be a snore-a-thon if it is not full of conflict, tension, and emotion.

A great climax is more nuanced than a "yes, the protagonist achieved the story goal," or a "no, they failed." A truly satisfying ending is one that has all four must-haves.

Where to Find the Climax

The climax is found at around the ninety percent mark of the story. It will be a single scene or a sequence of scenes that build up until the story goal is achieved or not achieved. The story's journey stops as soon as the story goal is achieved or not. This is why answering it too early in the book is a risk, and the readers will put your book down.

The ten percent remaining after the climax is the place for all the loose ends to be tidied up. Everything after the climax scene is the resolution.

Perfecting the Climax

Let's look at actionable advice to give when an issue with the climax is found.

NO CLIMAX

This happens when it's not clear in the story if the protagonist achieved their main story goal.

Editing Advice: Go back to the blurb and find the story goal. Then reread the inciting incident scene. The climax scene should mirror the inciting incident, so this will give you ideas on what to suggest for the climax scene. Remember, at this stage, we're editing and not revising.

WEAK CLIMAX

If there is a scene in the story that is faster paced and tenser than the climax scene, this means the climax scene is weak.

Editing Advice: Revise the scene, amping up the missing story elements. Use the advice given in chapters 9 through 12.

IRRELEVANT CLIMAX

This means there is a climax scene, but it is not related to the blurb and doesn't show the reader if the story goal was achieved.

Editing Advice: Revise the scene to make the climax relate the action to the blurb and clearly show the story goal resolved. This means the scene must show the protagonist either achieving or failing at the story goal.

Where to Next?

Editing the five story arc scenes gives the foundation to answer the question: Is there a story in the manuscript?

Let's go to the next chapter and create a skeleton synopsis. This is the most powerful tool to prove to yourself, and to anyone who will listen, that there is a story in the draft you're editing.

Chapter Six:
Meet the Skeleton Synopsis

"The Fictionary Synopsis is a brilliant tool for both author and editor, ensuring that a solid story arc has been written."
—Kara Henderson, Fictionary Certified StoryCoach Editor

The Skeleton Synopsis

We have the story arc, so now it's time to write a skeleton synopsis. Writing a skeleton synopsis at this stage will highlight any structural issues missed when you edited the story arc scenes in the previous chapter.

A skeleton synopsis is rough. It's for your eyes only to check that the story works. You'll use the story arc to list the key action in the five Fictionary Story Arc scenes.

> **Skeleton Synopsis = Skeleton Blurb + 5 Fictionary Story Arc Scenes + Resolution**

Writing the Synopsis

When we use the 38 Fictionary Story Elements, they all work together to build meaning. We're going to show you how to build meaning. The creative story editor's method is a gift that keeps on giving.

Some of you might not love writing a synopsis. Not yet. With this creative story-editing method, you can produce a skeleton synopsis that will flow.

With your creative story editor's hat on, let's start writing that skeleton synopsis.

STEP 1: PERFORM A HANDS-OFF READ-THROUGH

A hands-off read-through means you read the story without making any changes.

STEP 2: NAME EVERY SCENE

You can do this when you're performing a hands-off read-through. A hands-off read-through means you read the story without making any changes, but you can and should make notes and name every scene.

When naming the scenes, find and label the inciting incident, plot point 1, the middle plot point, plot point 2, and the climax.

In addition to the Scene Name story element, list the POV Character, POV Goal, Scene Middle, Scene Climax, and Impact on POV story elements for the five story arc scenes. See Chapter 10: Learn More Plot Story Elements for an explanation of these elements.

Briefly, the scene middle is what happens in the middle of the scene that changes the scene's direction.

The scene climax is the event that is the climax of the scene, not the story.

AFTER-DRAFT OUTLINE

By listing the scene name, POV character, POV goal, scene middle, scene climax, and impact on POV character, you'll have created an after-draft outline that is essential to the success of a story edit.

After-Draft Outline

You've created an after-draft outline, and depending on the point you're at with your draft, you'll do one of the following:

1. Test the structure against the story arc and know you have a story.

2. Use the story arc to build the structure.

This after-draft outline is going to lead you right to a skeleton synopsis.

After you've created an after-draft outline:

Let's assume there is a story. To write a skeleton synopsis at this stage, the following story elements for each Fictionary Story Arc scene will help you set it up.

1. Scene Name

2. POV Character

3. POV Goal

4. Scene Middle

5. Scene Climax

6. Impact on POV Character

And you'll need the story arc.

Now there are four clear steps to getting that skeleton synopsis done:

1. Reference the skeleton blurb.

2. Find the five Fictionary Story Arc scenes on the story arc.

3. List scene name, scene middle, scene climax and impact on POV character for each of these scenes.

4. Summarize the ending showing the story's resolution.

Write a Skeleton Synopsis

As with the blurb, you're writing the synopsis for you, the creative story editor. No one else gets to read it unless you want to share it. The prose doesn't have to be perfect. This is your first pass at the synopsis. You'll update it after you perform a scene-by-scene edit.

The synopsis will help you determine if there is a story or not. You'll find that if you can't write the synopsis at this stage, then most likely the story is not finished. The attempt at writing a synopsis will highlight which portions of the story still need to be written.

Paragraph Breakdown of a Skeleton Synopsis

PARAGRAPH 1: SETUP

Insert the skeleton blurb here. It shows that the protagonist must do something to achieve the story goal or there will be consequences.

PARAGRAPH 2: INCITING INCIDENT

Write out the scene name, POV character, POV goal, scene middle, scene climax, and impact on POV character for the inciting incident.

PARAGRAPH 3: PLOT POINT 1

Write out the scene name, POV character, POV goal, scene middle, scene climax, and impact on POV character for plot point 1.

PARAGRAPH 4: MIDDLE PLOT POINT

Write out the scene name, POV character, POV goal, scene middle, scene climax, and impact on POV character for the middle plot point.

PARAGRAPH 5: PLOT POINT 2

Write out the scene name, POV character, POV goal, scene middle, scene climax, and impact on POV character for plot point 2.

PARAGRAPH 6: CLIMAX

Write out the scene name, POV character, POV goal, scene middle, scene climax, and impact on POV character for the climax.

PARAGRAPH 7: RESOLUTION

Show how the end of the story mirrors the ordinary world at the beginning of the story.

IS THERE A STORY?

The synopsis you just wrote will help you answer this question.

If the answer to this question is yes, you're ready for scene-by-scene editing.

But how do you know if the answer is yes or no?

Look at each paragraph. Does each paragraph fulfill the duties of each story arc key scene as defined in Chapter 5: Meet the Story Arc?

If you're not sure, reread each of the story arc scenes and add more detail to the synopsis. Do this until you know a story exists.

Where to Next?

Let's look at the working synopsis for Evolution, as this is the novel, we'll use to share editors' advice throughout this book.

Working Synopsis Example

Let's look at Evolution. This is for the pre-edited version. We have a skeleton blurb, the draft includes all five Fictionary Story Arc scenes, and there is a written resolution.

First, we've listed the five Fictionary Story Arc scenes with three story elements: the Scene Name, POV Character, POV Goal, Scene Middle, Scene Climax, and Impact on POV Character. You'll notice these are very short points that highlight the story element but don't go into too much detail. We're building a skeleton synopsis to show if we have a story.

EVOLUTION WORKING SYNOPSIS

INCITING INCIDENT

Scene Name: Saving Daisy

POV Character: Jaz Cooper

POV Goal: Commit suicide.

Scene Middle: Daisy through the ice. Daisy scratches Jaz.

Scene Climax: Daisy is rescued, and she rescues Jaz in return.

Impact POV Character: Decides she wants to live.

+

PLOT POINT 1

Scene Name: Nick was murdered.

POV Character: Jaz Cooper

POV Goal: Reconnect with high school friend, Alyssa.

Scene Middle: Alyssa leaves and Jaz crawling

into bed with three big dogs.

Scene Climax: Jaz sees Poppy's nightmare in a vision.

Impact on POV Character: Terrified Nick was murdered.

+

MIDDLE PLOT POINT

Scene Name: Dinner with Tom.

POV Character: Jaz Cooper

POV Goal: Not feel guilty about dinner with another man.

Scene Middle: Tells Tom Alyssa's dog was in car that chased Nick off the road.

Scene Climax: Jaz reveals she's pregnant but not her secret ability.

Impact on POV Character: Emotionally drained from revealing secret.

+

PLOT POINT 2

Scene Name: Transhumance revelation

POV Character: Jaz Cooper

POV Goal: Find out what Nick was researching.

Scene Middle: Nick believed he changed his gene structure and should never have children.

Scene Climax: Jaz hides Nick's journal and keeps her secret.

Impact on POV Character: Terrified her unborn child is in danger.

+

CLIMAX

Scene Name: Alyssa attacks Jaz.

> **POV Character: Jaz Cooper**
>
> **POV Goal: Confirm Alyssa killed Nick.**
>
> **Scene Middle: Alyssa reveals she killed Nick by accident.**
>
> **Scene Climax: Physical battle that Jaz wins.**
>
> **Impact on POV Character: Regret.**
>
> **Then we add a final paragraph with the resolution. Jaz's baby is born and has the same abilities as Jaz. Jaz overcomes her fear of crowds but has the secret of her baby's abilities to hide.**

This means we used the skeleton blurb to start the synopsis and give an overview for the first paragraph. Then we added a paragraph for each of the five Fictionary Story Arc scenes, and we ended with a resolution that addresses the plot.

The Working Synopsis for Evolution

You'll notice below a working synopsis contains the key information needed in a final synopsis. It's written in sentence form but not polished. The skeleton expands on the story elements listed above. It's enough to know a story exists, so we can edit using it. It's not enough to use to share with anyone but the editor. Not yet.

Setup (from the skeleton blurb): After her husband and dog die, Jaz Cooper, a woman with a debilitating fear of crowds, discovers she has a special connection with dogs. If she touches one, she can see into their minds. She uses this talent as an excuse to draw further away from human interaction. Her estranged friend, Alyssa, reconnects and inserts herself in Jaz's life.

Inciting Incident: Jaz doesn't want to live without Nick. During a winter storm, Jaz rescues Daisy, a Great Dane, from drowning. While Jaz is pulling Daisy from the ice, Jaz gets cut, and Daisy licks her wound. Jaz decides she wants to live but doesn't know Daisy infected her and she can now see into the mind of a dog.

Plot Point 1: Jaz crawls into bed with Alyssa's dog. By seeing the dog's dream, she witnesses Nick's murder but not who killed him. Nick's research and her ability to see into a dog's mind are related. She must find out who killed him or never learn the truth about her abilities.

Middle Plot Point: Jaz shares the dog's nightmare with Tom and that she's pregnant with Nick's child. This is a big step in trusting another. She'll work with Tom to figure out who murdered Nick.

Plot Point 2: Jaz discovers Nick didn't want children because his genes had been altered from a dog bite. She's terrified her unborn baby is infected. She also discovers Alyssa's husband had a child with Nick's colleague.

Climax: Jaz discovers Alyssa killed Nick by accident because Nick had information about her husband's child. Alyssa attacks Jaz, and Jaz wins.

Resolution: Jaz's baby is born and has the same abilities as Jaz. Jaz overcomes her fear of crowds but has the secret of her baby's abilities to hide.

This is a very loose synopsis, but it gives us a way to focus on the overall story.

Now we'll be able to see where the rest of the scenes fit and whether they are related to the overall story.

Suggestions from an Editor

Let's check out what the editors of Evolution had to say.

One of the thirteen editors made the following comment about the story arc:

I have started with the story arc. After all, if there is an issue here, then it needs to be sorted out. It is the ultimate macro edit.

Let's do a quick review of what should happen in each key scene of the story arc.

The story arc is the structure of your story and the timing of the events in that story. The simplest form of the story arc includes the inciting incident, plot point one, the middle event, plot point two, the climax, and the resolution.

To create a story readers love, the events must occur in a timely and sensible manner.

The story arc will help you see the structure of your manuscript and decide on the best placement of the plot events. If they are not in the right place, readers can feel they are holding their breath for plot points that are too far apart, or they feel that the story is rushed if they are too close together.

That was the opening. The editor explained four of the five Fictionary Story Arc scenes were in place in the novel. The scene with the problem was plot point one. Here is what the editor said.

Plot point one is the point of no return. The character can't back out of the central conflict. The character's desire to engage with it overrules all else. This marks the end of act I.

Plot point one should be around the 25 percent mark in the story.

Plot point one is quite late in the story. I marked scene 37: Nick was murdered as plot point 1. It occurs at circa 41 percent. I marked the scene as plot point 1, as this is when Jaz knows that Nick was murdered. In the scene notes of scene 37, there are notes about how to move this scene to make your story structure stronger.

TEA with Kristina

I'm going to keep this in mind as I revise Evolution. Since I work in Fictionary, the story arc for Evolution will redraw as I revise each scene. I'll make revisions after the story edit is complete. I'll use the 38 Fictionary Story Elements to help me determine if the scenes are the best length for the story, whether they can be cut or shortened, and whether they have a purpose. The story arc will update, and I'll know if I'm on the right track.

Note that the story doesn't have to be perfect at this stage. If the story follows the general form, you're good to start scene-by-scene editing. I thought Evolution's story arc was close enough, so I began the next step of the revision journey.

If you're the writer self-editing your own story and you found that a story-level issue exists, then don't start scene-by-scene editing. Fix the story-level issue first. Then move on to scene-by-scene editing.

Fixing a story-level issue may change the structure, and it's best to make sure the story arc still works and that other scenes don't need to be added or deleted. Then you can come to scene-by-scene editing.

For the editor editing someone else's story, write the summary letter, giving the writer actionable advice on how to fix the story-level issue. You'll recommend they do this before revising the story at a scene level.

Where to Next?

The next chapter is the beginning of act 2 of this book. Remember, plot point 1 means the protagonist accepts the story goal, and you're the protagonist here. The next chapter will motivate you, propel you, and give you the editing momentum you need to get you through your edit.

At this moment, you realize you have a story in the draft, and now you want to structurally edit that story to be the best story it can be.

You have just accepted the story goal of performing one of the world's best story edits.

Meet　　Learn　　Action

Chapter Seven:
Learn Scene-by-Scene Editing

"I used to try and edit my novels all in one go, laboring under the misapprehension that tackling all things character, plot, and setting at once was the best way to revise. When I first discovered the power of scene-by-scene editing (tackling one scene at a time in sequential fashion) I knew I was wrong. Editing scene-by-scene ensures you tackle both macro and micro story issues, and helps you produce a first-rate novel." —Shane Millar, Fictionary Certified StoryCoach Editor

Scenes in a Story

When you edit a draft at the scene level, you're evaluating each scene and making sure it has all the elements of a great scene. This book shows you how to edit best by combining the 38 Fictionary Story Elements. You don't need every one of the story elements in every scene, but you do need enough of them working together to keep the reader engaged.

What Is a Scene?

A scene is a part of your novel in which characters engage in action.

A scene is a mini story with a beginning, a middle, and an end.

A scene is a moment in the character's life in which something happens that matters. Something related to the story goal. Or something that creates consequences for the protagonist and the POV character.

Scenes are a big deal. They are the bricks that build up the story edifice.

The simplest structure of a scene is:

- A scene starts with a hook
- A POV character has a scene goal
- A scene has a middle
- A scene has a climax
- A scene ends with a hook

If a scene is missing any one of these parts, then look at the scene to see if it works. If a scene has these five parts, then it has the potential to be a strong scene.

These units of story need to be individually strong. They need to be vivid. And every scene must impact the protagonist, whether the protagonist is in the scene or not. We'll get to this last one later.

Scene-by-Scene Editing

Word choice, style, and grammar are all important, but if the story isn't strong, it doesn't matter if it's copyedited and proofread to perfection. Excellent prose alone won't sell books. A powerful story will.

And a powerful story is made up of powerful scenes. This book will show you that power comes from the story elements working together, and we'll give you actionable advice to achieve that power.

You are the artist. You are unique. Only you can bring your story to life. What we're talking about is form and not formula. You'll use scene-by-scene editing as a technique similar to the way a painter mixes paints to get a desired effect. Some blue mixed with some red creates magenta. That's the craft. How the painter uses the color, that is the art.

Stories follow a structure: that's the craft.

How a creative story editor uses the 38 Fictionary Story Elements within scenes, organizes the scenes within chapters, and creates a strong story arc, that's the art.

You will know there is a new scene in the draft when one or more of the following happens:

- A change in POV
- A change in time
- A change in location
- A scene break character
- A chapter break

We are strong believers in using scene break characters between scenes. These are symbols like *** or ~.

In fact, Fictionary was designed to require scene break characters, because that's the first step in the formatting process that helps a writer create a stronger story.

With today's technology, a writer cannot know where a page break will occur. Scenes separated by a blank line can cause problems. What if a scene ends at the bottom of a page on an e-reader, the reader clicks or swipes to the next page, and a new scene starts? They haven't been given a visual clue that a new scene is starting, and they might get jarred from the story. This would present another opportunity to put the book down.

Getting a Scene to Work

A scene won't work unless the story elements are working together. There can't be Character story elements without Plot story elements. There can't be Plot elements without Setting elements. There can't be Setting elements without Character elements.

Pretend we have a scene with a great battle, but the POV character for the scene has no goal. Will anyone care about the battle? The character must want something, and there must be consequences if they don't get it. Remember, the skeleton blurb will help you when editing this.

Story elements connect scenes over the length of the story, helping the story flow from one scene to the next, from one chapter to the next, from one act to the next, until the ending mirrors the beginning, and the reader is satisfied.

Scene placement

No matter what genre a story is written for, all stories have a beginning, a middle, and an end. The beginning includes everything from the first word to the beginning of plot point 1, including a prologue, if there is one. This makes up act 1.

The middle includes everything from plot point 1 to plot point 2. This makes up act 2.

And the end is everything from the start of plot point 2 to the final word, including the resolution.

Scenes fit into one of the three buckets (act 1, act 2, and act 3): the beginning, the middle, and the end.

Risk Assessment

Creative story editing means you edit the overall manuscript structure first, then edit each scene within the structure based on character, plot, and setting, and finally edit the overall structure again.

When you are in the middle of a creative story edit, things can feel messy. It might feel as though plot points and plot holes are monsters looming over you. But they aren't if you focus on this method.

A creative story editor looks for areas at risk—in particular, the risk that the reader will put down the book.

The first scene that isn't structured well is the first time a reader might put the book down.

The end of every scene and the start of the next are places the reader might stop reading. Hence, these are places at risk.

But how do you make each scene great? You work your way through the 38 Fictionary Story Elements.

Before we get to scene-by-scene editing using the 38 Fictionary Story Elements, we are going to look at the story-level risks.

Creative Story-Editing Efficiency

By working through the process in this book, you'll avoid revising scenes that you might end up deleting.

When you are at the scene-by-scene editing stage, the overall structure is sound. You know this because you've already named every scene, made sure the five key plot points exist, ensured they are generally in the right place, and are performing the five duties of a story arc scene.

With that done, it's time to focus on the scenes. You will come back to the structure again after the scene-by-scene edit is complete.

If you're the writer, you'll make your scene revisions after the scene-by-scene edit. Then you'll check the structure. You'll never know whether the revisions altered the structure in a good or bad way unless you check. Luckily, that's easy with the Fictionary Story Arc. It redraws while you revise the story.

If you're the editor, you'll edit on a scene-by-scene basis, make your suggestions, and conduct a final review of the structure before sending the edit to your client.

When you edit on a scene-by-scene basis, you must always keep the skeleton blurb in mind, or the story could end up being a group of scenes following one after the other without any focus. A risky strategy. The blurb helps you stay true to the story's intent. What you don't want to create is an episodic story (this means having scenes that aren't related in some way to a story that builds as the reader progresses).

Then, when you have finished each of the scene-by-scene edits, you go back to the overall story structure and look at it again.

This way of editing also helps with the scene flow. When you look at each scene, there will be elements you can look at that stop the story being episodic.

Where to Next?

You know what a scene is. We've taught you how to write a skeleton blurb and a skeleton synopsis. This means you now have the tools and knowledge to start a scene-by-scene story edit.

The story goal is what propels the protagonist through the story. To help you connect the scenes to the story goal, we'll look at the supergroups of story elements: Character, Plot, and Setting.

Meet Learn Action

Chapter Eight:
Learn the Supergroups

"Analyzing character, plot, and setting as you self-edit can be a daunting task. Having a clear path forward makes it so much easier." —Sherry Leclerc, Fictionary Certified StoryCoach Editor

Where Did Fictionary Come From?

TEA with Kristina

When Lucy asked me, "Kristina, how did you manage to find the clarity in the complexity of creative story editing?" I was flattered. And then I started thinking about the years it took me to create and finalize the list of story elements and then organize them into supergroups.

I read hundreds of books, took courses, talked

> with writers and editors around the world, and worked with mentors, which all led to creating the Fictionary supergroups of story elements.

Each group has a heavy responsibility...

When a story remains in your mind long after you read or saw the story, what do you remember?

Most likely it's a compelling character, an intriguing plot, or a fantastic setting.

And there we have the three supergroups.

- Character
- Plot
- Setting

Without characters, there is no story.

Without a plot, there is no story.

Without a setting, there is no story.

And we all really, really want a great story to emerge from the draft, so we need characters, plot, and settings.

The three supergroups must all work together.

One group may have a stronger presence in a story than another, and that's okay, as long as story elements from each group exist and the elements are interwoven throughout each scene.

With the structure for the groups, we researched the story elements that belonged in each group. That meant narrowing down the elements to the ones that would provide the most help to a creative story editor.

Each story element had to be designed in a way that gave the editor actionable advice. Theory is great, but how does it help an editor make a story better if the theory is abstract and hard to take action on?

On top of that, the three supergroups and the 38 Fictionary Story Elements had to work with the Fictionary Story Arc. And that led us to performing story edits by first looking at the structure, then the scene, and then the structure again.

When you have a handle on the three supergroups, you can choose to do two types of edits.

How Deep a Story Edit?

> **How deeply are you going to edit? Because that makes all the difference.**

You might be at the start of your journey, or you might be far into that journey. Either way, this book will be here for you every step of the way. We don't want you to be asking yourself whether you can manage an edit. That is a yes-or-no question. We want you to answer how deeply you will edit.

As we want everyone to edit well.

> **How to Edit Using the Fictionary Story Elements**
>
> **In the next chapter, we discuss each of the 38 Fictionary Story Elements. And when you go through the book, you can choose to edit each scene with all the Fictionary Story Elements, or you can edit using one Fictionary Story Element at a time, read each scene, and edit the Fictionary Story Element in each consecutive scene.**
>
> **Many editors choose to be somewhere in between. They choose to pick a handful of similar Fictionary Story Elements and read the draft about eight times.**
>
> **Our best advice is to edit the way that feels best for you.**

Does it matter how you use the 38 Fictionary Story Elements?
No. It matters that you are performing a robust creative story edit.

A Creative Story Edit Is an Investment

With creative story editing, you're working on an investment. The draft is getting the best investment around. The 38 Fictionary Story Elements are the biggest editing investment you can give to the draft. Your editing time, your editing artistry means you are making the story stronger.

And the editing investment will pay off.

A Creative Story Editor's Actionable Revision Plan

A revision note is a note the editor keeps for themselves or for their client when they are creating a revision plan. This can be actionable advice at the story element level, the scene level, or the manuscript level.

The revision plan starts at the story level, moves to the scenes level, and ends back at the story level. This includes the story element evaluation, notes per scene, and, if you're using Fictionary to edit, the Fictionary Visual Insights. We'll cover the insights in Chapter 13: Action Visual Insights.

The writer will use the revision plan to revise their story. That is the gift the editor gives to the writer.

Where to Next?

You'll recall every story has a beginning, a middle, and an end. Every story should include the five Fictionary Story Arc scenes. These are the inciting incident, plot point 1, the middle, plot point 2, and the climax. The manuscript you're editing is made up of these scenes, plus all the connecting scenes. We're about to embark on a journey to make sure every scene belongs in the story, is strong, and flows from one to the next to create a great story.

Keep reading and you'll get a deeper look into the story elements that belong in each supergroup. We'll give you a process to use each one!

A Creative Story Editor Needs Tools

How does a creative story editor edit a story to ensure reader engagement? There is an avalanche of information on how to edit and trying to stand up against all the story theories is tough going, no matter if you're new to editing or are a seasoned professional. It's tough going when you don't have a process that is robust.

Many books and courses give you the theory, and that's great, but you might find it daunting to try to remember everything. You might be repeating under your breath, "How do I remember it all? How do I remember it all?" Over and over again.

Every editor needs a process, that helps them remember and apply everything they've learned about story editing.

The 38 Fictionary Story Elements
A creative story editor edits the major components of the story. We call these components the 38 Fictionary Story Elements. These Fictionary Story Elements show you whether you've created and linked great scenes.

And the snowball effect of editing scene after scene is that the more great scenes add up, the greater the story will be.

Imagine how hard it is to perform a story edit without a process and a tool. There are 38 story elements that should be considered for each scene. Let's say an eighty-five-thousand-word novel has sixty-five scenes. That means there are 2,470 story elements to edit. So, we're back to how do you remember it all and how do you use the knowledge efficiently?

We'll give you the knowledge AND a process so you feel comfortable knowing where you are in your editing journey. We love the process. Editing each scene against the 38 Fictionary Story Elements will transform the draft, scene by scene, into the finished novel.

The Fictionary story-editing method results in actionable advice and is an actionable way to edit.

WHAT IS A STORY ELEMENT?

A story element is an essential section in each scene in a story. Atoms join to make molecules, just as scenes join to make stories. Atoms are made of sub-atomic particles, and scenes are made up of sub-scenic sections. These are the story elements.

But not all atoms are the same. In school, we learned atoms are made up of protons, neutrons, and electrons. But wait! Doesn't that sound like three supergroups?

An atom is unique because it is made up of a different number of protons, neutrons, and electrons—just as every story and scene is unique because it is made up of different combinations of the 38 Fictionary Story Elements within the three supergroups: Character, Plot, and Setting.

Once you see how intuitive the 38 Fictionary Story Elements are, you will be singing their praises. Their story power comes from interweaving the elements.

If a story element is missing throughout the entire story, the reader will feel there is something lacking. Imagine a story without any objects. Just as the story elements' story power comes from the buildup and interweaving of story elements, scene after scene, missing story elements weaken the story's power. That weakening accumulates, too, with every missing element throughout the whole story.

And we don't want that.

WHY THIRTY-EIGHT?

What every reader gets from a story will be different. What every creative story editor asks of a draft manuscript will be the same: the same 38 Fictionary Story Elements, in each and every scene.

TEA with Kristina

I organized the editing process into thirty-eight story elements using over ten years of research. I interviewed many writers, publishers, editors, and agents. I brought together the information I gathered into the most important story elements that are going to help you.

The interpretation of these 38 Fictionary Story Elements is where the artistry comes in.

Artistry with action. Artistry in motion.

A creative story editor should finish their edit with actionable advice for themselves and/or for the author.

The 38 Fictionary Story Elements

The 38 Fictionary Story Elements are sorted into three supergroups:

- Plot
- Character
- Setting

The Character, Plot, and Setting story elements must be in balance or the story won't work.

The knowledge of a great story plus the balance and use of the story elements, the ways they support and build on each other, and the ways they relate to the story arc will help you create a great story.

This method allows you to improve a story quickly without wasting unnecessary time.

When the legs of a stool are the same length, the stool is balanced and strong.

When one leg is shorter than the others, the stool is unbalanced and falls flat.

When one leg is longer than the others, the stool is unbalanced and falls flat.

Using the story elements in an unbalanced way causes the story to fall flat.

And the fourth part of the stool, the seat, is the overall structure of your story, which, of course, is important to story editing.

Imagine a stool without a seat. Ouch!

Where to Next?

The three supergroups await!

The 38 Fictionary Story Elements are all interrelated. When you work on one, you'll often find it influences another. The story elements are checkpoints. We'll show you how to edit a story against each element and how to combine the elements so you become one of the world's best editors.

Without a plot, there is no story.

Without characters, there is no story.

Without setting, there is no story.

Let's start with the Fictionary Plot Story Elements first. Then we'll look at the Fictionary Character story elements, and finally the Fictionary Setting story elements.

Meet   **Learn**   Action

Chapter Nine:
Learn the Plot Story Elements

"**A good entry hook is absolutely magic for ensuring readers keep turning the pages.**" —**James Gallagher, Fictionary Certified StoryCoach Editor**

Plot First

We will look at the Plot elements first.

Why?

Remember, no one part of the 38 Fictionary Story Elements is more important than the others; rather, if you follow a route, then each element that you edit will inform the next element.

Plot is a good place to start as it answers what happens in the story.

Let's Get Plotting

The plot is what happens in a story. It's part of what keeps the reader turning the pages. It's also probably what the reader found intriguing in the blurb. Remember that promise? We're going to help the story keep that promise.

The structure of the plot frames the story.

MEET THE FICTIONARY PLOT STORY ELEMENTS

The Fictionary Plot Story Elements are there to ensure the plot flows and contains no plot holes. The plot story elements ensure the plot is tight and not confusing. These Fictionary Plot Story Elements sweep the reader into the story world and keep them in the midst of the story.

Some of the Plot elements are used at the story level, and some are used at the scene level. The plot's meaning builds up scene after scene.

THE FICTIONARY PLOT STORY ELEMENTS:

- Scene Name
- Story Arc
- Purpose
- Opening Type
- Closing Type
- Anchored
- Entry Hook
- Exit Hook
- Tension
- Conflict
- Revelation
- Backstory
- Flashback
- Scene Middle
- Scene Climax
- Action/Sequel
- Reader Knowledge Gained

Structural Plotting Suggestions

After you've answered the story test question—Does the manuscript have a story? —with a yes, you'll be able to edit the plot structure of the story by asking key questions.

The Fictionary Story Elements will show you what questions to ask.

We're going to talk about structural editing later. For now, here are questions about structure to illustrate what we're aiming for when we start scene-by-scene editing.

- Are the story arc plot point scenes written with higher word counts than the scenes near them?

  Hint: they should be.

- Are there flashbacks or backstory in act 3?

  Hint: there shouldn't be.

- Are there scene entry and exit hooks in every scene?

  Hint: there should be.

- Are there too many repetitions of scene opening or closing types?

  Hint: there shouldn't be.

The Fictionary Visual Insights will make it easy to answer these questions and give specific, actionable advice to the writer—even if the writer is you.

Once you get into the swing of editing, the story elements will become second nature to you as you edit. And you will start to see patterns in a draft. That's part of the editing process, seeing the plot's patterns and asking, "Is this the strongest the plot can be?"

Where to Next?

It may seem like a lot of elements to remember already, but we're giving you a process to connect the elements and make it easier to apply them to any edit.

Let's work through the plot story elements starting with the scene name.

Fictionary Story Element: Scene Name

Naming each scene is the first step in a story edit. If you can't name a scene, then you don't know what the scene is about. And if you don't know what a scene is about, you can't edit it. That is why we're starting with the scene name as the first element to apply to the story.

Naming each scene first helps you in many ways. The Scene Name story element helps determine the purpose of the scene and guides you to find scenes that need work.

To name scenes on the first read-through, the editor references the blurb, so they can link the scene name to the story's intent. The bonus is that naming all the scenes creates an after-draft outline. When you create an after-draft outline by naming scenes, your edit will take less time, because you're organized and have a list that acts as the story outline.

At this stage, you have the skeleton blurb and the skeleton synopsis to work with.

You'll recall the three questions a skeleton blurb must answer:

1.   Who is the protagonist?

2.   What is the story goal?

3.   What is at stake?

And then you created the skeleton synopsis:

Working Synopsis = Skeleton Blurb + 5 Story Arc Scenes + Resolution

Now you're adding an after-draft outline to your editing box of tools.

It's almost impossible to edit a story without a list of scene names.

Naming a scene does not mean you're adding a title to every scene. A scene name is an editing tool for your reference while editing.

Definition

A scene name represents the main theme or action in the scene.

Scene and Story Level

Naming the scene happens at the scene level. For editing insight, it is used both during scene-level and story-level editing.

At the scene level, you are looking to see how easy it is to name each scene. If it is not simple, the troubleshooting section below will help you figure out why.

At the story-level review, the scene names show the patterns in the content of the scenes. If a scene needs to be moved to make the themes work within chapters, or to have the meaning build up in an order that adds tension, make a revision note. Make a note, keep naming scenes.

Perfecting the Scene Name Story Element

Your fun editing task is to read each scene in the story and name them.

There is a three-word-or-fewer rule to naming a scene. If you can name the scene in three or fewer words, brilliant. Try to name the scene by what is shown in the scene. Not what you think it shows. Not what you would like it to show. But what is actually there in the scene.

When you can't name a scene, or if you can't name the scene without using too many words, then you will need to look at the scene structure. It could mean the scene lacks focus. Or it could mean the scene needs to be split into two scenes. Or it could be that the scene should be cut from the story.

Naming the scenes is closely linked to the purpose of a scene. If you can't name a scene, it might be hard to find its purpose. And this is a problem. If too many scenes in a row don't have a purpose, then this will show up in the naming of the scene. We'll cover the purpose of a scene soon.

Naming scenes also helps organize chapters, because the main theme is mentioned in the scenes. Chapter 13: Action Visual Insights, covers scenes per chapter.

Troubleshooting

If you have trouble naming the scene, it is time to look at the scene in depth.

Does the scene have the following?

1. A clear POV character

2. A clear POV character goal

3. A middle

4. A climax

Remember

> **MARCS: the answers to these questions help the editor recommend how to Move, Add, Revise, Cut, or Split a scene.**

All this from naming a scene! We said the 38 Fictionary Story Elements were powerful. It is not just understanding what each one is but also the action a Fictionary Story Editor will take. If you recommend splitting the scene into two, this can be the first place you justify the advice; then you can also use other Fictionary Story Elements to back up the recommendation.

The scene name may resonate with the writer, or the scene name may be a surprise. If the name is a surprise, this alone tells the writer whether what they thought they were showing the reader is actually what they showed.

Suggestions from the Editors

When an editor names a scene, they give the writer the gift of an outline. For an editor to name a scene in three words or fewer, they have to understand what the scene is mainly about.

In Evolution, one editor named a scene "Katie Pregnant," but she's not. This is a big clue the wrong meaning came out in the scene. It showed that the scene needed work.

TEA with Kristina

When you get to the naming section, if you cannot name the scene, then there will be a too-many/too-much issue. Either there are too many themes going on in the scene or there is too much action going on in the scene.

When editing using the 38 Fictionary Story Elements, you gain confidence that you know what you are looking for in every scene. If you can't name a scene, then you know this is a red flag and there is an issue in the draft. When you know where an issue is, you can edit a draft and

> create actionable advice. As you're editing, the troubleshooting section for the relevant Fictionary Story Element will show what the draft needs.

Where to Next?

We are going to explore Fictionary Story Arc plot points. These are the inciting incident, plot point 1, middle plot point, plot point 2, and the climax. When naming the scenes, it's a good idea to mark the scenes that are one of the five story arc scenes.

Without the five Fictionary Story Arc scenes, there isn't a story yet. A story must contain an inciting incident, plot point 1, the middle plot point, plot point 2, and the climax.

If you accepted the fun editing task, the great news is the scenes are named. If not, we recommend stopping the edit now and naming the scenes. You are building the foundation of the edit.

Fictionary Story Element: Story Arc

You can't confirm the five Fictionary plot point scenes without reading the story. And if the story doesn't contain the five plot point scenes, there isn't a story.

Luckily, you read the story as you named each scene, and you probably have a good idea if these scenes exist.

Understanding the five Fictionary plot points of the Fictionary Story Arc is imperative to know how to edit the highest level of a story.

Review Chapter 5: Meet the Story Arc if you need a refresher on the five story arc scenes.

The Fictionary Story Arc scenes are the first place to start when determining whether the draft contains a story.

If the five Fictionary Story Arc scenes are not present, then there is no story yet.

Let's repeat that, as it's one of the most important things you'll learn in this book.

> **If the five Fictionary Story Arc scenes do not exist, there is no story yet.**

If you're the writer performing a self-edit, this means there is more work to do on the draft before scene-by-scene edits should start.

If you're an editor working on a client's manuscript, start writing the summary letter, beginning with an overview of the story's structure.

Definition

The Fictionary Story Arc is a set of five specific scenes that must be present in a draft to show there is a story:

- Inciting incident
- Plot point 1
- Middle plot point
- Plot point 2
- Climax

These scenes all have story duties that we will look at below. Just as a reminder, the duties are to:

1. Contain new information

2. Change the story's direction

3. Raise the stakes

4. Be full of tension

5. Be written in the protagonist's POV

Scene and Story Level

At the story level, make sure all five scenes exist and are in the right place. This is the starting point for knowing if a story exists.

At the scene level, make sure the scenes accomplish what they must for a story arc scene. We will cover this in the upcoming section, "Fictionary Story Element: Purpose."

If the scenes exist, are in the right place, and accomplish what they should, you have proof a story exists.

Perfecting the Story Arc Story Element

The editing task is to find the five Fictionary plot point scenes and ensure they are located in the best place in the story and that they are doing everything they must do.

Before completing a scene-by-scene story edit for all the Fictionary Story Elements, it's important to check that the story arc scenes exist and appear in the right place.

The skeleton blurb helps find the story arc scenes, as these scenes must all have the protagonist in them and relate to the story goal in a specific way.

REMEMBER THAT THE FOLLOWING ARE THE FIVE STORY ARC SCENES:

1. Inciting incident: the story goal is revealed to the protagonist.

2. Plot point 1: the protagonist accepts the story goal.

3. Middle plot point: the protagonist goes from reactive to proactive in addressing the story goal.

4. Plot point 2: the protagonist fails to answer the story goal and must change mentally.

5. Climax: the protagonist answers the story goal that was asked in the inciting incident (this scene should have the most emotion).

When you've found one of these scenes, make sure that it fulfills the criteria listed in the five duties.

The Fictionary Story Arc scenes should be written as dramatic scenes, not as backstory or a narrative summary, and they therefore let the reader experience the event alongside the protagonist.

The protagonist must be in each of the story arc scenes; even better, the protagonist should be the POV character driving each of these scenes.

Use the blurb when looking for your Fictionary Story Arc scenes, and if the protagonist relates to the story goal in that way, then you have found it! If you cannot find them, then the writer needs to know this, too.

The story arc is reviewed at the start of an edit and at the end of the edit or revisions.

If you're the writer, after you've edited and revised the story against all the 38 Fictionary Story Elements, it's important to recheck this story arc and ensure the scenes are in the best place.

Troubleshooting

If one of the story arc scenes is not in the draft, the story needs to be revised.

If one of the story arc scenes is not in the right place, the story needs to be revised.

If one of the story arc scenes does not fulfill its duties, the story needs to be revised.

When you look at the Story Arc insight, you can see the perfect placement and the ranges these scenes need to be in. Now look at your story arc. If two plot points are too far apart, then the story can drag.

When you look at the Story Arc insight and two plot points are too close together, then the story can feel rushed. See Chapter 13: Action Visual Insights, to learn how to read insights.

Suggestions from an Editor

In scene 2 of Evolution, one editor made the following comment regarding the inciting incident. Although the overall note is encouraging, it doesn't help the writer take action.

EDITOR 1:

This is an excellent inciting incident. We understand Jaz's depression, the depth of her pain at losing both her husband and her dog. Having the neighbor's dog be in peril is intriguing and I'm interested to see where it goes.

TEA with Kristina

The editor provided no actionable advice. In addition, the writer may not know what an inciting incident is.

To make the note more helpful, the editor could

have explained what an inciting incident is. If the following were added, the writer would have the opportunity to learn from the editor.

The inciting incident is the moment the protagonist's world changes in a dramatic way, giving them a goal or motive they simply can't ignore.

Write your inciting incident as a dramatic scene, not as backstory or narrative summary, and let the reader experience the event alongside the protagonist. This will increase your chances of getting the reader emotionally involved.

If you don't have an inciting incident in the first fifteen percent of your novel, you need a strong reason for delaying it. Readers expect something to trigger the protagonist to act.

As the writer revises the story, they'll also know to keep this in mind in case they decide to move the scene to later in the story or add other scenes before this one.

Where to Next?

Here you get to choose what element to work on next. Naming the scene and knowing you have a basic story arc means you know you have a story. Now it's time to make the story great.

The story elements are ordered in the way they appear inside Fictionary. We'll give you recommendations on the order to process them, but you need to take the path that works for you and the story you are editing. Always remember you are the artist. And story editing is an art form.

In this book, the story element Purpose comes next. This is a great place to go next, simply because the purpose tells you if the scene should be in the story or not. There's no sense in editing a scene further if it should be cut from the story.

Fictionary Story Element: Purpose

Some craft book writers recommend finding the purpose of a scene before the scene is written. We're looking at the purpose of a scene after the scene is written and making sure all the story elements support the purpose.

With each new scene, the reader either trusts the author more or trusts them less. If there isn't a purpose of a scene and a reason the scene exists in the story, the reader loses trust in the writer, and you know what that means. They start losing interest in the story.

The purpose of a scene is not a long description of what the scene accomplished.

Definition

The purpose of a scene is the main reason the scene exists in the story, and it must be related to the story goal stated in the blurb.

There are many reasons a scene deserves to be in a story, and some of these are below.

Whatever the purpose, every scene must either bring the protagonist closer to reaching the story goal or further away. You'll know by now to have the skeleton blurb handy, so it's a continual reminder of what the story goal is.

The placement of the scene in the story also influences the purpose of the scene.

In the beginning (act 1): these scenes are introductory scenes. They are enticing scenes that show the protagonist in their ordinary world (including their main flaw) and draw the reader into the story using action that creates conflict and tension.

Purposes such as character introduction and establishment of setting will be used more often in act 1 than in act 2 or act 3.

In the middle (act 2): the protagonist should be changing from reactive to proactive, the obstacles put in their way should be bigger and more difficult to overcome, and their main flaw is definitely causing problems.

In act 3 (starting at plot point 2): the protagonist is at a low point where everything looks bleak, but they must move forward. The scenes need to honor their position in the story.

Purposes such as building suspense and intensifying conflict will really come into play in act 3. What shouldn't be in act 3 is the introduction of characters or backstory that could have come earlier.

Scene and Story Level

At the scene level, the Purpose story element is used on a scene-by-scene basis for every scene in a novel.

When evaluating each scene, list the purpose of the scene.

If the purpose is not clear, we recommend editing the scene using the story elements: Scene Name, POV Goal, What if Goal Fails, Scene Middle, and Scene Climax. This will help you determine if there is a purpose. If you still can't find one, mark the scene stating you don't know, and come back after this pass at editing the entire story. This will help you decide if the scene should be cut from the story or revised.

> **In Fictionary, the drop-down menu beside Purpose gives you the option of selecting "Don't know yet." Use this if you want to check scenes for a purpose and then come back to edit the scene you're working on.**

At the story level, when you've listed every scene's purpose, it's time to evaluate the purpose against the novel structure.

Perfecting the Purpose Story Element

Your editing task is to list the purpose of each scene—and we feel like a drum roll should be sounded here—in three words or fewer.

PERFECTING THE PURPOSE OF THE FIVE FICTIONARY STORY ARC SCENES

The definition of the five Fictionary Story Arc scenes is the purpose of those scenes.

HERE'S A RECAP FROM THE STORY ARC SECTION:

- Inciting incident: the protagonist's world changes in a dramatic way and the story goal is revealed.
- Plot point 1: the protagonist can't get out of the central conflict and accepts the story goal.

- Middle plot point: the protagonist moves from reactive to proactive.
- Plot point 2: the protagonist feels failure because they have not changed to answer the story goal.
- Climax: the protagonist answers the main story goal.

For more details on the Fictionary Story Arc, see chapter 5, Meet the Story Arc.

PERFECTING THE PURPOSE OF NON-STORY ARC SCENES

If a scene is not a story arc scene, here are eight ways the purpose of a scene can drive the story forward.

- Build suspense.
- Introduce characters.
- Develop characters.
- Establish mood.
- Establish setting.
- Intensify conflict.
- Move the story forward.
- Show clues or red herrings.

The purpose should inform all other story elements. Identify the purpose of each scene early in your story-editing process. Later you can check that all the other story elements are in line with the purpose of their scene.

Any scene created will have a particular setting, with a set of elements and objects that contribute to it. All these can work toward the purpose of the scene—or detract from it if they're chosen haphazardly.

For example, in Evolution, the main character, Jaz, has just had her dog die, so the purpose of one scene is to show how she feels about the loss. The setting is the hallway where her dog used to sleep. The polished wooden floor looks drab and cold to Jaz. Sunlight streams through the windows in cruel contrast to her misery. She focuses on her dog's empty bed and climbs into it, tears falling down her cheeks.

Everything in the scene contributes to the purpose of showing Jaz's feelings of loss and sadness, establishing the mood, and setting the stage for the story to move forward—perhaps she gets another dog, for example.

Troubleshooting

If a scene in a story does not have a purpose related to the main story goal, it should be cut from the story or revised. A scene without a purpose will distract the reader from the main story: it may even bore the reader. And the reader might put the story down, all because the scene lacked purpose.

Once you know the purpose of each scene, make sure every other story element used in the scene relates to that purpose. Because all the elements use the purpose, it's important to list the purpose for every scene early in a story edit.

Be honest with yourself. If you can't define the purpose of a scene, the scene must be cut or revised. There is no other choice.

Suggestions from an Editor

The following comment refers to a scene in Evolution where the editor didn't know what the purpose of the scene was. The editor first marked the purpose of the scene in Fictionary as "Don't Know Yet." They then went on to say the following:

EDITOR 7:

This is another scene with a bit too much going on, which makes it hard for the reader to follow. There's tea making, and dogs moving around on beds, and self-defense courses, and Tom, and reopening the case, and visiting Alyssa, and renewing their conversation about whether or not Daisy infected Jaz, and Katie's health, and how Jaz can be a better friend. Whew! It's all good info, but it's also hard to follow. Revise it down a bit, or consider splitting it into two scenes and adding more emotion to ramp up the tension.

> **TEA with Kristina**
>
> **What I took away from this comment was that the scene lacks purpose because it's not focused. The editor also gave me advice on how to fix the issue.**
>
> **I liked the editor's voice. You can feel the rush in the sentence that describes everything in the**

scene, and this showed me how accurate the edit was.

The first sentence in the advice ("This is another scene with a bit too much going on, which makes it hard for the reader to follow") tells me there are other scenes lacking a purpose. This might be an overall issue I have to deal with.

After your first draft, you may discover scenes that don't seem to serve any purposes. This happens to me when I get so involved in writing a scene that I forget how it fits into the overall story.

Where to Next?

Now that we've convinced you to make sure every scene has a purpose, we're going to move on to structural level story elements. The next story elements show you how to find patterns in a story. The information you collect when editing a scene will be used to make suggested revisions at the story level.

Let's take a look at the Opening Type and Closing Type Fictionary Story Elements.

Fictionary Story Element: Opening Type

The first sentence of a scene contains an opening type. If it's really good, it contains an entry hook too. It is the sentence that draws the reader into the scene.

You've probably read that the first sentence of a book is important to hook the reader. We're upping that statement. The first sentence of every scene must hook the reader, so they keep reading. We're starting with the opening type and will build on that later with how to anchor and hook the reader.

Definition

The opening type is the method used to create the first sentence of the scene.

There are four scene opening types:

- Action
- Dialogue
- Thought
- Description

Action means the character or characters are in motion.

Dialogue means a character is speaking.

Thought means a character is thinking.

Description is everything else, including narrative.

And the key to a novel that flows is to ensure the following:

- All four types are used throughout the novel.
- All are relevant to the purpose of the scene.
- The balance of the opening types works for the genre.

Let's look at some examples for Evolution that illustrate each type. Jaz is the "I" in the examples. These examples show how closely opening types and entry hooks are related.

ACTION:

I shut the refrigerator door for the fifth time. Food wouldn't solve my problems.

Hook: What problems is the protagonist having?

DIALOGUE:

"How many times have you been out of the house since Nick died?" Katie asked.

Hook: Why is Katie concerned Jaz hasn't left the house?

Let's reorganize the sentence to start with "Katie asked," and see what the impact is.

Katie asked, "How many times have you been out of the house since Nick died?"

The opening type is still dialogue.

Having Katie at the end puts the emphasis on the question. Having Katie at the beginning puts the emphasis on who is asking the question.

THOUGHT:

Nervous, yup, I was nervous about introducing Rose to Daisy.

Hook: Why is Jaz nervous and what's at stake if the dogs don't get along?

DESCRIPTION:

Doctors' offices across the country all looked the same.

Hook: Why is Jaz in a doctor's office?

Note that if a sentence is not action, dialogue, or thought, then it's description.

Scene and Story Level

At the scene level, check if the scene opening types throughout your novel work for the purpose of the scene. If not, suggest a revision.

As an editor, not only are you looking for a balance in the opening types, but you're also looking to see if the opening type fits with the scene's purpose.

The type of scene helps determine the best opening type for the scene. Here are some recommendations an editor can give to a writer:

- Action: if the scene is a high-action scene, start with action. This will keep the pacing fast.
- Dialogue: if two characters are going to have an important discussion, try starting the scene with dialogue.
- Thought: if the scene is a character reacting emotionally to a previous event, try using thought to slow pacing and give the reader a breather.
- Description (includes narrative): if the setting is driving the scene and emotional impact of the scene plays a huge part, then try using description.

Perfecting the Opening Type Story Element

Your editing task is to list the scene opening type for every scene. Then edit them for how many of each type is used and the order in which they are used. Then check they aren't repetitive and that all four types have been used.

Repetition, unless done on purpose, bores a reader. Some repetition is obvious and easy to fix. Other types of repetition hide in a manuscript and need a method to find them. Scene opening types fall into the latter category. It's important to avoid boring the reader by starting each scene in the same way. Bored readers put books down.

With the skeleton blurb, Chapter 3: Meet the Story Promise, in mind—considering the protagonist's story goal and the stakes—you can ask whether the POV character would open a scene by acting/speaking/thinking/describing in the way they did.

When a scene starts with:

Action: make sure the action is relevant to the scene's goal and is a powerful draw into the scene.

Dialogue: check how quickly the reader can tell who else is in the scene. Waiting too long to let the reader know who the character is talking to can be confusing.

Thought: make sure it is appropriate to the scene. If it is a high-tension scene, a thought about the color of the wallpaper is not something the POV character would be thinking.

Description: make sure the scene is described from the POV character's senses.

Troubleshooting

When editing, determine whether any scene opening types are repetitive. Not just one of the four types, but if they start in the same physical place.

ISSUES TO LOOK OUT FOR:

- Dialogue: make sure the dialogue is relevant to the plot, is interesting, and makes the reader want to read on. Also ensure that the people who are talking are quickly identifiable to the reader.

- Thought: if the scene's purpose is not correct for the thought energy, then the reader can get disconnected from the story world.

- Description: if the description is story relevant, does it meander and slow the reader down? Look at why the description is necessary plot-wise, character-wise, and setting-wise. The description must be driving the story forward.

- Action: if the scene is an action scene, then the action might be relevant, but it might not be in a reflective scene.

Suggestions from an Editor

We chose a comment from two of the thirteen editors working on Evolution to illustrate the importance of opening types.

EDITOR 1:

All opening and closing types are used. There could be more use of thought in the opening types, but overall this is fine. And there could be a little more description in the closing types. When revising the story, remember to check all four types are still used.

Remember, when advising revisions, the final draft will need to be rechecked, so there is enough variety with the opening types once all the revisions are done.

EDITOR 2:

For scene 22 the opening sentence is "Nervous..." A direct thought that gets the reader quickly into Jaz's headspace.

Scene Name: Dogs meet
Purpose: Establish mood
Opening Type: Thought
Notice how thought goes well with establishing the mood.

TEA with Kristina

The first editor's advice for this element is spot-on. After the edit, the manuscript will be extensively revised, so it's important to do a quick check and make sure all four opening types are used and balanced.

> The second editor gave a specific example to show that opening the scene with a thought set the mood for the scene. Note how the editor used three of the story elements to discover this. Also note that the editor is showing me something I did well and is teaching me how to edit scenes using multiple story elements after I've done my revisions.
>
> The second comment is from an editor who chose to show me something I was doing well. All great editors share this type of knowledge.

Where to Next?

So far, you've named each scene and understand that a scene name keeps you focused. Then you started the scene-by-scene edit. You've edited a scene and understood its purpose and whether it deserves to be in the story.

You just looked at the opening type, so it seems appropriate to cover closing types right after opening types. Let's take that journey.

Fictionary Story Element: Closing Type

The last sentence in a scene is the magic that draws the reader forward into the next scene. The scene closing type and scene exit hook work together to make the reader turn the page. We'll explain the exit hook soon.

What you have just read for scene opening type applies to scene closing type.

As with the scene opening type, it's important to vary the closing type. Once you have listed each closing type, you can see if the draft is too repetitive.

Definition

The closing type is the method used to create the last sentence of the scene.

Action means a character or characters are in motion. This relates closely to the Character in Motion story element.

Dialogue means a character is speaking.

Thought means a character is thinking.

Description is everything else, including narrative.

Let us show you how using different closing types can give a reader insight into your characters. In this scene, one character is severely injured. The POV character has found the person unconscious in a puddle of mud. Here are four ways they could react.

- Dialogue: "How much longer?" I pressed the phone tight to my ear.
- Thought: Hurry up! The sirens seemed so far away.
- Action: I pounded his chest thirty times, blew two breaths, and started over.
- Description: Mud surrounded the man's body; his blond hair stuck to his forehead; sweat covered his cheeks; his chest remained still.

Each example reveals a personality trait, and each closing type leaves an open question. When you vary the closing types, you can stress different character traits. As the preceding examples show.

The dialogue and thought examples show the character is relying on help.

The action shows a proactive character taking charge.

The description shows a hopeless character observing someone.

The closing types are now working twice as hard. It's showing a character trait and creating an exit hook. The exit hook leaves the reader wondering if the man will survive.

Scene and Story Level

Keeping track of closing types at the scene and story level will improve the flow and pacing of the story.

At the scene level, check that the closing type works with the POV character's goal, the purpose of the scene, and the exit hook. We'll cover these elements later in the book. For now, you're building your knowledge in stages.

At the story level, check that all four closing types were used, that they are balanced, and that there aren't too many of one type in a row. Only when you can see the pattern for the whole story, can you edit it.

Perfecting the Closing Type Story Element

Your editing task is to list the scene closing type for every scene. Then check that they aren't repetitive and that all four types have been used in a balanced fashion.

If you're not happy with the balance of the closing types, think about what the writer could show with the closing types, how it links to the POV goal, the purpose of the scene, and the scene exit hook.

Then recommend the writer practices ending scenes with the different closing types and see what works best.

In opening and closing types, if the POV is very close, as in a first-person narrative, then the narrator is probably the protagonist. This means that the thoughts and the actions are sometimes more difficult to figure out. Here, the best path is to choose a way that shows differences. Action and description could be used when the protagonist is narrating about concrete things. When they are thinking about emotional thoughts or abstract things, then these are thoughts.

Troubleshooting

Ending each scene with the same closing type will become repetitive and, hence, boring to your reader.

Try to vary the scene closing types throughout your novel while still taking into consideration the goal of the scene.

Suggestions from the Editors

Suggestions from a summary letter from two of the thirteen editors:

EDITOR 7:

One form of repetition we often don't pick up on is the opening and closing of scenes. Of your eighty-seven scenes, sixty were closed with description of some form or another. I'd consider reviewing how you open each chapter to see if you can mix up the closings with dialogue, action, and thought more.

EDITOR 4:

After having a look at the opening and closing types for each scene, I made the following analysis: for closing types, "Description" opening types dominate the scenes, while there is a distinct lack of "Thought" opening types. For opening scenes, "Action" and "Dialogue" closing types dominate, while "Description" and "Thought" opening types are used much less frequently.

To correct this issue and, consequently, improve the overall flow, I suggest going through each scene and noting the scenes that share matching opening and closing types. If you find any scenes that match, it would be good practice to change the opening or closing type to another less frequently used opening/closing type. For example, if a scene uses both "Action" opening and closing types, then I would suggest using a "Thought" opening type instead; this way, you would have a wider range of opening/closing types and an improved flow.

> **TEA with Kristina**
>
> One editor pointed out an issue with scene closing types and was very specific. The other editor pointed out an issue with both closing and opening types and gave a process for how I could fix the issue.
>
> Stating that sixty or eighty-seven scenes end with description shows there is an imbalance in the opening/closing types. This statement convinced me I need to fix the opening/closing types.
>
> This is an easy task for an editor and is one that can make a huge improvement on the flow of the story.

Where to Next?

Can you feel the sizzle of story elements coming together? I bet you can, and it's getting exciting, so let's keep going.

What happens if your reader gets disoriented? You can guess that's not good, right? Next we'll look at how to anchor a reader early in a scene, so they don't get disoriented and put the book down.

Fictionary Story Element: Anchored

If the draft starts every new scene where the POV character, the setting, and the time are all anchored, the reader is oriented quickly and jumps into the scene.

If the scene is not anchored, then the reader is adrift at the start of the scene. Scene anchoring is tightly linked to scene opening type and entry hook.

Scene anchoring does not stop or distract the reader. Scene anchoring must be written so the reader doesn't notice it's happening.

Definition

There are three parts to scene anchoring. The reader must know the following:

1. Who is the POV character for the scene?

2. Where is the scene happening?

3. When is the scene happening?

The start of a new scene can mean the POV character has changed, the setting has changed, or the time has changed; hence every scene needs to be anchored with those three, so the reader isn't lost.

There are scenes where none of the three changed from the previous, and that's okay, too. Sometimes it's just time for a scene break, and, you guessed it, this is where the artistry comes in.

Scene and Story Level

This is a scene-level story element. You're checking the first few paragraphs of each scene and asking if the reader understands who has the POV, when the scene takes place in the context of the story, and where the scene takes place. We'll get into the POV character, location, and timing later in the book.

Perfecting the Anchored Story Element

Your editing task, which you can do at the same time as the opening type and opening hook, is to check and note whether each scene is anchored in POV, time, and setting.

Scene anchoring is tightly linked to the story elements of POV character, opening type, and opening hook. To perfect this story element, you must also perfect the others.

Troubleshooting

When you review scene anchoring, look at every scene's Anchored story element for the whole story. Perhaps two of the three anchors are well used, but the draft lacks the third.

When this happens, let the writer know. Your suggestions will give the writer actionable advice that will improve the flow and pacing of the story.

Suggestions from the Editors

EDITOR 1:

I've used the Story Map to show you which scenes have an issue with being anchored in POV, location, or time.

> **The Story Map is an insight in Fictionary that shows all the story elements in one place. Because the editor worked in Fictionary, they can show this to the writer.**

The start of a new scene means the POV character has changed, the setting has changed, or the time has changed; hence every scene needs to be anchored, so the reader doesn't get confused. A confused reader may put the book down and go do something else.

For each scene where I've set the element to "No," please check the scene opening. You're always anchored in POV because you're writing in the first-person POV. However, the area of anchoring that needs the most work is the timeline. I rarely knew when something was taking place. Secondary to that was the location. Please check each scene and make sure they're anchored in POV, time, and location.

POV:

The reader needs to know who has the POV within the first few paragraphs.

LOCATION:

You know where the character is because you wrote the scene. If the reader can't figure out where the character is within the first couple of paragraphs, you may lose them—the reader—I mean, and not the character.

There are exceptions to this. If your scene is about a character waking in a dark place and confused about where she is, then it's okay for the reader to be confused about where they are too. This will add to the tension. The reader needs to understand the lack of setting is done on purpose.

TIMING:

The timing the reader needs to understand depends on the scene you're writing.

The reader may need to know only if the scene is happening during the day or at night. If several years or several seconds have passed in a character's life, then the reader needs to understand that. If you are jumping back in time or forward in time, the reader needs to understand that, too.

The quicker the reader gets the timing, the quicker they will be drawn into the scene.

EDITOR 9:

Occasionally in the story, scenes would begin without any indication of how much time had passed since the last scene. One of the first examples of this is the first scene in chapter 2—it's not entirely clear how much time has elapsed since the funeral in chapter 1. In this case, the amount of time that has lapsed is important because she [Jaz] left the funeral in such a state of emotional distress—it's important to know how much time she's had to settle down, so the reader can know how much it is influencing her actions in the scene with Daisy.

When I felt that there was too little information about when a scene is occurring, I've left "Too Little" in the field for the Date/Time story element.

> **TEA with Kristina**
>
> **Two editors provided the following feedback on my work, and there was a hole in my writing: I did not consistently add a time anchor at the**

start of scenes.

The first editor used some words that could be improved. They wrote words like "You're always anchored in POV because you're writing in the first-person POV."

To soften the feedback, "You're" could be removed from this sentence: "You're" sounds accusatory, and it's not me as the writer who is unanchored; it's the scene.

This sentence could be rewritten to be more motivational: Every scene is anchored in POV because the story is written in first-person POV.

The difference is subtle but important. The same applies to the advice given below.

The feedback from the second editor is better. Not only does the editor give a specific example, but they showed how they were going to proceed through the edit.

My preferred way to proceed is to look at the scene opening type, entry hook, and scene anchoring all together. I look for issues first. Then when I'm revising a scene, I know what parts to keep and what to cut, all the while keeping the story elements in mind.

Where to Next?

Your knowledge of how to edit a scene is growing. Naming the scenes gave you an after-draft outline you'll reference throughout the edit. The purpose showed whether the scene deserves a place in the story. The opening and closing types will help you give advice to the writer regarding the flow of the story.

Scene anchoring makes sure the reader doesn't get jarred out of the story.

Let's continue amassing your knowledge by bringing these story elements together with the Entry Hook story element.

Fictionary Story Element: Entry Hook

When a new scene starts, the reader may be tempted to put the book down. Entry hooks tell the reader: Don't put the book down. Just read on to find out if . . .

The entry hook must happen quickly at the beginning of each scene. When a reader receives a clue that a new scene is starting, it's a place where they might stop reading. You don't want the reader to read a line or two and put your book down.

An entry hook is not something that happens 250 words or later in a scene.

Definition

The scene entry hook is the part of the scene that keeps the reader reading beyond the first paragraph or two.

Change (or the threat of change) that forces a character to act is an entry hook. It's stronger if the change forces the protagonist or the POV character to act. Next best is if it forces another character to act, because that action will impact the protagonist. And every scene must impact the protagonist or their main story goal, whether the protagonist is in the scene or not. See Impact on Protagonist story element.

Scene and Story Level

This story element is mostly reviewed at the scene-level. You'll make sure every scene has a strong entry hook that draws the reader into the scene.

At the story level, make sure to check for repetition.

Perfecting the Entry Hook Story Element

Your editing task is to read every scene opening and look for an entry hook. To edit each scene, read the first one or two paragraphs and list the entry hook. Showing the writer their entry hooks will help them as they revise the story. They will know what to strive for.

If there is an entry hook, write √, plus what it is. We'll explain the √ later in this section, so be patient.

If there is no entry hook, write "none."

If the entry hook is weak, write "weak."

If the entry hook is there but it's too far into the scene, write "too late" plus what it is.

This may be the place where the action starts. The editing advice might be to cut everything before the first action, and then the scene starts at the entry hook. When the text before the action is important, suggest weaving it into the scene after the hook. Don't forget about the scene opening type and scene anchoring when you're editing with this story element.

Troubleshooting

The entry hook makes the reader ask, "What happens next?" And if at the start of the scene, in the first paragraph or two, there is nothing that gets the reader asking, "How will that pan out?" then there is no entry hook.

As your confidence grows as an editor, noticing that an element is not there becomes easier. To start with, you might second-guess yourself. But if the entry hook is not easy to find, then advise the writer to focus on the element during the revision process.

Entry hooks need to be varied. If each scene starts with a question using dialogue, the entry hook might be strong on a per-scene basis, but the repetitiveness of the entry hook format will bore the reader. See "Opening Type" for more on this.

Check each scene for entry hooks, create a list, and review the list you created to determine whether there is a problem at the macro level. Reviewing the list shows you if this is a big problem or a small problem.

If only one or two scenes need revising, then it's a small issue.

If many scenes need revising, then it's a big issue, and there needs to be a revision plan so the entry hooks are created with purpose and aren't repetitive.

Suggestions from an Editor

The editors all used Fictionary StoryCoach to perform the edit, and that's why there is repeated reference to the Fictionary Story Map.

EDITOR 5:

Entry and exit hooks in/out of the scenes were sometimes excellent. At other times, they could do with some work.

These have been marked in the Story Map to show you where there is no hook at the beginning of the scene to make the reader want to keep reading, and none at the end of the scene to keep the reader turning the pages.

Where I've noted there isn't an entry hook, or it's weak or repetitive, you might consider how you could rewrite the scene opening to entice your reader further into the scene.

Use the Story Map (Visualize page) to see which scenes I've noted. There are some suggestions in those scenes.

TEA with Kristina

Entry Hook is the final story element belonging to the scene opening. One method to review each scene is to use one editing pass to review only the Scene Opening story elements.

These elements are Opening Type, Anchored, and Entry Hook.

You can rip through a manuscript at speed by reading only the scene openings and updating the Scene Opening story elements.

To get really jazzed, when you're updating the elements on the Evaluate page in Fictionary, put a $\sqrt{}$ everywhere the element is done well. Staring at a Story Map with a ton of $\sqrt{}$s is truly motivational—first, because you can see all the good bits in one place. And second, because you've quickly highlighted the areas that need work. This means you've shown the writer what to review and possibly revise. How cool is that!

Where to Next?

Exit hooks are just as important as entry hooks. In the next section, we'll look at the exit hooks.

Fictionary Story Element: Exit Hook

Hooks are ways to keep a reader from putting a book down, and the end of a scene is another likely place to lose a reader.

Why? Because it's a natural break in the story. It's the moment a reader decides whether they want to spend more time with the book.

A scene exit hook's magic keeps your reader wanting to begin the next scene. It's what will stop them from putting the book down, which means it's critical for writing a suspenseful and successful story. Note that the exit hook will be written in one of the closing types: Dialogue, Thought, Description, Action.

Definition

The exit hook shows the question the reader is left with at the end of the scene.

The ending of a scene should feel unfinished. If the scene feels finished, it doesn't have an exit hook. The reader must wonder what will happen next. This will keep them engaged in the story because it's exciting.

Here are some common types of exit hooks:

- Dramatic cliff-hanger: perhaps the protagonist's life is at risk.

- Revelation: shows the reader something that will change the course of the story.

- Setback for the protagonist or antagonist—remember POV goals? Use them here and present the characters with realistic, suspenseful obstacles.

- A secret revealed: reveal either a full secret or only part of a secret.

- A question left hanging: this will tease the reader, making them crave the answer.

- An unexpected plot twist: this will keep the reader guessing.

Scene and Story Level

Like the entry hook, the exit hook is mostly a scene-level story element. You'll check every scene has a strong exit hook that draws the reader to the next scene.

At the story level, check for repetition.

Perfecting the Exit Hook Story Element

Your editing task is to read every scene ending and look for an exit hook. To edit each scene, read the last one or two paragraphs of the scene and mark the state of the exit hook.

- If there is an exit hook, write √, plus what it is.
- If there is no exit hook, write "none."
- If the exit hook is weak, write "weak."
- If the exit hook is there but it's too soon into the scene, write "too soon" plus what it is.
- If you find an exit hook doesn't appear in the final paragraph of the scene, but appears earlier, recommend rearranging the text so the hook comes later in the scene.

Carefully consider the final scene of a story. By the end of the book, the main story question posed in the blurb must be answered. If it's not, the reader won't be satisfied and most likely won't read the next book by the author.

The ending can have exit hooks that lead to the next book in the series. But, and we really mean this, an exit hook at the end of a book cannot be so big that the reader feels frustrated.

Troubleshooting

The ultimate aim is to get the reader to resist going to bed, or making dinner, or whatever might take them away from your book, even for a few minutes. Make it impossible for them to stop turning the pages. Varying exit hooks makes the story more interesting. As intriguing as it sounds, ending every scene with a cliff-hanger will get old quickly.

The lack of an exit hook means the scene is not connected to another scene. It can mean the story is

episodic.

Look at the exit hooks through the whole story. Do they repeat, and are they strong enough for the energy needed to get the reader to start the next scene?

Suggestions from an Editor

EDITOR 1:

When reviewing the Story Map, select Scene Name, Entry Hook, and Exit Hook. This will show you the scenes where there is an issue. When you revise the opening hook scenes, make sure the scene remains anchored in POV, time, and location.

> ## TEA with Kristina
>
> **Studying the entry hook and exit hook together is interesting. The question that comes to mind is, "Do they work together to draw the reader in?"**
>
> **This editor made me think about more than exit hooks alone. To improve the advice, adding whether this is a large issue would help me better understand how much work I have to do in the revision process.**

Where to Next?

Now we're really making progress. We've just covered the basic Fictionary Story Elements for plot.

One option is to stay with the Plot elements.

The other option is to move to editing the Character story elements and then come back.

The choice is yours.

YOU'VE EDITED A SCENE FOR THE FOLLOWING:

- The scene name
- Its purpose in the story

- What type of opening and closing type is used
- Whether the reader is anchored
- Whether the reader is hooked at the beginning of the scene
- Whether the reader is driven to read the next scene

But what keeps the reader reading within a scene? What keeps them turning the pages? If the tension is too much for you, and you want to know how to edit for that, turn the page and start the next chapter.

Meet   Learn   Action

Chapter Ten:
Learn More Plot Story Elements

"Characters can only act on what they know. POV Knowledge Gained is priceless in avoiding annoying plot holes." — Lisa Taylor, Fictionary Certified StoryCoach Editor

Edit for the Reader

We have covered eight of the 38 Fictionary Story Elements, and we hope you have seen a pattern. Have you noticed something that all the elements are doing? Have you noticed how so many of the story elements are looking at the story element from the reader's POV?

A writer writes, so their perfect reader can enjoy their story. An editor edits so the writer can expand their reader base.

Readers fall on a spectrum, and creative story editors know we have to look out for places where a reader might put the book down. And that's part of the beauty of the 38 Fictionary Story Elements. They make the story stronger by asking questions about the story. And they consider where the reader might put the book down.

A Page-Turner Edit

Let's look at our definition of a page-turner:

A book a reader wants to read in a single sitting.

Notice the reader is mentioned. A quiet literary book can be just as much of a page-turner as a high-action thriller.

The wonderful question all writers want the reader to ask is, "How will the story turn out?"

When the reader asks how the story is going to work out, then the reader is invested, be it a literary page-turner, a genre page-turner, or a narrative non-fiction page-turner.

The Secret to a Page-Turner Is a Well-Edited Book

A page-turner is a book in which the reader wants to turn the page. It says what it does, doesn't it?

A book that has been edited with the 38 Fictionary Story Elements is a well-edited book.

A creative story editor uses the story elements to avoid plot holes, create characters readers connect with, and set up a meaningful setting. So far you have seen the power of the first eight Plot Story Elements. And you have seen how each one of the elements builds on the meaning of the one before. When you edit the first, you then use that to edit the next story element.

Where to Next?

As a creative story editor, when you are looking for each element in each of the scenes, think about how a reader would respond to the text. And when you think about the reader, remember you are an editor and a reader.

If you find yourself skipping text, putting the draft down because you need to make a cup of tea, or getting confused about a character introduction, then look at why.

There will be a reason for your reaction. When you edit using the 38 Fictionary Story Elements, you can pinpoint exactly what needs to be looked at. It can be small, or it can be something that needs a big revision. Both constitute great news. Your editing advice rescues stories from being drowned by reader confusion.

Onward we go to the next level of depth with more Plot story elements.

Fictionary Story Element: Tension

We promised to show you what keeps a reader reading within a scene.

The answer is tension.

A scene without tension will not keep a reader engaged, so there must be tension in every scene. Yes, we said every scene. Without tension, the reader stops reading, and that is not the reader reaction we're looking for.

Tension is the reader's anticipation that something will or won't happen.

That could be the threat of something bad happening in a thriller or the anticipation that something good could happen, such as sexual tension in a romantic story.

Tension is in every genre.

Answering the anticipation is not tension; paying out the threat is not tension; lovers getting together is not tension. When the threat is gone, so, too, is the tension.

We'll show you how tension is not the same as conflict in the next section.

Definition

Tension is the anticipation something bad or good will happen.

Tension is built from a reader's hope, worry, and care for the story. Readers tense up when they have hopes for the POV character and they worry that the POV character might not achieve the scene goal. These hopes and worries keep the reader engaged.

When a reader picks up a story, they hope the story will keep them glued to the page; then, as they get to know the protagonist, they have hopes for the protagonist. They hope the character will succeed at their story goal. And they read on to see if those hopes will come true. This is the anticipation.

A reader must worry about the protagonist in order to carry on reading. And the reader worries only when they are invested and empathize with the protagonist.

The reader must know what the protagonist stands to lose if they fail to achieve the story goal. These are the stakes.

Scene and Story Level

Tension can be both big and small. Big tension spans the entire story, and there must be smaller scene-level tension in every scene.

At the story level, the story's main story goal being answered positively is at stake for the protagonist. The unanswered story goal keeps the tension throughout the story. Story-level tension won't be resolved until the end of the climax.

The story blurb is helpful when editing for tension in a story. The blurb shows the main story goal. If the structure of the story is set up to follow the story arc, and the main story question is not answered until the story's climax, the story is structured to have tension throughout. We come back to the blurb again. You can see by now that the blurb is important to the creative story editor.

At the scene level, use the POV character's goal together with the Tension story element.

At the scene level, if an element of tension is resolved, there must be something else that causes tension to keep the reader engaged. Scene-level tension can be resolved in one scene, over multiple scenes, or over the entire story.

You should be able to relate the scene-level tension back to the blurb and the bigger story question. If you can't, revisions are required.

Perfecting the Tension Story Element

Your editing task for this story element is to look for tension in each scene using the story goal found in the skeleton blurb and the POV goal for the scene. Look for places where the POV character is at risk or where the protagonist is closer to or pushed further from the story goal, even if they are not in the scene.

If there isn't a main story goal, there will be no tension in the story.

Refer to the writer's skeleton blurb.

The protagonist _____

must _____(story goal)

otherwise _____(story stakes)

Reaching or not reaching the story goal as defined in the skeleton blurb creates tension.

Then go to scene 1 and edit the scene for tension. To do this, look for places in the scene where the protagonist is at risk of not achieving the main story goal—even if they are not in the scene—or the POV character's goal for the scene is at risk.

For each scene, look at the POV Goal and What if Goal Fails story elements—more on these later. If there are no consequences if the goal fails, there is no tension.

> **If there is a clear POV goal and if there are consequences if the POV character fails at achieving the scene goal, then there will be tension.**

If you're editing someone else's manuscript, you will have already asked your client for a blurb. This is often a big ask, as the writer may not have one.

Make them feel comfortable by telling them it's for your own use and doesn't have to be perfect. Give them a few guidelines stating it must show who the protagonist is, what their goal is, and what's at risk if they don't achieve the goal.

The section "A Super-Fast Skeleton Blurb Method," Chapter 3: Meet the Story Promise, shows you how to do this.

Troubleshooting

One caution.

If tension is set up in one scene and solved by the end of the same scene repeatedly, the reader will start to think the protagonist always achieves their goals and will assume the protagonist will achieve their main story goal. Then they'll lose interest in the whole story because it lacks tension.

We mentioned how to use the Fictionary Skeleton Blurb for story tension, but if you need help, write a quick scene-level blurb.

> **A scene-level blurb:**
> **The** _____ **(POV Character)**
> **must** _____ **(POV Goal)**
> **otherwise** _____ **(What if Goal Fails)**

Then use these story elements to edit the scene and make sure the tension works at the scene level. These elements are covered in Chapter 11: Learn the Character Story Elements.

Suggestions from the Editors

EDITOR 1:

Next up was scene 58. Fantastic tension and the ending to this scene was fabulous. There's no way any of your readers will put the book down after that scene. Again, I'd look at this scene ending and see if you can replicate some of the tension.

EDITOR 3:

This is a good scene at building tension. What will they find? Who is rattling the door? Will Dan catch them?

While the POV character goal for the scene isn't that defined—just to look through Dan's things—the consequences of getting caught doing that could spell trouble for either character, so this is well handled.

TEA with Kristina

When you read a story element that has been done well, make a note of it. If you are editing for someone else, they need the good pointed out so they can carry on with their strengths and build on them.

When you are self-editing, notice and comment on the parts you are doing well. That is one of the secrets to self-motivation when self-editing.

Kristina's thoughts on the feedback from Editor 1:

This feedback was motivating. The editor is telling me I should use this scene as an example of how to create strong tension in a scene. It's important to show a writer where the writing is strong, but it's just as important to show them how to replicate the effect.

> Let's get some better advice on the same scene. Kristina's thoughts on the feedback from Editor 3:
>
> Can you see the difference? This editor demonstrated why there was good tension in the scene by showing the open questions. They also showed there isn't a clear POV character goal, but that it might not matter. This, again, is where artistry comes in. Fictionary is there to guide an editor but not be restrictive.
>
> Using more than one story element helps show how to make a scene better.

Where to Next?

Tension and conflict are interrelated. Conflict can create tension, and we're going to find out how.

Fictionary Story Element: Conflict

Conflict controls pacing. No conflict means a slow . . . boring . . . story. But if there's too much conflict, the reader loses interest because they haven't been given time to connect with the characters and see how the characters react to the conflict.

We also must care about the character, or the conflict doesn't matter, and that's the reason for introducing the ordinary world of the character. The reader is given time to get to know the character.

Conflict increases tension only if it creates uncertainty about the character reaching their goal and only if it's related to the story.

Tension and conflict are two Fictionary Story Elements that must work together.

Definition

Conflict is the action that is actually happening in a scene and that pits two or more characters against each other.

A physical fight, an argument, a battle to win a race. Conflict is only valuable if it hinders or helps the characters in relation to their goals.

Conflict can be internal or external. External conflict happens to a character. Internal, or inner, conflict brings about a fundamental internal struggle that needs to happen for the story goal to be resolved.

No goal, no conflict.

Remember, tension is the reader's anticipation that something will or won't happen. It's not the event actually happening.

Conflict must cause an emotional response in the character. If the character doesn't have an emotional response, the reader won't either. We care when the character cares. We care when a character is motivated. We care when the conflict stands in the way of something the character wants or needs. We care when the character cannot ignore the conflict.

Scene and Story Level

Before reading the first scene of the novel, list the overall story conflict. This conflict must span the entire story and can be called the primary conflict, as it's the main conflict the protagonist is dealing with throughout the story. This shouldn't get resolved until the climax of the story.

If the protagonist isn't up against something for the entire story, the story can come across as episodic (meaning a series of scenes that don't appear to be related, meaning the reader might put the book down). We are repeating this because we're trying to help the editor pinpoint every place a reader might put the book down.

The main conflict brings us back to the skeleton blurb. The blurb shows the reader what the overarching conflict of the story is. By looking at the story goal and what's at stake in the skeleton blurb, you should be able to list what the story conflict in the scene is.

At the scene level, you're looking to see if the conflict is related to the main story goal and stakes. If it's not, it could be conflict for the sake of conflict, which is not good for the story.

Perfecting the Conflict Story Element

Your editing task for this story element is to list every conflict on a scene-by-scene basis. To locate the conflict, find the places in the scene that stop the POV character from achieving their scene goal.

As conflict is the action in the scene, you'll know if there is conflict in a scene when you can answer the question, "What if the POV goal fails?" If nothing happens when the goal fails, there is no conflict. These scene stakes are the Fictionary Story Element is What if Goal Fails. Here we are interweaving the story elements again.

It could also mean the goal is weak or not related to the story. Conflict for the sake of conflict is boring, so it must be related to the POV character's goal for a scene. Remember to use the skeleton blurb to see if the scene conflict relates to the main story in a relevant way.

Delay may cause tension, but it's not conflict. Tension is necessary in every scene, and there is nothing wrong with using delay as a technique to create tension, as long as it doesn't go on too long or come across as contrived.

Ask what is causing the POV character to fail at achieving the scene goal or making it difficult to achieve the scene goal.

Conflict can be caused by the antagonist (if there is one), a character who is not an antagonist but is in direct conflict with the protagonist, an inanimate object (such as a storm), or the protagonist themselves.

Remember, the first step in finding the protagonist is to think of the protagonist as an entity that can be made up of one or more characters.

We're going to think of conflict in terms of an entity too.

The entity creating conflict can be one of the following:

1.   An antagonist

2.   A character in direct conflict with the protagonist

3.   An inanimate object

4.   The protagonist (inner conflict)

Try listing the conflict entity for every scene, and you'll quickly see whether there is conflict in the scene.

Not all scenes must have conflict, but they must have tension. If you find a scene with no tension and no conflict, revisions are needed.

Troubleshooting

For the scenes where you can't list the conflict, use the following to figure out where the issue is. Make a note for each scene based on the choices listed below.

- No conflict: check to see if there is enough tension, or if the conflict is happening off the scene.

- Too little: the scene needs more paragraph real estate on the actual conflict.

- Too much: the scene feels melodramatic, perhaps figure out where the scene is related to the big climax. If this scene is not the climax, it should have less conflict than the climax scene.

- Unrelated: the conflict is unrelated to the story goal, or the scene goal, so it feels manufactured.

- Misunderstanding: this is not conflict. If it can be cleared up, it won't count. Misunderstanding can cause tension, so you might want to use it as a technique to cause tension.

Suggestions from an Editor

EDITOR 13:

Jaz doesn't tend to have much emotional reaction in some scenes or inner conflict. As a result, she can come across a little flat sometimes and not as multidimensional as she could be. For example, she seems to have no emotional reaction when Tom tells her the story of his dead wife, or when Tom tells her he has stopped investigating Nick's case.

Similarly, it's sometimes unclear, beyond cues in the dialogue, if other characters are worried, scared, enraged, livid, bright red in the face, calm, ice-cold, etc.

> **TEA with Kristina**
>
> **From this advice, I can see that I have a hole in the draft manuscript. And the advice is actionable. I need to look at the conflict at the scene level. The editor also marked scenes that lacked tension or had low tension.**

> With this information, I can see where I need to revise the story.
>
> With this feedback, I can see that my dialogue might be overwhelming the conflict action in the scene.
>
> The lack of conflict is coming from a lack of emotional response by Jaz. I'm going to use the story element Impact on Protagonist first to determine how the scene could affect Jaz. For a deeper look, I'll review the story element What if Goal Fails. These together will spark my creativity, and I'm confident I'll get ideas to fix the lack of conflict issues.

Where to Next?

We've revealed why tension and conflict are needed and how they relate to each other. The Revelation story element is the obvious next choice.

Fictionary Story Element: Revelation

The power of a character learning something new is that the new information forces them to make a decision, increases tension, and increases conflict. A revelation must be like adding fuel to the fire. The anticipation or the action that follows a story critical revelation is a hook for the reader to read on.

Revelations are important because they add tension and conflict to a scene, if done right. Done poorly, it's information the reader doesn't need, leaving them wondering if the author has control over the story.

Partial revelations add to a reader's uncertainty, which also increases tension. Uncertainty means the reader can't predict what's going to happen. Revelations give the story power and momentum. Revelations are an opportunity to think of all the different ways characters could react. Then where the revelations occur in a story should be carefully considered, so the action in the story is propelled forward.

A revelation is different from backstory because the character knows the backstory, so it's not a revelation for them.

Definition

A revelation is something the reader and a character learn that is meaningful to the story and that they didn't know before this scene. It is usually a critical discovery.

Scene and Story Level

Editing for revelation happens at the scene level and story level.

At the scene level, the revelation should be related to the story, getting the protagonist closer or further away from their story goal. The revelation must also be the spur that gets the action in the scene going.

At the story level, evaluating the placement of revelations is key. The number of revelations after the middle plot point should decrease. There should be no revelations after plot point 2. If this happens, the revelation appears contrived and placed for convenience.

Perfecting the Revelation Story Element

Your editing task for this story element is to list all the revelations and see if they are well placed for the plot to work.

On the first editing pass, you can use this element to remind yourself of when information was revealed. For example, let's say too much is revealed early in the story and it's reducing the tension. Make a suggestion of where the revelation could be better placed.

Whatever you list for the revelation of a scene, you also list which character knows this information. We're particularly interested in the POV characters and the protagonist.

If you're using Fictionary, copy the information you listed in Revelation to POV Knowledge Gained.

If the POV character is NOT the protagonist and the protagonist is not in the scene, list the information under Reader Knowledge Gained. This way you can keep track of what the reader knows but the protagonist doesn't. The protagonist cannot act on the information they don't know.

Troubleshooting

If there is a revelation not related to the plot or character development, this can mean a revelation doesn't make sense, because it comes out of nowhere. There must be breadcrumbs leading to all major revelations or the reader will lose faith in the story, and maybe even in the writer.

A plot hole occurs if a character references a revelation, but they weren't in the scene where the revelation occurred. Keep track of which characters know about the revelation and if the reader knows, too.

When something is revealed either too early or too late, the editor will recommend moving the revelation to where it is better suited to the story or reveal the revelation in parts.

Another problem occurs when there are too many revelations in a row, and the reader doesn't have a chance to take in the moment, or the characters don't have a chance to react. That is one reason why revelations should not be in the last third of the story, when the pacing picks up.

If there are revelations that are not addressed by the end of the story, the editing recommendation should be to follow up on that revelation.

Suggestions from an Editor

EDITOR 6:

Revelation of Information

This is handled quite well throughout—you have done a masterful job with many setups and payoffs (my favorite being the grandfather clock, which plays a critical role in the climax).

There is one area of the story, though, that could still use some work in this respect: the Lady subplot with Christopher.

There is no mention of Jaz's plan to find a guide dog for Christopher until she tells Vicky that she already has a guide dog lined up and ready to meet him—in scene 81. Because we don't find this out until then, it feels convenient and contrived. Ideally this would be set up in the first half of the novel—perhaps with Jaz discovering that Lady has become available as a therapy dog but not realizing what she can do with that information until chapter 25.

> ### TEA with Kristina
>
> **Let's talk about Jaz finding a therapy dog. Lady is a dog. A revelation is something I could use early in the book. Perhaps Jaz has the revela-**

tion she needs a guide dog and then has another revelation that Christopher needs one and she can help him get one. The key is to keep track of the revelations, so they make sense from a story perspective.

I need to revise earlier scenes to make this revelation flow in the story and not appear unexpectedly.

Where to Next?

We're going to cover character motivation next. Why? Because tension keeps the reader worried. Conflict keeps the reader engaged. But why is the character going through such a tension- and conflict-filled life?

The Revelation, Backstory, and Flashback story elements are used to show character motivation. This is the "Why?" of what the character does. Without motivation, the character's actions will lack meaning. And without meaning, the reader won't connect with the character.

Now let's time travel to the past and search for character motivation.

Fictionary Story Element: Backstory

Without backstory, a reader won't connect with a character.
Period.

Backstory creates the character's motivation in the story. And once the reader understands where the motivation comes from, then the reader will have huge empathy for the character.

Reader empathy gets the reader invested to keep reading.

Without a backstory, characters may come across as flat, and too much backstory is called an info dump.

Backstory is not the same as revelations or flashbacks. We'll cover flashbacks soon.

Definition

Events that happen before the story begins are the backstory. Sometimes during the story, you need to inform the reader of something that happened earlier in the life of a character, because the backstory creates motivations or reasons for character flaws.

Backstory should make the story flow, highlight motivations, and show why a character ended up with their inner flaw. A good backstory is an event that affected a character before page one.

Scene and Story Level

This story element is covered at both the story level and the scene level.

At the story level, check there is minimal backstory after the middle plot point. From the middle on, the readers should already know the characters' backstory and what motivates them. There should be no backstory after plot point 2. This is where high-action takes place, and slowing things down to add backstory will take away from the forward motion of the story.

At the scene level, you're checking if the backstory is needed yet or at all. Backstory must relate to the purpose of a scene. The question is, "How is any given backstory supporting the purpose of a scene?" Without an answer to that, it may mean the backstory is not needed or the backstory should be moved to another scene.

Perfecting the Backstory Story Element

Your fun editing task is to list the backstory for every scene. Try to list this in three words or fewer. You're going to use the information to edit at the story level.

Ask yourself if any of these questions are answered:

- Is the draft revealing the backstory in an engaging way?
- Is the backstory plot relevant?
- Does the backstory show a character's motivation, the "why" of the character goal? This character motivation is a strong emotional connection that the reader has with the story.
- The backstory can help the reader understand why the character is willing to go through with the story's ordeals.

The writer may have files upon files of information that helped them complete the draft. But that is all the underwater part of the research iceberg. The reader needs to know only what helps them with the plot. And that is the tip of the backstory iceberg.

Some drafts are over half backstory. In this case, you will be editing using a technique where the draft bounces between the present and the past. As you are editing, you can use this element to determine whether the draft has given the present and the past a fair balance.

Troubleshooting

Sometimes during the story, there is the need to inform the reader of something that happened before the story started.

If a novel has a small amount of backstory, then the draft should not have too much backstory early in the manuscript. The information should be doled out as the reader needs to learn it. The characters need to do something interesting before too much backstory is included.

Curiosity is what drives the reader forward. If the character has a past that's driving their motivation, then don't show the reader too soon. Keep the reader curious by doling out parts of the backstory.

There should not be too much backstory at one time. If the reader is jarred out of the immediate story, this can cause them to lose interest. To make a scene active, backstory can be shown in a flashback. More on that later.

When recommending that large portions of backstory be cut, suggest that the cut text from the scene is saved somewhere else. The backstory might be repurposed in the current book or in another.

Look for revelations, backstory, or flashbacks that occur after plot point 2. These are most likely causing story problems, and the writer needs to know this.

As with revelations, depending on how you like to edit, you can list the backstory in three words or fewer for each scene. This will give you an after-draft outline for the backstory.

Try keeping the following notes on a per-scene basis when you discover backstory issues:

- Too much: this usually means the backstory is not meted out strategically.
- Too little: this usually means the reader might get confused or not understand a character's motivation.
- Irrelevant: the backstory isn't related to character motivations, the protagonist's inner flaw, or the story goal.

- √: the backstory is excellent.

> **You can also combine the process by listing the backstory along with a comment such as "Too early." This way you get an after-draft backstory outline.**

Suggestions from an Editor

EDITOR 4:

As the editor, we look for areas where there is too little backstory, too much backstory—also known as an info dump—or where it is irrelevant to the story. The backstory in Evolution seems to include Jaz's story about the scar on her face, and the conflict between Alyssa and Jaz.

There are a few instances where I have listed the backstory as being too late or too little. This usually means I was confused or didn't understand a character's motivation. To some degree it can be beneficial not to give too much away too soon. In the Story Map, you will find the scenes I have marked are usually related to the relationship between Jaz and Alyssa, which seems to be only alluded to for a long time without any real/full explanation. This could be an area of the plot that you may wish to review, to see if there is any way of giving more to the reader without removing that tension.

I didn't find the backstory about how Jaz got her scar to really play an important role in the plot. The scar is not mentioned a lot, and it doesn't seem that her scar really is an issue for her. It's more like a sideline to the anxiety and grief over losing her husband, plus the suggestion he may have been murdered. To some degree, these elements feel like enough for the character to deal with, and this scene about the scar feels like a distraction about what else is going on. It's also never really referenced again. I, therefore, suggest a review of the role of the scar. Either work it further into the plot so it's clearly a source of anxiety or stress for her that she can overcome or remove it altogether.

> ## TEA with Kristina
>
> **This is great advice. The editor is showing me I have an issue with backstory. The issue occurs throughout the story, and I've been given a plot line to work on with Jaz and Alyssa. I have something very specific to revise, and that's**

great news.

Let's talk about the scar the editor mentioned in the feedback for Evolution. In my mind, the scar was a major motivation for Jaz's character flaw. Clearly this didn't come out in the story, and I need to make revisions. The advice is specific and actionable, which I love.

Where to Next?

If backstory is extremely important, it can be written as an active scene in the past. This is what we call a flashback. Let's go look at flashbacks.

Fictionary Story Element: Flashback

Is there something that happened in a character's past, before the start of the story, that has a significant impact on character motivation or actions? Did you answer yes? Then perhaps it's time to use a flashback.

A flashback takes the reader from the current time to a previous time. This usually happens quickly, and the reader is then returned to the present.

Flashbacks are different from backstory, as they are shown in an action scene and not a narrative summary or part of the current scene. A reader lives a flashback along with the POV character.

If the event happens during the current story, it's not a flashback. That's a story told out of chronological order.

Definition

A flashback is an action scene that shows an event that happened in the past.

It must do the following:

1. Be related to the story being told.

2. Have tension.

3. Be written in active form.

Scene and Story Level

Editing the flashback is important at the scene level and the story level.

At the story level, ask yourself if the flashbacks are clustered together or spread throughout the story. If too many flashbacks occur close together, the reader may find it difficult to return to the present story.

Normally we recommend that a story does not have a flashback in the first scene of a novel. This is asking a reader to start a new story before they are connected to the main story. It's difficult to do well and keep the reader engaged.

At the scene level, the way the flashback is entered is crucial for its success.

When editing for flashbacks, look at how the flashback is entered and exited. A sound or loud noise can jar the character into or out of the flashback. Any of the senses can work for this.

Perfecting the Flashback Story Element

Your editing task for this element is to note every flashback in the story and look at how each flashback is entered into and left by the POV character.

The draft should save flashbacks for the most important backstory. Flashbacks should be used sparingly.

Flashbacks can be a sentence, a paragraph, a scene, or an entire chapter.

This is where the edit comes in. There may be a flashback in which a murder occurs and solving the murder is the driving motive for the protagonist. In that case, the draft should give the flashback time to develop on the page. The reader won't want to be shortchanged with only a few sentences.

Part of the success of a flashback depends on taking the reader back into the present scene after the flashback ends. This means a hook in the flashback that will make the present more interesting. It also means anchoring the reader in the present quickly.

Treat the flashback as a scene and edit it using the Fictionary Story Elements the way you would any other scene in the story. Anchoring and hooking a reader at the beginning of a flashback is extremely important.

If there are no issues with flashbacks, give a $\sqrt{}$ if the flashback is great, along with naming the flashback in three words or fewer.

Troubleshooting

The importance of a flashback should influence its length. So, look at each flashback and ask, "How important is it to the story?" If a flashback is too long relative to its importance, think about what needs to be cut from the flashback.

If a flashback is too short relative to its importance, think about how to show more action in the flashback scene.

Here are some tips on how to keep track of flashbacks.

IF THERE ARE ISSUES WITH A FLASHBACK, LIST THE FLASHBACK NAME ALONG WITH THE FOLLOWING:

- Too long: the flashback is too long relative to its importance to the plot.
- Too short: the flashback is too short relative to its importance to the plot.
- Not active: the flashback is not written in an active style. This can either be turned into backstory or be rewritten as an active scene.
- Unclear entry: this is when it took you a moment to figure out you'd entered a flashback.
- Unclear exit: this is when it took you a moment to figure out you'd returned to the present time.
- Too early: Try not to have a flashback before the inciting incident. If you must, do it with care, as Louise Penny did in The Madness of Crowds.

THERE ARE TWO REASONS AN EARLY FLASHBACK WORKS IN THE MADNESS OF CROWDS:

1. The blurb has set up the tension for the story, so the reader is engaged before the flashback happens.

2. The flashback jumps to the very near past, so it doesn't feel like a new story is starting.

If you must use a flashback early in a novel, read scene 1 of The Madness of Crowds and study how to do this well.

When it comes time to revise the novel, the writer will have enough information to make every flashback earn its place in the story.

Suggestions from an Editor

EDITOR 6:

You don't have any flashbacks, so I was wondering if you did that on purpose—for example, not flashing back to Jaz and Nick together to show "how they were." But the book certainly doesn't need it. Reading the journals, messages, and files are great. And the visions are pure genius for giving hints of the past that accelerate the story forward—an inspired source of clues!

TEA with Kristina

From the editor's feedback above, I can see how readers could think I have a hole in my writing. I will go back and look at the book in its entirety and see if flashbacks would give my story more depth, or if I like the story without any flashbacks. This clear advice is something I can work with to make an artistic decision. It also showed me what is working in the book, so I won't remove the visions.

Where to Next?

So far in this chapter, we've learned tension keeps the reader worried, conflict keeps the reader engaged, and a character's history, whether told through a revelation, backstory, or flashback connects the reader to the character.

We're doing well keeping the reader turning the pages, but there's still more. The structure of a scene is just as important as the structure of the story, and we're going right into the middle of the scene now, to the Fictionary Story Element: Scene Middle.

Fictionary Story Element: Scene Middle

A scene without complications is a scene a reader can walk away from. The scene middle is the place to add complications to renew the reader's excitement about the scene.

Every scene has a scene arc. Just like the full story, a scene will have a beginning, middle, and end. What happens in the middle must propel the plot forward, develop characters, and create tension. The scene middle is where those complications happen for the POV character.

The Scene Middle story element helps you determine if the scene is well structured, just as the middle plot point helps you determine if the story is well structured.

Definition

The scene middle is everything after both the scene's opening hook and POV goal and before the scene's climax.

Scene and Story Level

At the scene level, this story element helps you figure out if a scene has a structure that is engaging for the reader.

At the story level, look at the story elements Scene Name, Scene Middle, and Scene Climax together. These provide a detailed outline of the story.

We use this combination all the time to test the strength of a story. Remember how important the scene middle is for creating the skeleton synopsis.

Perfecting the Scene Middle Story Element

Your editing task is to list the scene middle in no more than three words for every scene.

Using the skeleton blurb, look at the POV character's actions after the entry hook and up to the scene climax.

The scene middle should be a turning point for the characters, and after the scene middle the POV character should have a purpose, which is pursuing the scene goal or pursuing a new goal.

Things will either get worse or better in the scene middle, but the POV character should be driving the action forward until the climax of the scene.

Remember, a novel is made up of chapters, and chapters are made up of scenes. The better the scenes are, the better the chapters, and hence the better the novel.

LOOK FOR EVENTS IN THE SCENE MIDDLE THAT DO THE FOLLOWING:

1. Drive the plot forward.

2. Develop characters.

3. Create tension.

Troubleshooting

Can you describe the scene middle in no more than three words? You've named the scene in no more than three words, so this is your challenge. If you can do this, the scene middle is focused.

The next challenge is to figure out if the scene middle has tension.

The middle of a scene is where the draft might have entered the world of too much description. There might be a meander where the story goes off track. The scene middle might have added a mini story that is not related to the plot. All of these can make the story lag, meaning it gets boring, and the reader is tempted to skim.

Uninteresting stories are littered with scenes where nothing happens to the characters. When bad things happen, or there is the threat of bad things happening, or there is the anticipation of good things, then the reader cares. And a caring reader reads on.

The scene middle needs editing if you skim whole paragraphs in the middle of the scene.

To tighten the middle, look for the following:

- Information that can be withheld until later.
- Repetition from a previous scene that could be cut from the scene.
- Descriptions that are not character or plot relevant.

IF THERE ARE ISSUES WITH A SCENE MIDDLE, LIST THE SCENE MIDDLE DESCRIPTION YOU CREATED, ALONG WITH THE FOLLOWING:

- Lags: this is when you start to skim the middle of the scene.
- No complications: this part of the scene needs a complication; if it is not there, then recommend to revise the scene to include a complication.

Suggestions from an Editor

EDITOR 5:

The scene middle should be a turning point for the characters. Things will either get worse or get better, and either way the POV character should be driving the action forward until the climax of the scene. Vicky and Daisy meet again, but there's a lack of tension and conflict. This is why I put "No complications" in the Scene Middle element. To heighten this, make Vicky have a stronger reaction to seeing and petting Daisy, or maybe Daisy has a stronger reaction to seeing Vicky.

TEA with Kristina

Nobody likes to admit that they drift off or that they skim parts of stories. As a creative story editor, we can admit it, as we have actionable advice on how to revise drafts out of their drift-offs.

The advice from editor 5 is showing me I have a drift off moment in the scene middle. This scene takes place in chapter 3 of Evolution, so it's very early in the story.

I love that the editor suggested ways to fix the problem. I've got a creative place to start my revisions.

Where to Next?

Since we talked about the scene climax in this section, it only seems right to cover that next.

Fictionary Story Element: Scene Climax

Without a scene climax, the scene is not a mini story. It's an episode. Too many episodes lead to an episodic story. An episodic story is one where the scenes are not connected to the main story.

A scene is a story in miniature, and it has a scene climax that is a smaller version of the story climax. If you think of the classical three-act story structure, a scene can be modeled in the same way. The climax must happen in act 3 of the scene. There can be a sentence or two after the climax but keep it short and make it an exit hook.

The POV goal is the POV character's goal for the scene, and at the climax, the reader finds out if they succeeded at achieving the scene POV goal.

An unsatisfying scene climax is when the scene POV goal has not been addressed.

Definition

For a scene, the climax is a mini peak or escalation in the drama and the action. Notice, it's a mini peak. It cannot be more extreme than the climax of the whole story. There can be closure in some scene climaxes, but it can't happen at the end of every scene.

Scene and Story Level

The scene climax story element is looked at both at the scene level and the story level.

At the scene level, the scene climax must show the reader whether the POV character achieved their goal. That doesn't mean it's always a win for the POV scene goal; rather, the POV scene goal must be dealt with in some way. And together with the exit hook, this leads the reader to want to read the next scene.

At the story level, look out for too many happy resolutions in a row. The reader will get bored if there is no adversity in scene climax after scene climax.

Perfecting the Scene Climax Story Element

Your editing task is to list the scene climax in no more than three words for every scene. And note if the scene climax addresses the scene POV goal. If it does not, then the scene needs to be revised.

The scene climax together with the exit hook is what ensures the reader wants more.

In the scene climax, the POV character does one of the following:

1. Achieves the POV goal.

2. Achieves part of the POV goal.

3. Fails to achieve the POV goal.

Troubleshooting

The scene climax cannot be more extreme than the climax of the novel. When the POV goal is addressed in the scene, this should open the story to the inevitable but surprising scene goal in the next scene.

The easiest way to discover if there is an issue with the scene climax is if you can't describe it in fewer than three words.

This tells you the following:

1. There isn't a scene climax.

2. The scene climax isn't focused.

3. The scene climax is not related to the POV character's goal.

IF YOU CAN'T DESCRIBE THE SCENE CLIMAX IN THREE WORDS OR FEWER, YOUR EDITING TASK IS TO USE ONE OF THE FOLLOWING SUGGESTIONS:

- None: there is no climax to the scene.
- Weak: the climax of the scene exists, but it is weak.
- Extreme: the climax of the scene is over the top and it risks being more dramatic than the climax of the novel.
- Happy: the climax ended in a happy place. This is a check that not too many happy scene climaxes happen one after another.
- Unrelated: the climax is unrelated to the POV goal for the scene.

- And, of course, we can't forget to motivate the writer. The √ is always welcome when a job is well done.

Suggestions from the Editors

EDITOR 4:

The middle of the scene, where we are introduced to Mr. Wheaten Terrier, and the climax, where we find out Mr. Wheaten Terrier is a police officer who was at Nick's funeral, is a very good complication if it is an introduction to a character we'll be seeing more of and foreshadows future action.

EDITOR 8:

[This advice is from a different editor about a different scene in Evolution.]

Jaz knows Dan slept with Irene because of the vision in scene 13. Then it is revealed in chapter 9, scene 27, that the woman is Irene. But Jaz knows who the woman is and she doesn't tell us, nor does she have any reaction when she sees Irene in person in this scene. That is why I have written "weak" in the scene climax. This would be a perfect place for Jaz to have an inner conflict about seeing Irene while having lunch with Alyssa.

> ### TEA with Kristina
>
> Here with Editor 4, we get to see what an editor thought about the structure of a scene in Evolution. They stated why they liked the climax and gave a condition that shows me what I need to pay attention to as the story moves forward.
>
> In Fictionary, the editor left the note above in the notes panel and a √ in the Scene Climax story element. So that made me happy!
>
> Editor 8 shows me I have revision work to do on chapter 9, scene 27. Notice how specific the editor is when referring to scene and chapter numbers. This makes it easy for me to reference. The editor also gives suggestions on how to fix the scene.

> I've shown the good and the bad examples in the same manuscript, so it's clear a writer might be very good at a story element in one scene but have trouble with it in another scene. An editor must always be on the lookout for trouble with any story element.

Where to Next?

When you get to the scene climax, the only place left to go is the next scene. And the big question as an editor is what type of scene should that be. Should it be a high-octane action scene, or should it be a more reflective sequel scene?

In the next section, we will learn how each type of scene is important to add depth to a story.

Fictionary Story Element: Action/Sequel

The mix of action scenes and sequel scenes is a balancing act, and when a story is perfectly balanced, the tension, flow, and pacing are kept throughout the story.

The levels of conflict or tension help determine whether the scene is an action scene or a sequel scene.

An action scene ends with a conflict-filled scene climax; a sequel scene is where a character reacts to an action scene. They pause and take stock.

The conflict scenes are higher-energy scenes. The sequel scenes are the quieter energy scenes. A sequel scene can be about internal reactions to the previous scene, or it can be external with quiet dialogue.

Definition

An action scene is where something happens, mostly written via movement and dialogue. Usually description and character internalizations are kept to a minimum. The POV character's goal drives the action and the story forward.

A sequel scene is where a character reacts to the events that happened in the action scene. This can be an emotional reaction, a decision made, or simply thoughts. If done well, the reader will feel a greater connection to the character.

Scene and Story Level

At the scene level, when you read through the story, list whether a scene is mostly an action scene or mostly a sequel scene. You'll do this at the scene level but review it at the story level.

At the story level, look at groups of all the same scene types. If there are lots of action scenes in a row, that is a signal these need to be read together to determine whether the reader might need to see the POV character reflecting on the action.

For too many sequels in a row, the creative story editor investigates if there is not enough happening in these scenes.

Perfecting the Action/Sequel Story Element

Your editing task is to decide whether the scene is mostly an action or mostly a sequel scene. List this for each scene and look for patterns.

Most scenes will be some combination of an action scene and a sequel scene, so look for the main intent. Or look for the one the scene ends with. Is the climax a conflict and not a decision? Then the scene is most likely an action scene.

Troubleshooting

Pacing and how a reader reacts to the work need to be considered. Too many action scenes in a row and the POV character and the reader cannot react to what is happening in the story. The reader might put the book down because they need a breather from all the conflict.

> **The biggest risk is too many scenes in a row that are sequel scenes.**

Sequel scenes show a character reacting to an action scene. Too many sequel scenes in a row means there is not enough action to react to. The excess of sequel scenes could get boring or make the character appear as if they are not doing anything—also boring.

Suggestions from an Editor

EDITOR 3:

There are a lot of action scenes in the story, which I think is connected to the issue raised earlier that Jaz's emotions aren't always that clear in the scene. If they were, or she were more self-reflective, this might balance out the Action/Sequel scenes.

Too many action scenes in a row can tire a reader. A reader needs to see how the characters react to the action scenes, and this is what sequels are for. A sequel can occur as a whole scene or as part of an action scene.

> ### TEA with Kristina
>
> Action scenes are the power, they are the extrovert scenes, going out looking for excitement. And the sequel scenes are introvert scenes, looking inward and questioning themselves. There are some scenes that are a little bit of both, and that works too.
>
> I love the editor's advice above because it tells me what the overall issue is with the action/sequel scenes and how to fix it. As I make my revisions based on the editor's comments, I'll add more sequel scenes.

Where to Next?

The next element is helpful for stories written from multiple POVs where the protagonist is not in every scene. It is also helpful for first-person narratives that have an unreliable narrator.

If the draft is a multiple POV story or the narrator is unreliable, it's important to keep track of what the protagonist knows and what the reader knows. Done well, keeping information from the protagonist but giving it to the reader is another way to create tension.

Let's move on and see how.

Fictionary Story Element: Reader Knowledge Gained

Information is power, and that power creates a huge tension-filled hook for the reader.

Part of the appeal of a multiple POV narrative is the reader knows more than the protagonist. This is powerfully addictive for the reader.

Part of the appeal of a first-person narrative is the intimacy. But if the narrator is unreliable, then this element can be used as the reader can use their knowledge of how life works compared to how the first person narrates the story.

A reader wants to read on because of the tension in the story. And that tension is driven by how much the reader knows. Too much knowledge and the reader has no desire to read on. Not enough knowledge and the reader will get lost. As with all the story elements, balance is important.

Reader Knowledge Gained is different from Revelation, Backstory, and Flashbacks, and it must be used in combination with those elements.

Definition

The Reader Knowledge Gained story element is a record of the amount of story critical knowledge the reader has gained in a scene that the protagonist doesn't know.

Scene and Story Level

At the scene level, as a creative story editor, you need to look at when in the scene the reader gets their knowledge.

At the story level, this Fictionary Story Element adds depth to the draft, no matter the POV style used. When the reader knows story critical information, the tension builds up, and this keeps the reader reading.

During revisions, scenes can get moved around. By having a list of the key items in Reader Knowledge Gained, the writer can keep track of when the knowledge was shown to the reader. This is important to check at the story level.

Perfecting the Reader Knowledge Gained Story Element

Your fun editing task for this story element is to look at the scene's beginning, middle, and end. Then note what is revealed to the reader. Keep a note of any information the reader gains, but the protagonist doesn't. Check for scenes where the protagonist is not in the scene and list the key information the reader learned.

> **Refer to the writer's skeleton blurb, and check if the reader knowledge gained is important to the story and whether or not the protagonist will achieve their story goal.**

When we edit, we like to see where the reader gains the knowledge. If that is perfect placement for that information level, great. We recommend moving it, if we think it needs to have more impact in a more obvious place.

IN A SCENE, THERE ARE THREE PLACES WHERE THE INFORMATION CAN BE GIVEN:

1. Scene climax

2. Scene beginning

3. Scene middle

If the knowledge is given at the scene climax, the reader will pay the most attention. The second-most potently memorable place is at the start of the scene. In the middle part of the scene, the reader knowledge gained can get glossed over by a careless reader. That might be the intention, and as a creative story editor, your artistry comes into play again.

Troubleshooting

Reader Knowledge Gained is great for sorting out information a reader might know but that the protagonist doesn't know.

Let's say the character hid a diary in the glove compartment of her car, and the protagonist goes to the car to steal it, but the protagonist was not in the scene where the character hid the diary. The reader will know the diary is there, but the protagonist won't.

Meaning. . . the protagonist can't act on the information they don't know.

Suggestions from an Editor

EDITOR 5:

Jaz is the first-person POV and this can limit the reader to only seeing what the POV narrator sees. And yet, you have achieved something very clever in your story. The dog visions allow Jaz to see things that she was not there for. This creates tension, as she does not see everything. Great stuff. There are places in the scene notes that I have discussed that the visions should be earlier or later, notably Poppy's nightmare vision, and subsequent ones.

> TEA with Kristina
>
> **This story-level feedback from the editor shows**

me where the editor thinks I should give information at a different time, and then there are specific notes in each scene that I can look at and see how they can improve my story's tension.

This is an advanced element and hard to track, but it is indicative of a larger issue.

I recommend addressing this element once the other story elements are complete. You'll be familiar with the story by then, and it will be easier to understand the Reader Knowledge Gained.

Where to Next?

Reader Knowledge Gained is all about the reader's knowledge compared to the knowledge that the protagonist has. The logical next set should be Fictionary Character story elements. And by happy happenstance, that's exactly where we are going after we have a quick summary of all the Plot elements!

Plot Elements Summarized

You've already made sure there is a story in the draft by checking the story arc scenes. Now we're focusing on the scene-by-scene edit. The following story elements are used to start the scene-by-scene edit.

- The scene name
- Its purpose in the story
- The opening type
- The closing type
- Whether the reader is hooked at the beginning of the scene

- Whether the reader is driven to read the next scene
- Whether the reader is anchored

After that you learned tension keeps the reader worried, conflict keeps the reader engaged, and a character's history, whether told through a revelation, backstory, or flashback connects the reader to the character.

Then you learned how to structure scenes using Scene Middle, Scene Climax, and Action/Sequel story elements. We ended the Plot story elements by understanding what a reader learns as compared with what the protagonist learns.

That means we've covered all the Fictionary Plot Story Elements, and perhaps you're wondering how these are going to work with the Character and Setting story elements. Perhaps you're wondering what steps to take next. We're going to show you.

For the editor working on someone else's book, keep going on the scene-by-scene edit. You'll use everything you do in this phase to create the best editing package possible for your client.

For the writer editing their own novel, you have a choice. Some writers like to revise the scenes now based on the Plot elements, and some like to keep going on the scene-by-scene edit, working their way through all the story elements. You are the artist, and the choice is yours.

We recommend you don't start revising if you haven't edited using all the Plot story elements. There won't be a full plan yet.

Assuming you've done a full edit of the Plot story elements, take a look at all the scenes where you marked the scene as not having a purpose. These are the first to revise or cut.

Once that's done, you know every scene has a place in the story. You can quickly work your way through the rest of the scene-level story elements.

For easy reference, here is a quick view of all the Plot story elements and how to edit using each one.

SCENE NAME

Have you named every scene in three words or fewer? Yes? Woo-hoo! Go to the next step.

NO?

If you have trouble naming the scene, it is time to look at the scene in depth.

Does the scene have the following?

1.   A clear POV character

2.   A clear POV character goal

3.   A middle

4.   A climax

If not, it's time to revise the scene and make sure each of the above is there.

SCENE PURPOSE

Does every scene have a purpose? Yes? Woo-hoo! Go to the next step. No?

If a scene in a story does not have a purpose related to the main story goal, it should be cut from the story or revised. A scene without a purpose will distract the reader from the main story: it may even bore the reader. And the reader might put the story down, all because the scene lacked purpose.

SCENE OPENING TYPE

Have you marked every scene with an opening type? Yes? Woo-hoo! Go to the next step. No?

Finish doing this for every scene. When you're ready to review the structure and balance of the story, you'll need this information.

SCENE CLOSING TYPE

Have you marked every scene with a closing type? Yes? Woo-hoo! Go to the next step. No?

Finish doing this for every scene. When you're ready to review the structure and balance of the story, you'll need this information.

SCENE ENTRY/EXIT HOOKS

Does every scene start with an entry hook and end with an exit hook? Yes? Woo-hoo! Go to the next step. No?

In the first one or two paragraphs of the scene, is the entry hook missing? In the last one or two paragraphs of the scene, is the exit hook missing?

When you have noted the entry and exit hooks for every scene, you'll have a strong view of whether this is done well, is a minor issue, or is a major issue.

Keeping track of these two elements during the scene-by-scene edit gives you information to use at the story-level edit.

SCENE ANCHORING

As the writer, editing your own story, if you've already revised your story based on the earlier list, we recommend revising the Anchored element next. With the entry and exit hooks done, you're close to knowing the scene starts and ends in the right place. An anchored scene helps draw the reader into the scene, helping the story flow.

Was every scene anchored? Yes? Woo-hoo! Go to the next step.

No?

Look at the three types of anchoring: POV Anchoring, Scene Time Anchoring, and Scene Setting Anchoring.

Does the draft have an overall issue with anchoring? Then this is a major issue the writer needs to know about.

SCENE TENSION

Does every scene have tension? Yes? Woo-hoo! Go to the next step.

No?

Using the story goal found in the skeleton blurb, look for places where there are no consequences if the POV goal fails or where the protagonist is closer to or pushed further from the story goal. This is a revise-or-cut action. And if there is no tension, it could mean the scene should not be in the story. Or if the scene is relevant, look at making the editing advice to revise.

SCENE CONFLICT

Does every scene have enough conflict? Yes? Woo-hoo! Go to the next step.

No?

Refer to the scenes that you marked as lacking conflict. Find the scene goal. Suggest actionable advice to revise places in the scene that stop the POV character from achieving their scene goal. A scene with no goal could be the reason the scene has no conflict.

SCENE REVELATION

Are the revelations in the scene needed just then? Yes? Woo-hoo! Go to the next step.

No?

Review the revelations from a story level. Are the revelations grouped together? Then the actionable advice is to spread out the revelations.

BACKSTORY

Is the backstory used evenly across the story up to the end of act 2? Yes? Woo-hoo! Go to the next step.

No?

Review the concentration of backstory. Does the backstory overwhelm the story and stop the story from moving to the story goal? Then some of the backstory should be cut.

Any backstory in act 3 should be moved or cut.

FLASHBACKS

Are the flashbacks plot relevant, and do they occur before the end of act 2? Yes? Woo-hoo! Go to the next step.

No?

Reread every flashback.

Suggest moving flashbacks if there are too many flashbacks grouped together. In act 3, recommend cutting or moving flashbacks.

The reader should be asked to invest only in flashbacks that are story critical.

SCENE MIDDLE

Has every scene middle been named in no more than three words? Yes? Woo-hoo! Go to the next step.

No?

Reread scenes where the scene middle could not be described. Remember MARCS. This is cut, revise, or split decision time. For each scene middle that was not named in fewer than three words, decide if that is because the scene should not be in the book, and if that is the case, then advise to cut the scene.

Perhaps the scene needs revising, so look at the POV scene goal and at the middle and make sure the POV character is proactive.

If the scene is too long or has two locations or two scene goals, split the scene, and then the naming should be easier. Some revisions might be necessary after the splitting.

SCENE CLIMAX

Has every scene climax been named in no more than three words? Yes? Woo-hoo! Go to the next step.

No?

Reread scenes where the climax was not described. Cut, revise, and split are the actionable advice for this story element. For each scene climax that could not be described, check if there is a clear scene goal. If it has a clear goal, then suggest to the writer that they revise the scene to address the scene goal in the climax.

If there is no scene goal, then advise they cut the scene or revise both the scene POV goal and the scene climax. If the scene has two scene goals, recommend splitting the scene into two.

ACTION/SEQUEL

Have all the scenes been named as action or sequel? Yes? Woo-hoo! Go to the next step.

No?

If you cannot choose whether a scene is an action or sequel scene, look at the climax, which will tell you how the reader will remember the scene if it is too close to call. Then look at the rest of the scene.

READER KNOWLEDGE GAINED

Are you happy with the Reader Knowledge Gained? Yes? Woo-hoo! Go to the next step.

No?

At the story level, review the reader knowledge gained for each scene until you're sure you can give the writer clear recommendations on how to handle this element.

Where to Next?

Onward through this scene-by-scene edit. It's time to get intimate with the characters.

Chapter Eleven:
Learn the Character Story Elements

> "The character story elements ensure my characters are never flat, but always motivated and connected to the story." — Ryan Rivers, Fictionary Certified StoryCoach Editor

Fictionary Character Story Elements

Characters have a heavy responsibility in a novel.

> **Readers must connect with and care about the protagonist so they will follow them through the whole length of the novel.**

If readers do not care about the protagonist or how the protagonist will negotiate the conflict, they will not read on.

As a creative story editor, our job is to get the reader to read the book, from the first page all the way through to the last. And the cast of characters, with extra focus on the protagonist, is where we need to put a lot of our editing time.

A creative story editor knows who the protagonist is, who is in the story, and who is in each scene.

This is only the beginning.

After you've listed all the characters in the novel and listed them for every scene, there's more to do.

This is the only way to fully edit the character in the context of the story structure.

What's great about being a Fictionary Story Editor is that the Fictionary software makes these steps simple.

While you're editing the story, here are some questions to ask yourself:

1.   Is there enough page time for each character to give the reader time to connect to them?

2.   Is the protagonist—we will talk more about this in the next section—in each of the five story arc scenes?

3.   And better yet, does the protagonist have the POV for each of the five story arc scenes?

4.   Does every character have a unique purpose at the story level and at the scene level?

5.   Are any of the character names too similar?

THE CHARACTER STORY ELEMENTS:

- Character List (per scene)
- POV (Point of View)
- POV Goal
- Character Arc
- POV Goal Internal
- Goal Related to Plot
- What if Goal Fails
- Impact on POV Character

- Impact on Protagonist
- POV Knowledge Gained
- Character in Motion

Scene and Story Level

Some of the Character story elements are used at the story level, some at the scene level, and some for both. As we cover each element, we'll show you how to use each element for maximum effect.

Perfecting the Character Story Elements

You may find that you spend more time evaluating some elements than others. That's okay.

All draft stories are strong in some areas and weak in others.

You may also find that by evaluating the story and each scene using the Fictionary Story Elements, some elements will require large revisions and others no revisions at all.

The goal is that you'll know you've covered all important elements of a story, and the story will be strong because of that. We guarantee the story will be better.

TEA with Kristina

Let's say you've just heard the news that thousands of people died in a tsunami. While incredibly sad, it's hard to connect the event to strong feelings, because you can't connect it to a person.

Now let's say you hear a story of a young woman on her way home to see her family for the first time in five years. Her name is Hannah. She has a one-year-old daughter in her arms. She arrives moments before the tsunami, just in time to see her family at a distance, but she doesn't

> get to hug them before the water kills them all. That has more of an impact because you see Hannah as a person with a goal.
>
> But what if Hannah has been your neighbor for the last five years? You've babysat her daughter, Samantha. Because you're more connected to Hannah, your feeling of loss is stronger.
>
> And it gets only stronger the more you're connected. What if Hannah was your spouse? Now the effect on you is horrific.
>
> This is the goal. You want the death of Hannah to affect readers in the strongest way possible. And the Fictionary Character story elements will sort that out.

Where to Next?

It's time to put in the work to make sure the characters live up to the responsibility they've been given, so let's look at the Fictionary Character story elements.

Fictionary Story Element: Character List

Too many characters in a scene will confuse the reader. If a character isn't properly introduced in a scene, the reader will get confused. You get the idea.

The excitement of using the character list to edit is seeing how the characters are woven through the story. This section and the next show how using a character list will add depth to the edit.

For now, we're evaluating the characters on a per-scene basis and not at the story level. A story-level review of the character list will come later.

Definition

The character list is split into two: the characters who have a role in the scene and the characters who are spoken or thought about in the scene. So as a creative story editor, knowing who's in and who's mentioned in a scene is important for creating a comprehensive edit.

We're going to split the character list into the quick fixes and the more sophisticated character list editing fixes.

Scene and Story Level

The character list is used to strengthen the reader's ability to connect with the cast of characters through the whole story and in each scene they are in.

The fewer characters in a scene and in a story, the more time a reader has to get connected with each character.

And it's important because your readers want to cheer for somebody or cheer against somebody, depending on the story. So the number of characters is going to influence that.

And, of course, there are exceptions. Having a scene with a large list of characters, such as basketball teams playing each other, is fine.

Perfecting the Character List Story Element

Your fun editing task is to list every character in every scene. Then list every character mentioned in every scene.

In Fictionary this is easy. Once you click on View Character List, you can add a character to a scene or one who's mentioned in a scene.

Troubleshooting

TOO MANY CHARACTERS

Are you worried there are too many characters in a scene?

The first step is to review who is in the scene. Since you've made a list for each scene, this is easy.

When reviewing the names, ask yourself, "Does every character have a unique purpose in the scene?"

If the answer is no, recommend the writer think about combining two characters into one.

The fewer characters, the more time there is to develop each character and the more time a reader has to grow to love the characters.

CONFUSING NAMES

Once you have listed the character names in all the scenes, review the names when listed together. We call this list the Cast of Characters. Readers can be confused by having names that are too similar. For example, Sherry and Shirley. Both start with the sh sound and end with a y.

As an editor, if you ever stumble over who a character is or refer back to previous pages to figure it out, there is a problem. This is what we're trying to avoid.

INCONSISTENT NAMING CONVENTIONS

With the list of characters, review naming conventions.

The following is good advice to ensure your drafts are clear to the reader:

1. Don't change a character's name.

2. Don't use nicknames.

3. Don't alternate between first and last names.

All these actions make it hard for a reader to keep track of names. There are cases where a character is referred to using more than one name by other characters in a book. For example, there may be an aunt whose niece refers to her as Auntie. Recommend the writer make it easy for the reader and call her Auntie Sarah, or whatever the character's first name is.

Suggestions from an Editor

EDITOR 7:

Quick note: This is the one and only time Jaz's assistant has been mentioned. Delete her character!

IMPACT OF EDITING ADVICE:

Let's look at the ending of scene five of the original version (115 words) of Evolution.

My assistant popped her head back in the room and snapped chewing gum. Her purple hair hung almost to her waist, and a soft roll swelled over her jeans. "Do you need anything else tonight? I'm on my way out."

"Nope. You can go." I strode to the door, and Mr. Wheaten Terrier had no choice but to follow me. I didn't like talking to strangers, especially ones with hidden agendas.

We exited, and I locked the outer door.

"Gotta go," I said and hoofed it through the dark parking lot to my car. I was seated with the ignition running before he could say anything more.

I had an empty home to go to.

> **By using Fictionary software, the editor can quickly check the number of scenes a character is in. So, this editor knew the character was in only one scene and didn't serve a purpose—and maybe even reduced the tension.**

Note there are other changes not related to character name, so these are in here, too

This was an easy fix. The new version of the ending was shorter (74 words) and ended as follows.

"Do you need anything else from me today? I'm on my way out." I strode to the door, and Mr. Wheaten Terrier had no choice but to follow. I didn't like talking to strangers, especially ones with hidden agendas. He could have mailed me Nick's things.

We exited, and I locked the outer door.

"Gotta go." I hoofed it to my car and was seated with the ignition running before he could say anything more.

I flipped on the wipers and sped out of the parking lot. The man faded to a blur in the rearview mirror.

TEA with Kristina

The editor's advice was only two sentences, and it helped me revise the scene and make it better just by removing one unnamed character.

I'm going to share an example from a book that I recently edited. The protagonist has two brothers with families in the story, and both families play a supporting role in helping the protagonist. Does there need to be two brothers? Is his one brother doing something different from the other brother? In this case, the answer was no. The protagonist had a nice family.

> Kinda boring.
>
> I recommended the writer cut one of the families altogether and revise the scenes with the second brother to include the first brother instead.
>
> What happens now is that the reader doesn't get confused between which brother is in a scene. They can get closer and more connected to one brother and his family, and it makes it easier for the reader to remember. It makes the readers happier, as they're more engaged with the character.

Where to Next?

We are just at the start of the character list. This section is to be used for the first editing pass. In the next section, we will explore how to use the character list after the initial editing pass. We'll cover when the characters enter the story, when they leave, and how to edit with those moments. Let's take a deeper look at using the character list after the first pass after scene-by-scene editing is complete.

Fictionary Story Element: How to Edit Using the Character List

After you've read through the draft and created the character list for every scene, you get to have more fun with the characters.

We love looking at the major and minor characters and how they are introduced into a draft. When a character is introduced to a story, the editor must evaluate if the page time given to the introduction is in sync with that character's importance.

The character list helps get the balance right for each character.

Definition

Post-read-through list of characters is the final list after the novel has been edited. This list was updated every time a scene was edited during the first pass.

The list of characters per scene helps you discover the following:

- When each character enters and exits the story.
- If the page time given to each character is right for the story.
- If the reader can keep track of characters from one scene to the next.

Scene and Story Level

At the scene level, find the first scene a character appears in.

> **Read the introduction of the character. Does it work in the scene?**

At the story level, the character introduction needs to be equal to the weight that the character plays in the story. There is no point introducing a character for three pages if they don't appear in the story again. Major characters deserve the page time.

At the story level, an editor will look at when major characters enter and exit the story. The protagonist must enter the story early and must not leave before the climax.

Perfecting Character List Story Element

Your fun editing task is to find the first scene each character appears in and check if the time spent on introducing the character is appropriate.

Troubleshooting

When you first read the story, were there any moments when you had to flip back to earlier in the story to figure out who a character was? Look at how they were first introduced.

Did any of the characters seem to jump out of nowhere? This will entail recommending scene revisions, so it's clear how the character got in the scene.

Here are areas to check.

MAJOR VERSUS MINOR CHARACTERS

Major characters should get a more detailed description than minor characters when they first appear. The level of description signals to the reader whether the character is important to the story.

OVERUSE OF CHARACTER DESCRIPTION

Use the Scenes per Character insight after you've read the story once and updated the characters per scene. If you feel the draft spends too much time describing characters, you can check this now. Look for characters who are in fewer than three scenes. If a lot of time is spent describing these characters or showing their backstory, recommend the descriptions and backstory be shortened. Go to the Cast of Characters and click View Character's First Scene. If the draft has spent too much time describing the character, then put a note on the scene on the Evaluate page.

KEEPING TRACK OF CHARACTERS

If a character is in one scene and the next scene is in the same location at the same time, then either the character must still be there, or their exit must be shown in the scene. This element will keep the draft from having disappearing characters.

CHARACTER ENTRY AND EXIT

Character entry is the first time a character appears in a novel. The character introduction is the beginning of their character arc. When a character exits the story, it's the end of their character arc.

Major characters will probably exit the novel later in the story.

Minor characters can exit anytime.

The more major a character is, the longer the introduction.

For the minor characters, not as long an introduction is needed. So once the reader is engaged with the character, not only do you need to know when they enter the story, but you need to know when they exit the story.

If there is a protagonist and they enter the story early, which they should, they shouldn't exit early. The protagonist must be in the climax scene, and they must also be in the five Fictionary Story Arc scenes.

When you're editing a story, you want to be looking at the following:

- Who is the protagonist?
- Are they in the key scenes?
- Are they in the majority of scenes?
- When did they enter the story?
- When do they exit the story?

Then you have a strong understanding of what the characters are doing scene by scene, but also throughout the story.

CHARACTER ENTRY AND EXIT RELATIVE TO OTHER CHARACTERS

The number of scenes a character appears in should increase along with how important the character is in the story.

The protagonist should be in the highest number of scenes.

Minor characters should be in the lowest number of scenes.

MAJOR EVENT

You'll want to check the protagonist is in the major scenes, such as the inciting incident, plot points, and climax. Without the protagonist in the climax scene, the reader will be disappointed. You'll also be able to keep track of which characters are in the scenes where major events occur. This will help fix any plot holes.

1. Check when key characters enter and exit the story.

2. Check when characters enter and exit the story relative to other characters.

3. Determine which characters were present for a major event.

Suggestions from an Editor

EDITOR 6:

You have a nice flow of characters across the scenes. The number of scenes per character matches their importance well.

And Nick is mentioned by Jaz in almost every scene! This is a great way to show he is always on her mind! He's central to the story.

Not much time is given to Jaz's family in the plot. This is fine, as it's not necessarily important. However, the scene in which her sister Olivia comes to visit is never fully closed off. Does her sister leave or stay the night? She seems to vanish completely in the next scene with no mention made of what happened.

> ## TEA with Kristina
>
> The editor's advice about Nick shows how important the mentioned characters are. It's great reinforcement that the characters and their time in scenes matches their importance to the story. Nick is the character murdered in Evolution, so he's very important to the story and to Jaz's motivations.
>
> The editor references Jaz's family. This is a good catch of a plot hole. I know to look at the sister, Olivia, to see how to fill in this plot hole.
>
> In this case, I left two sisters sitting on a veranda with no scene exit hook. I'm thinking a reader might put the book down and not pick it back up.

Where to Next?

The story elements are all interconnected. Once you know who is in each scene, you can decide if the best character was chosen as the POV character for that scene. Let's go on to find out if the right character was chosen as the POV character on a per-scene basis.

Fictionary Story Element: POV (Point of View)

A story needs to have a perspective, and that perspective comes from who is telling the story.

When a reader asks: "Who is telling this story, anyway?" they are asking whose perspective they are experiencing the story from.

Before we get into POV, let's look at the style of the story. A draft can be written from the choice of the following:

1. First person, such as Charles Dickens's David Copperfield.

2. Second person, such as Jay McInerney's Bright Lights, Big City.

3. Third person, such as George R. R. Martin's A Game of Thrones.

This is an overall story choice. Once that's made, readers want to know who is telling the story at the beginning of every scene. Yes, every scene.

The feelings, actions, and senses of the scene are all derived from the POV character's experiences.

A novel can be written from one character's POV, such as in Kristina Stanley's Evolution, which we're using as an example in this book, or from multiple POVs, such as in George R. R. Martin's A Game of Thrones. There are eight POV characters in the first book in that series.

Definition

The POV character is the character who is telling the story at any given moment. Their life experiences color how they see their story world, which may or may not be the same as what the reader sees. And that is the beauty of understanding POV and how to get the reader to read between the lines to see the real story being filtered by the POV character.

Scene and Story Level

At the scene level, the POV story element is edited on a scene-by-scene basis, looking for consistency.

When evaluating each scene, note the POV character. Scenes are mini stories, and the reader wants to know who's giving their opinion on how that scene plays out.

At the story level, when you've listed every POV character, it's time to edit the POV choices against the story structure.

THERE ARE QUESTIONS AT THE STORY LEVEL A CREATIVE STORY EDITOR MUST ASK:

- Is every Fictionary Story Arc scene written from the protagonist's POV? If not, why not?
- How many POV characters are there?
- Is the best balance used?

Perfecting the POV Story Element

Your fun editing task is to list the POV character for every scene. This will help you see the structure of the story.

The POV Characters insight shows the order, balance, and number of scenes each POV character has.

When a writer chooses a POV character for a scene, they promise the readers they will experience the scene from that character's perspective.

But how do you know if the writer kept that promise? You must edit the entire story against the list of POV characters.

The moment you think you know who the POV character for the scene is, list that character and then read the scene to make sure the scene stays true to the POV.

Troubleshooting

If the writer has expert control of POV, your job as an editor is easy. But if the POV is uncontrolled, then make sure the story doesn't switch to a different POV character by mistake.

If a scene is "following" the character of the police detective, suddenly switching to the POV of the suspect can be disorienting. This is called head-hopping and can jar the reader from the spell of the story.

In a multi-POV story, check the majority of the scenes are written from the protagonist's POV. If more time is spent on secondary characters, it's possible the wrong protagonist was chosen.

> **If a POV character changes within a scene, it must be done efficiently and without confusion.**

A reader needs time to connect with characters. The fewer the POV characters, the more time readers have to bond with each individual character, and the more invested they'll feel in the story.

> **If there are seven or more POV characters in a story, it's time to look at each one and recommend ways to reduce the number.**

Suggestions from an Editor

EDITOR 4:

The novel is told in first-person POV from Jaz's perspective. However, in scene 7 (the first scene in chapter 4), the POV shifts to third-person limited (still from Jaz's perspective). This should be rewritten in first person to match the rest of the novel.

TEA with Kristina

The editing advice shows I didn't notice I'd switched perspectives. This is a great catch by editor 4.

If a writer is struggling with POV control, recommend starting a new scene every time there is a change in POV characters. You can also sug-

> gest how to cut portions of a scene that contain head-hopping. This gives the writer something to practice.

Where to Next?

We previously covered the purpose of a scene. You know why the scene is in the story. And now you can decide whether the best POV character was chosen to match the purpose of the scene. This is one more example of how the story elements are interrelated.

Writing from a character's POV won't help the story be great if the POV character doesn't have a goal. Let's find out how goals can improve tension, pacing, and everything else in a story.

Fictionary Story Element: POV Goal

A character without a goal is boring.

The POV character goal is what the POV character wants during a scene. It must be something external to them. External goals drive a story forward.

Goals create proactive characters, and proactive characters are interesting. Without a goal, there's no one for the reader to cheer for or against, no meaningful obstacle to put in the character's way—and no reason for your reader to keep reading. If a character doesn't have a goal, then what are they doing?

The external goal is what a character wants in the story, not what they want in life. For this element we're evaluating the scene goal and not the overall story goal found in the blurb.

Definition

The external goal is the goal a character shows the story world and the reader. It's what the POV character strives to accomplish in a scene.

Scene and Story Level

The element is important at both the story and the scene level. At the scene level, you must edit each scene and determine what, if anything, is the POV character's goal.

The scene level is where we break up the big story goals into smaller ones, enabling the reader to track the progress of the goal.

The POV goal at the scene level sets up the opportunity to create conflict in the scene. Great stuff.

Remember to refer to the Conflict story element for details. Conflict in the scene should hinder the character in their attempt to achieve their goal.

At the story level, the goals must become stronger as the story progresses. The consequences of not achieving the goal should get worse as the story progresses. Keep track of the goals for every scene so you learn how they change over the course of the story.

Perfecting the POV Goal Story Element

Your fun editing task is to list the POV character's goal for every scene.

Review the goals in the scenes immediately after the inciting incident, plot point 1, the middle plot point, plot point 2, and the climax. These are good places for the protagonist's goal to change or be altered because of what happened in the plot point scenes. This activity will ensure the Fictionary Story Arc scenes are transformational.

A character with a goal related to the overall story goal found in the blurb is a driving force within the story. To check if the goal is related to the overall story, ask, "Does the goal help or hinder the main story goal outlined in the blurb for the story?" If it's neither, it's the wrong POV goal.

A three-dimensional character should have both internal and external goals.

We will discuss the internal goals in the "POV Goal Internal" section.

External goals are tangible.

Make sure the external goal relates to the main plot and to the character's overall goal for the novel. For example, in a murder mystery, the protagonist's goal for the novel is to solve the murder.

Troubleshooting

If you can't list the goal for the scene, there is an issue with the scene that must be addressed.

Always remember the $\sqrt{}$. If the POV character's goal is clear, motivate the writer and let them know. List the goal beside the check mark. This is invaluable information for the writer.

If they think the goal is something different than what you listed, the scene is not doing what they intended it to do.

Edit each scene.

1.   Does the POV character have no goal? Mark it "No Goal."

2.   Does the POV character have too many goals, causing the scene to lack focus? Mark the scene "Too Many Goals."

3.   Are the goals inconsistent with the POV character's personality? Mark "Inconsistent."

4.   POV goal is solved too quickly and bores the reader. Mark "Too quick."

Suggestions from an Editor

EDITOR 4:

At times, the POV Goal or the POV Goal Internal of the scene is unclear, or there are too many goals. At other times, it's crystal clear. The difficulty seems to arise when the main protagonist is not really directing the scene through any inner monologue and simply seems a passive player in a conversation with someone else that is informing her of events. In other words, she can seem passive in the scene also. This issue may be resolved by projecting more of Jaz's thoughts into each scene so she is seen to react to the events around her, thereby enabling the reader to see what her desire or goal is in that scene.

TEA with Kristina

The editor's notes showed me I didn't have full control over Jaz, the protagonist and the POV

character in every scene.

POV goals break down the main story goal, so that the reader can believe the protagonist is ready to face the main story goal in the climax.

An external goal must be tangible. To know if a goal is tangible, ask yourself whether the reader knows when the goal is reached. If it's clear a goal is reached, then the goal is tangible.

If the goal is to be happy, how does the reader know it's been accomplished? Not tangible.

If the goal is to get a puppy, the reader knows if the character got that puppy. Very tangible. And I love puppies, so I used this example.

Where to Next?

At this stage of the edit, we know who is in each scene, who the POV character is, and what the POV character goal is. Now we're going to figure out how that relates to the story.

In every scene, the protagonist is either further away from reaching the main story goal, the one promised to the reader in the blurb, or closer to achieving the goal. The character arc helps edit this. We're going to look at a character arc in terms of the character's goals and not in terms of their personal development.

Fictionary Story Element: Character Arc (in connection to the Story Goal)

The Fictionary Character Arc shows you if a scene is needed in a story.

That's a complicated task, but you're going to see how easy it is to accomplish.

You'll remember that the purpose of a scene also shows if a scene is needed. The character arc and the purpose of a scene make a powerful combination.

> **It's important to keep track of the protagonist and whether they are moving away from or toward achieving their main story goal.**

Every story has one entity that is the protagonist. And they must get closer to or further from the story goal. Readers need to follow someone—a character, a group—to the end of the story. In Chapter 3: Meet the Story Promise ("The Fictionary Protagonist" section), we show how to identify the protagonist. Before editing using this story element, make sure it's clear who the protagonist is.

Definition

We have a different way of looking at a character arc. We're using the protagonist and the story goal to determine whether the protagonist is closer or further away from the story goal by the end of a scene.

> **A change in the character arc creates movement in the story.**

The character arc should either be positive, meaning the character is moving toward the story goal, or negative, meaning the protagonist is further away from their story goal. Never neutral, as that means the story has stopped moving forward.

Scene and Story Level

At the scene level, this story element keeps the story interesting.

Keep track of this for every scene in the book, even if the protagonist is not in the scene. Their goal should either get easier or harder to achieve based on what other characters do. Otherwise, why is the scene in the story?

After you've noted whether each scene moves the protagonist closer or further away from their story goal, you'll draw the character arc.

> **If you're using Fictionary, this draws automatically for you.**

Once you've drawn the character arc, review it at the story level to ensure there are ups and downs in the character arc.

Remember, if you have a flat character arc, the reader might get bored and put the book down.

Perfecting the Character Arc Story Element

Your fun editing task is to read each scene and mark the character arc as positive, neutral, or negative.

Cause and effect: the forward motion of a scene can be assessed if you know how the scene impacts the protagonist's main story goal.

> **No matter what type of protagonist the story has, the impact on the protagonist must be strongly positive or negative in each of the five Fictionary Story Arc scenes.**

The story arc scenes have a big impact on the story, so they must have a big impact on the protagonist. The impact should be stronger than in the other scenes. And in the climax scene, it must be the strongest.

> **Remember the inciting incident is the moment the protagonist's world changes in a dramatic way, and their story goal is stated.**

If the protagonist's state does not change in a dramatic way when their world changes in a dramatic way, there is a problem. Perhaps the wrong protagonist was chosen, or perhaps the inciting incident isn't related to the plot. Whatever the reason, the scene needs to be revised.

Plot point 1 is the point of no return. The character can't back out of the central conflict, and they accept their story goal. This is the moment when the setup of the story ends and act 1 is over.

Let's face it. If any one of us changes our lives and can't return to our previous life, we are going to feel different when that happens. The protagonist must too.

The middle plot point is when the protagonist changes from reactive to proactive.

Here again the protagonist is going to change their behavior, and the only way that happens is if their state changes.

Plot point 2 will be a low point for your protagonist. Their actions since the middle have caused disaster. At plot point 2, they become more determined to reach their goal.

> **Note the word disaster in the description.**

That shows you must take the protagonist from a positive to a negative state in this story arc scene.

Depending on the type of story written, the protagonist either wins or loses. They achieve the main story goal or they don't. And that must impact their emotional and physical state. Let me repeat that. The story arc scenes must impact the protagonist.

Let's get back to positive, negative, neutral, and your editing task.

It's important to understand the character arc across the entire novel. And this means you must draw it, or you can let Fictionary draw it for you. You have three choices for each scene, and each choice draws the character arc.

- Positive: the character arc rises.
- Neutral: the character arc stays flat.
- Negative: the character arc descends.

Troubleshooting

The character arc is the key movement in a scene and a key to keeping the story moving forward. If the scene is not related to the story goal, there are two choices: recommend the writer rewrite the scene or cut the scene.

As a creative story editor, advising a cut is difficult, whether giving that advice to someone else or to yourself. But when you know categorically that there is a reason for the cut, that the scene is not pulling its weight in the story, then the cut is easier to make.

Suggestions from an Editor

EDITOR 10:

Flat lines on the [character arc] insight mean the scene needs work. This means it's time to question whether the scene belongs in the story because the scene didn't have a positive or negative impact on Jaz in terms of the story goal. When there is no impact on her, the story isn't moving forward. Every scene must make it harder or easier for her to achieve their goal.

TEA with Kristina

The advice from editor 10 is okay but not great. It's missing the explanation of what I should do. This comment was in a summary letter and not in the notes per scene. It's unclear if it re-

> lates to a big problem in the story or a minor problem. It's also unclear what scene I need to address.
>
> Lucky for me, the edit was performed in Fictionary, and I could see how the editor marked the scenes for the character arc. This showed what scenes I needed to revise.
>
> The world's best creative story editors give specific, actionable advice.

Where to Next?

You're probably getting the idea that goals are very important. So let's tackle the internal goal of the POV character.

Fictionary Story Element: POV Goal Internal

Without internal goals, a character will come across as flat.

The internal goal of the POV character is usually a weakness the character must overcome. They may or may not be aware of this weakness at the beginning of the story.

The weakness will hinder the character and is something they must conquer to reach their external story goal.

If the reader understands early in the story that the character has a weakness—often referred to as the internal flaw—they'll be expecting that character to change based on that weakness. The character will have an internal goal of working on this weakness throughout the story.

Characters with flaws and weaknesses are not just interesting to read about; they make the story flow, as it is the connecting story thread that pulls the reader into the story.

Without an internal goal, the character stays two-dimensional.

Definition

An internal goal is related to a major character weakness. This weakness should make it difficult for the character to reach their external goal. The weakness is a personality trait or repeated behavior that has a negative impact on the POV character.

Let's dig deeper and figure out the internal goal in the story you're editing.

Scene and Story Level

At the scene level, the POV character's internal goal may not be known to that character, but the reader needs to know about it early in the story. Sometimes the inner goal is even shown in the story's blurb.

> ### Not all POV characters must have an internal goal.

Sometimes a POV character is used to pass along information to the reader, or make the protagonist's life difficult, or give a clue. If the character is not a major character, they must have an external goal for a scene if they are the POV character, but they don't need an internal goal for the scene.

At the story level, the internal goal belongs to the protagonist. It can be something that the protagonist might not know until the middle of the story, but the reader has to be aware of it at the beginning of the story.

Perfecting the POV Goal Internal Story Element

You have two fun editing tasks for the internal goal. The first is to determine the story-level internal goal for the protagonist. The second is to list the internal goal (if there is one) for each POV character.

The internal goal can be shown in backstory or a flashback but does not have to be.

One way to proceed is to make a list of the POV characters' internal goals and then ask yourself, "Is that goal something that character needs as opposed to wants?"

It's important for the reader to understand the emotional meaning each action has for the protagonist and POV character, and the emotional meaning must be driven by a strong internal goal. We'll get into this more when we cover the impact the scene has on the protagonist and on the POV character.

> **There might be only one internal goal per POV character, which can last for the entire novel, or if there's a strong protagonist, there might also be only one internal goal for that character for the entire novel.**

A beautifully written book that has a protagonist who has a story-wide internal goal is called The Woman in the Window by A. J. Finn. It's about a woman who can't leave the house. In the opening scene, she's watching people on her street, and she wants to go out, but she can't. And right away the author has not told the reader that this is the problem. They've shown it brilliantly in the opening scene.

Troubleshooting

Early on, if it's not clear what the internal flaw is, one option is to query the writer before you get too far into the edit. Another option is to keep editing and see the point in the story when it becomes clear.

Look out for two characters who have the same internal goal. This is perfect if the protagonist is a combined protagonist. If not, check whether both characters are needed in the story.

Suggestions from an Editor

EDITOR 10:

The main internal goals seem to be coping with the loss of Nick, dealing with her [Jaz's] anxiety, understanding what happened to Nick, and being a better friend and better connected to those around her. Coping with the loss of Nick and anxiety are interlinked. She doesn't have Nick to help her with the anxiety and therefore has to draw on other sources, including herself. Coping with the loss of Nick also leads her into seeking to find out and understand what happened to him. Her journey to redemption is also Nick's. This is a good parallel.

These are quite good internal goals, as they are more long-term in nature; therefore Jaz can't solve them quickly, and it prevents the story from becoming episodic. **However, some of the individual scene goals are probably solved a little too quickly at times.**

This can decrease the tension in the plot if she is seen to be achieving her goals too quickly. For example, when Jaz introduces Lady to Christopher, apart from one initial blip, it actually goes very smoothly, which, given Christopher was near a melting point earlier in the scene, may seem unbelievable. Please see notes and comments about these matters in the scenes.

> ## TEA with Kristina
>
> An editor's role is to look at each scene and guess, as you read through it, what you think the internal goal is. Sometimes editors get this right on the first pass through a story, and

sometimes they don't.

And so the advice to the writer at the beginning entails ways that you can rewrite the opening scenes to clarify the internal flaw, which drives the internal goal for the character.

In the editor's suggestions above, I put in bold the sentence that had the most meaning to me. Here it is again: However, some of the individual scene goals are probably solved a little too quickly at times.

I can see clearly that when a goal is achieved too quickly, it's a problem. My revision plan includes reviewing Jaz's internal goals and seeing how I can slow down her success.

The opening line of the advice is a concern to me. Just reading the number of internal goals made my eyes water. Seeing that from the editor's perspective showed me Jaz has too many internal goals. I'm going to figure out what the most important one is and make it clear in the story.

Where to Next?

Even though we know who is in every scene, we're still focusing on the POV character. This shows you how choosing the right character for this lead role is essential to creating a great story.

We've shown having a goal is important, so next we ask, "Is the POV character's goal related to the plot?" A scene goal that's not related to the overall story makes the story seem episodic, and readers find episodic stories easy to put down.

Fictionary Story Element: Goal Related to Plot

Linking scene goals to the plot makes the characters believable and the scenes fast paced.

Readers need to connect to stories with their hearts and minds, and the internal and external goals deal with just that. When the internal goal is in the scene, it appeals to the reader's emotions.

When the external goal is in the scene, the reader connects intellectually with the scene and wonders how the characters will achieve their tangible goal. By relating to the plot, the scene goals thread scenes together and pull the reader through the story.

What we're focusing on here is asking, "Is the external goal related to the plot?" This is a common way a writer can go awry with the story, and we want to keep them focused.

We're not evaluating the internal goal.

Definition

The external goal is what the POV character wants in a scene. The Goal Related to Plot story element is a reminder to edit the scene goal against the story goal stated in the blurb. So, yes, we're back to the blurb again.

Even though we're focusing on the external goal, we must remember that all elements are interrelated.

When either of the external or internal scene goals relate to the plot, then this link gives your character depth. The reader connects with the external goal intellectually, and the reader connects with the internal goal emotionally. These two connections are like story-reader superglue, and the reader sticks with the story to the end. And then once they put the book down, thanks to this story element, the story sticks in their memory.

Scene and Story Level

The Goal Related to Plot story element is analyzed for every scene.

You've listed the external goal under the POV Goal for the scene. You know what the overall story goal is from the blurb. So now you're checking that the external POV goal is related to the plot.

A way to test this is to ask if the goal will help the protagonist achieve their main story goal or make it harder for them. If the answer is no to both, the goal needs work.

At the story level, once the POV character's goal and how it is related to the plot is listed for every scene, review the list. Maybe this element is handled perfectly, in which case, let the writer know. If not, determine if any issues with this element are minor or major. A major issue may mean the story is episodic and needs major revision.

Perfecting the Goal Related to Plot Story Element

Your fun editing task is to list if the external POV goal is related to the plot for every scene. It can be as simple as putting "Yes" or "No" for the Goal Related to Plot story element. Or you can list why it's not related to the plot.

Troubleshooting

A goal can be expressed through dialogue, thought, action, or description.

Varying methods will make the story more interesting to the reader and add depth to the characters.

If the scene goals don't relate to the plot, then the story can feel episodic.

Let's look at an example of intensifying a scene by linking the goal to the plot.

The POV character's goal is to pick up her car from the service station. The antagonist is trying to find and kill the POV character, but he knows only what car she drives. He doesn't know where she lives, but he knows where she took her car for servicing. In this case, the POV character goal of getting her car from the service station puts her life in danger, gives an advantage to the antagonist, and builds suspense.

The reader needs to believe the actions the characters carry out could happen in the story world.

Giving a character a goal that is not related to the plot may make the reader wonder why the character has that goal. They may think the character's actions don't make sense in the context of the story. Once that happens, the risk is losing the reader.

Suggestions from an Editor

EDITOR 1:

Some good character development happens in the first part of this scene with Jaz making a concerted effort to get out of the house and go shopping. This shows the reader Jaz is making a progression toward her goals.

TEA with Kristina

The suggestion from the editor let me know that there is good character development in the scene. The first issue is that I'm not sure if the editor thinks the goal is related to the plot. The second issue is that I'm not sure if this was mentioned, because I have an issue in other places with relating the goal to the plot. The suggestion falls into the vague category and could be done better.

The smaller scene goals are manageable, bite-size goals that build up meaning for the reader. These scene goals also teach the reader that the writer knows how to build a story; they build trust between the reader and the writer.

A creative story editor needs to give advice that will make the reader–writer bond strong. Scene goals related to the main story goal provide one of the best places to look at this.

Where to Next?

We've covered the following Character story elements:

- The importance of knowing your characters in every scene
- Who the POV character is

- What their external goal is
- The character arc
- What their internal goal is
- Whether the goal is related to the plot

Now we're starting to tie these together. We know how to look for the scene goals and whether they are related to the plot goal for every scene. If the goal is not related to the plot, the post-edit options become revise or cut the scenes. But we are not through the edit yet! We need to keep looking at goals in every scene.

What if the goal fails? Does anything bad happen? Let's find out how to go even deeper into character goals.

Fictionary Story Element: What if Goal Fails?

If there are no stakes, there is no tension, and if there is no tension, the reader stops reading. This element is important, because if the scene goal fails and there are no consequences, it means there are no stakes, and it means the reader stops reading.

You get the idea. No stakes, no tension. No tension, no readers.

There are two parts to this Fictionary Story Element.

The first part: Are there any consequences if the POV character fails at achieving their scene goal?

The second part: If there are consequences, then how often does the POV character fail or succeed at achieving the scene goal?

As the creative story editor, looking out for the stakes is a major part of the edit. When there is nothing at stake, the reader will lose interest in the story.

When there is something at stake, the reader will stay in the story world.

A creative story editor always looks for moments when a reader might shrug and whisper the dreaded "meh" as they put the book down.

Then, once the consequences have been edited to be strong, the pattern of successes and failures needs to be edited. In some scenes, the character should reach the goal, and in others, the goal should not be reached. This will pull the reader through the story and keep them wondering what will happen next.

Also, be aware, that a consequence that is not related to the plot cannot be used to edit whether the scene goal fails. These unrelated consequences are not related to the plot, therefore not related to the story.

Definition

The Fictionary What if Goal Fails story element is all about consequences that will happen to the POV character if they do not achieve the scene goal.

Scene and Story Level

This scene-level element helps you edit each scene based on what is and isn't written. Yes, you read that correctly.

At the scene level, list what happens if the POV character doesn't reach the goal. The consequences will be greater in the five Fictionary Story Arc scenes and greatest in the climax scene. This is because the climax answers the question: Did the protagonist reach the main story goal?

At the story level, the creative story editor is looking for balance. Keep track of the number of scenes in which the POV character achieves the story goal and the number of scenes in which they fail to achieve the goal.

Perfecting the What If Goal Fails Story Element

You have two fun editing tasks for this story element. The first is to list the consequence if the goal fails, and the second is to keep track of the number of times the POV character fails to achieve their goal versus the number of times they succeed.

We like to list the edit as follows:

POV Goal: Find lost dog in the desert.

What if Goal Fails: F: Dog dies.

By using "F" before the consequence, you'll know if the POV character fails to achieve the goal. The reader will find out in the scene climax.

Note, you still list the consequence. In this case, if the dog is not found, it dies. What you're looking for is whether the reader feels tension as they read the scene. Not whether the dog dies or not.

The "F" and the "S" will be used to check for balance.

So far, we have looked at making sure there is a scene goal in every scene.

This element is the litmus test to see if that scene goal is good enough.

This doesn't mean the goal must fail. It means the reader must worry that if the goal fails, something bad happens. Remember the Plot story element called Tension? It's the fear of something bad happening.

Troubleshooting

When you find a POV goal has no real consequences when the goal isn't achieved, then either the scene needs to be revised or the scene needs to be cut. A goal in a scene is important, but it is important that this goal is good enough for the scene.

If the POV character's goal is to have a cup of coffee and she doesn't get it, will the reader really care? Probably not. But what if she wants a cup of coffee and there is poison in the coffee? Now there is a lot at stake, and there is tension in the scene, and the reader cares.

If the character fails every time, the story becomes unbelievable. The reader must question whether the character will succeed or fail at achieving the main plot goal.

When achieving a goal is causing a lack of tension or making a character unlikable, your client needs to know.

Suggestions from an Editor

EDITOR 12:

As a result of being unable to clearly identify some goals, it's also not possible to see if these succeed or fail. There are a number that also have no consequences (that is, it doesn't matter to the scene if the goal fails or succeeds). Often this is because the goal of the scene may also be a little weak.

TEA with Kristina

The editor is suggesting that part of the problem in Evolution starts with the scene goal being weak. The first step in my revision process for this element is to fix the problem with the goal; then I can work on what happens when the goal fails. In Fictionary, the editor also filled out the What if Goal Fails story element, so I know which specific scenes need revising.

Where to Next?

That's it for character goals. We've looked at the protagonist's story goal and at every POV character's external and internal goals to ensure all goals are related to the plot, every scene moves the protagonist closer to or further away from the story goal, and all the goals have consequences. By doing this for every scene, you're sure there are strong, focused goals to keep the reader reading.

There's still more to learn. Whether the POV character succeeds or fails at achieving the scene goal, that character will be impacted in some way. So, you guessed it: that's what we'll cover next.

Fictionary Story Element: Impact on POV Character

If a scene doesn't impact the POV character, there is a problem with the scene. Perhaps the wrong POV character was chosen. Perhaps there were no consequences if the POV character failed to achieve the scene goal. Perhaps the scene has no place in the story. This works well with the story elements: purpose of a scene and the character arc. We're getting strong knowledge to show us whether every scene deserves a place in the story.

The impact on the POV character can be emotional or physical. It can be something that causes the POV character to change direction or perform a new action. The point is that something must change.

The impact on the POV character either causes the character to grow or motivates the character to act. Characters like James Bond don't grow much internally, but they react and drive the story based on how a scene impacts them.

Characters who grow in a story do so to overcome their internal flaw, and this helps them reach the external story goal.

For single POV novels, you won't use this story element, and you can jump right ahead to Impact on Protagonist in the next section.

Definition

Impact on POV Character is how the POV character reacts to the actions in the scene. Every time they fail to achieve their goal, they react. Every time they achieve their goal, they react.

Scene and Story Level

This is a scene-level story element.

At the scene level, for the POV characters to feel real to a reader, that POV character must have realistic feelings and must react to events in a realistic way.

If the scene does not impact the POV character, the scene must be revised or cut.

Perfecting the Impact on POV Character Story Element

Your fun editing task is to list the impact the scene has on the POV character for every scene.

It's impossible to keep track of the emotional growth of a character without knowing how each scene impacts that character.

When you read a scene, you should know by the end whether the emotional impact on the POV character was positive or negative. This emotional impact will cause the POV character to take action.

Keep track of whether the impact is:

- Positive
- Negative
- Neutral, meaning there is no impact

For any scenes where there is no impact, recommend the writer revise the scene to show an impact. If there is no impact, there is no character reaction. And if the character doesn't react, nothing happens. And when nothing happens, a scene is boring.

Troubleshooting

If the character comes across as flat, or they don't ring true, look at this Fictionary Story Element. Stories are about characters, and if the characters don't learn from their experiences, then what is the point of the story?

This story element is tightly related to the scene goal. Reviewing the scene goal helps make recommendations for this element.

Suggestions from an Editor

EDITOR 5:

[The following refers to the scene in which Jaz visits the crash site where her husband died.]

This should be an emotional scene, but it's lacking a little. This is why I put "neutral" in the Impact on POV Character element. It shouldn't be neutral; it should be positive or negative. There needs to be more emotion in this scene regarding Jaz's reaction to things. Let the scene contribute to that emotion. She does have regret; she runs her hand over the stone and imagines Nick's last thoughts. This is a great start, but just push it further. Her husband died here. Does she hear his voice hanging in the air? Does she cry? Does her fear and anxiety almost take over and she can't even look at the rock/ stone, but she forces herself to not only look but to touch it?

TEA with Kristina

I love this story element because it helps me make sure the story goal is strong.

In the editor's suggestion, it's clear the scene in question has an issue.

The following is the opening line of the scene:

"I want to see where Nick crashed," I [Jaz] said.

That's a very clear goal. By this point in the story, the reader knows Nick was murdered and can understand Jaz's drive to find out who killed him and why.

The editor is encouraging me to go deeper and show Jaz reacting to where Nick was murdered. As an author, maybe I shied away from this because I've been happily married for a long time and don't want to think too hard about losing my husband. I'm going to face that fear and do a better job when I revise this scene.

Where to Next?

We just covered how the scene impacts the POV character. It's important not to forget the protagonist in all of this. The protagonist cannot be ignored. Every scene, as you already know from looking at the character arc, must bring the protagonist closer to or further away from achieving their story goal.

Now we're going to go deeper into the protagonist's world using the Impact on Protagonist story element.

Fictionary Story Element: Impact on Protagonist

The Impact on Protagonist Fictionary Story Element shows how the protagonist is affected emotionally and physically by the events of the scene even if they are not in the scene.

The protagonist and the POV character may be the same for some or even all the scenes of the draft. When they differ, you'll use both the Impact on POV Character and Impact on Protagonist story elements.

The protagonist must not change too early in the story; the change should be hinted at so there is growth throughout the story, and the internal flaw should not be solved until the climax scene.

When a protagonist is too early in their emotional growth for the story, then the pacing can feel off, and when they are too late, they might not be ready to face the climax, and the reader won't believe that the protagonist has the emotional resilience to face the climax.

Definition

Impact on Protagonist is how the protagonist reacts to the actions in the scene.

Every time they fail to achieve their goal, they react. Every time they achieve their goal, they react.

Scene and Story Level

At the scene level, read the scene and determine if the scene had a positive, negative, or neutral emotional impact on the protagonist. The protagonist might not be in the scene but must be impacted by every scene. Keep track of the ups and downs of the emotional reaction and use them for the protagonist's emotional growth.

Every scene must impact the protagonist, even if they are not in the scene.

This is not confusing, when you edit to see how the action would make the protagonist feel if they knew.

At the story level, the view of the positive reactions and negative reactions needs a holistic approach.

WE NEED TO LOOK AT THE WHOLE, AND TO FOCUS ON TWO ISSUES THAT CAN ARISE:

1. Are too many scenes impacting the protagonist in a positive way?

2. Does the protagonist go through enough negative reactions to prove to the reader that they have learned the emotional resilience the story teaches them?

Perfecting the Impact on Protagonist Story Element

Your fun editing task is to look at how the protagonist feels at the beginning of the scene and at the end of the scene and mark a + or a - if they end up feeling better or worse, respectively.

With the skeleton blurb—when the protagonist has a story goal with high stakes—would they emotionally react to the events in this scene in this way?

As the editor, if you feel the protagonist comes across as flat, this is a place to look for ways to fix that. We need to analyze each scene for how the protagonist feels at the beginning and end of the scene. Is there a change?

When you read a scene, you should know by the end whether the emotional impact on the protagonist character was positive, negative, or neutral.

Keep track of whether the impact is:

- Positive
- Negative
- Neutral, meaning there is no impact

At this point in the editing process, the control of what the character feels needs to be edited. Some authors say that when they are writing scenes, the characters control how things turn out.

A creative story editor's job is to give that control back to the author, even if you are both the editor and the au-

thor.

Troubleshooting

You may find a protagonist feels something that is not appropriate to feel until much later in the novel.

A protagonist must not feel an emotion in the wrong place for a story. If Elizabeth Bennet realizes in the first half of the book how wonderful Mr. Darcy really is, then perhaps Pride and Prejudice would not be such a great book. Getting the emotional timing of the protagonist is important; it builds up to the crescendo of the climax.

For example, if you have a protagonist whose flaw at the beginning of the story is fear of intimate relationships, and this is the flaw that will change by the end, you don't want to have a scene mid novel where the character has an intimate moment with another character.

Jane Austen hints at the second proposal by having Mr. Darcy declare his love right in the middle of the story. And Elizabeth Bennet is not emotionally ready to get married to him.

Suggestions from an Editor

EDITOR 9:

The other thing that stands out in this scene is that the protagonist does not seem to have an emotional reaction to the news of being pregnant. Her reaction seems to match the clinical, nondescript state of her surroundings, which may be deliberate. However, in the end all she does is get changed and leave. Is she happy, sad, overwhelmed?

> ## TEA with Kristina
>
> We all react emotionally to different situations. The editor is suggesting that a woman would react to being told she's pregnant. I believe any person would have an emotional reaction. So I know I must revise the scene being referenced to give Jaz an emotional reaction to the news. For this scene, the editor put neutral in the Im-

pact on Protagonist story element because Jaz didn't have a reaction.

I know I must revise the scene, and I'm excited to do so because I know what specifically needs to be addressed. This means the advice is actionable.

Where to Next?

We have looked at the emotional journey of each POV character and the protagonist throughout the story. We know who is in each scene, who the POV character is for each scene, whether each scene drives the protagonist closer to or further away from achieving the story goal, whether each goal is related to the plot, what happens if the goal fails, and, finally, how each scene impacts the POV character and the protagonist. Phew! That's a lot.

All of this is going to help with the next Fictionary Story Element. This is a plot hole–finding element. As an editor, our job is to note plot holes so the reader's journey through the story is the one the writer intended.

Fictionary Story Element: POV Knowledge Gained

Keeping track of what each POV character knows ensures the story is consistent and doesn't have plot holes.

A plot hole can cause a reader to lose trust in a writer. Once that trust is gone, as in real life, it's hard to get back. For example, a significant clue or revelation might be revealed in a scene that a character is not in. Later, that character references the clue or revelation, but they can't possibly know about it because they weren't in the scene where it was revealed.

A creative story editor must know what each POV character learns at what point in the story, because a character acting on knowledge they don't have will take the reader out of the story.

This element is not intended to cover minor revelations or events, that do not relate to the story goal.

Definition

POV Knowledge Gained keeps track of which POV character knows which revelation, or story critical information, so the POV character won't act on information they don't know yet.

Scene and Story Level

You'll keep track of this at the scene level but use the information at the story level.

Whatever you list for the revelation of a scene, you also list which character knows this information. We're particularly interested in the POV characters.

In Fictionary, copy the information you listed in the Revelation story element to POV Knowledge Gained.

If the POV character is not the protagonist, and the protagonist is not in the scene, also list the information under Reader Knowledge Gained. This way you can keep track of what the reader knows but the protagonist doesn't.

Perfecting the POV Knowledge Gained Story Element

Your fun editing task is to list any new information the POV character learns for every scene. You'll use this information to check for plot holes.

POV Knowledge Gained is closely related to the Revelation and Reader Knowledge Gained story elements.

A revelation is something the reader and a character learn that is meaningful to the story and that wasn't known before this scene. This is usually a critical discovery.

With practice, it becomes easier to know what to keep track of. While editing the draft, you might not know what's important. Do your best on the first pass. You can come back later and figure it out.

Troubleshooting

When reading the draft, consistency issues will sometimes pop up. This is the place to note them. A character referencing something the reader knows they don't know makes the reader put the book down.

When conducting the first pass of the draft, if you stop and pause at a character interaction or reaction to information they don't know yet, then this is a moment to write down this pause. If you flick back to look at what was revealed, this is an even bigger sign that a reader will be losing trust.

> **Plot holes are easy to sort out when this element is filled in.**

Suggestions from an Editor

EDITOR 2:

There are a handful of points in the story in which a character can't know something, as they don't have the knowledge. This includes Katie not knowing Rose is from the same lab as Daisy, and Tom and Vicky not knowing Jaz is pregnant (until later). These are plot holes to work on.

On the Story Map insight on the Visualize page, select POV Character and POV Knowledge Gained. You'll see where the POV character has referenced something in a scene that they can't know about.

Please review these scenes and consider rewriting the scene without the knowledge or revising a previous scene where the POV character has access to the information.

> ### TEA with Kristina
>
> The editor's suggestions are fabulous. The editor shows me exactly what is wrong and how to fix it. Again, they have an advantage because they performed the edit in Fictionary StoryCoach. That gave them the ability to see if the story elements are working together. It also gave them the ability to give me specific advice. I can't wait to revise that scene.

Where to Next?

Plot holes are bad, but so is a boring scene.

Let's get moving to the Character in Motion story element and find out how motion can keep a reader from being bored.

Fictionary Story Element: Character in Motion

For characters to come to life, they must move throughout the story.

A scene may feel flat if the characters in the scene are not doing anything. The motion can be rushing from one place to another, or it can be pulling weeds in the garden. Two characters sitting and talking, even if the dialogue is excellent, will seem less dynamic than if they are moving and talking.

A character in motion evokes emotion in the reader.

Characters who don't move are boring.

Definition

Having a character in motion means the character is physically moving.

Characters come to life as they move around the page; that motion makes them jump off the page and become real to the reader. For a character to jump off the page and into the imagination of the reader, they have to be jumping around in the scene.

Readers read as an escape, and one place the vibrancy of a story comes from the characters' actions.

Scene and Story Level

This is one of the elements that is edited at the scene level only. A character must be in motion in every scene.

For each scene, look at what the characters are doing. Are they doing anything? Are they interacting with the location? Are they interacting with other characters? Do they start in one place and move to another?

If they are not moving in every scene, it's time to recommend revisions.

Perfecting the Character in Motion Story Element

Your fun editing task is to mark each scene as characters being in motion or not, then see if this is a big issue for the story or only happens once or twice.

When you read a scene during the editing process, pay attention to whether the characters are in motion.

The Character in Motion story element allows the writer to do the following:

- Enhance characterization: the way a character moves shows characterization. For example, the way a character walks down the street: Are they nervous? Are they striding? Is that walk slivering through shadows? Just by changing a walk, a different personality comes to mind. Every action that a character has must be in keeping with who they are.

- Show a character's feelings: when a character steps around a person and gives them a wide berth, then bashes pots and pans, the actions show how the character is feeling.

- Increase tension: if a scene lacks tension, try adding motion to create tension. The story elements are all interrelated, and none work alone. A woman answering the door to a stranger takes a step backward as the stranger takes a step forward. Simple movements like this can add tension to a scene.

- Show an unreliable character: the character in motion shows a character in action. Those actions can be different from the words that they say. The Scarecrow from The Wizard of Oz says he has no brain, but he is always coming up with ideas. His actions of having apples thrown at him prepare the audience for the fact that he does not need a brain, as he already has one.

Troubleshooting

Characters not in motion sometimes happen in long pieces of dialogue. Dialogue is a great place to look for lack of motion. Note that shrugging or nodding don't count as motion if it's the only movement a character makes. The motion has to be interacting with the setting or another character.

When you find a scene without the character in motion, the story will feel slow. The meaning of the words on the page won't resonate.

Suggestions from an Editor

EDITOR 10:

I've noticed there are some scenes where characters are not in motion. Please view the Story Map insight and select Scene Name, Characters, and Character in Motion.

THESE SCENES INCLUDE:

Scene 19: Decides to Investigate
Scene 30: Vicky Apologizes
Scene 34: Jaz Makes Deal
Scene 39: (?) Unable to name as unsure of scene goal
Scene 40: Jaz Reads Journal
Scene 45: Jaz Stops Attack
Scene 51: Jaz Reads Logbook
Scene 52: Tom Updates
Scene 55: Jaz Snoops Socials
Scene 56: Jaz Interrogates Irene
Scene 57: The Winter Hat
Scene 59: Jaz Protects Alyssa
Scene 63: Jaz Next Steps
Scene 64: Investigates Nick's Belongings
Scene 65: Nick's Transhumance Theory
Scene 66: Nick's Germline Theory
Scene 68: Jaz's Party Story
Scene 69: Jaz Reflects
Scene 74: Tom Shares Findings
Scene 75: Alyssa Is Lying
Scene 76: Jaz Interrogates Dan
[The editor added per-scene notes.]

You can increase tension in a scene using motion. For example, a wife is telling her husband something important, and she wants his full attention. He walks around the room tidying things. A kettle boiling distracts him. He gives the dog a treat. Every movement he makes causes her anger to rise. You can use his motion to make her more and more agitated.

[You'll have noticed the editor shows the scene number and the scene name. This makes it easier for the writer to follow along.]

TEA with Kristina

Being busy for no reason does not mean the character is in motion. Just as any description must be story relevant, the movements that the characters have in a scene must advance the story.

Stories must build up in meaning, and small physical habits can be part of that buildup. We don't describe objects that are not relevant to the plot, and the character in motion must also be plot relevant. How is that motion showing their personality, their development, and their interaction with others? Do their actions reveal something in direct contrast to what they say?

The list the editor provided in the editor's suggestions shows me I have to take the advice seriously. Did you notice one of the scenes is called "Jaz stops attack"? You'd think that scene would have characters in motion.

When I reviewed the scene, the balance was too heavy on the dialogue, and there wasn't enough motion. When I wrote the scene, I thought it was full of motion. Now I realize that was me visually seeing the motion but not translating it to the page.

Where to Next?

We've come to the end of the Fictionary Character story elements, and it's time to move on to Setting. Before we do that, let's peek at the summary of all the Character elements.

Then we'll discover how to create an engaging plot through the power of description. A character cannot move in a vacuum—there must be a physical world that they live in.

Character Elements Summarized

In Chapter 9: Learn the Plot Elements, you learned to ensure you start the story edit from a place of strength, and we suggested using the story elements to edit a scene for the following:

- Scene name
- Its purpose in the story
- Type of opening and closing
- Whether the reader is anchored
- Whether the reader is hooked at the beginning of the scene
- Whether the reader is driven to read the next scene

After that, you learned tension keeps the reader worried, conflict keeps the reader engaged, and a character's history, whether told through a revelation, a backstory, or a flashback, connects the reader to the character.

Then you learned how to structure scenes using Scene Middle, Scene Climax, and Action/Sequel story elements. We ended the Plot story elements by understanding what a reader learns compared with the protagonist.

Now we've also covered the Character story elements. We started with a character list. Knowing who every character is and why they are important to the story is a solid foundation for editing characters.

Choosing the right POV character for every scene is a must for writers, and an editor's job is to ensure that was done. Goals drive the story forward, but only if they are related to the story and have an impact on the characters. We checked for plot holes and ended with making sure characters are in motion and keep the pacing fast. What happens next depends on who you are.

For the editor working on someone else's book, keep going on the scene-by-scene edit. You'll use everything you do here to create the best editing package possible for your client.

As with the Plot story elements, the writer working on their own novel has a choice. Revise the scene based on the Character story elements or keep going on the scene-by-scene edit, working your way through the remaining story elements. Remember, you are the artist, and the choice is yours.

If you want to revise now, here are some tips. You will have named every scene and have checked the story arc. You know you have a story, so you can start revisions at the scene level.

We're going to start with the characters in a scene, as they form the basis of a scene.

CHARACTER LIST (PER SCENE)

Have you reviewed the section called "Character List" and found there were no areas to troubleshoot? Yes? Woo-hoo! Go to the next step.

No?

Revise the scene and fix any areas you discovered in the troubleshooting section of the character list.

POV

This is a story element that you edit at the story level. You've captured the information you need, and when we get to the manuscript level edits, this is going to come in handy.

For now, just make sure it's clear who the POV character is. Hopefully you've done that in the "Scene Anchoring" section.

POV GOAL

Without a goal, a character has no reason to take an action. And without action, the story is boring.

Is there a clear POV character goal for every scene? Yes? Woo-hoo! Go to the next step.

No?

Revise the scenes based on the advice given in the "POV Goal" section.

CHARACTER ARC

This is a story element that you edit at the story level. You've captured the information you need, and when we get to the manuscript level edits, this is going to come in handy.

For now, just make sure you've listed whether the scene takes the protagonist closer to or further away from achieving the story goal or neither. Hopefully, you've done that in the "Character Arc" section.

POV GOAL INTERNAL

An internal goal gives the POV character depth. The character will achieve this goal slowly over the story.

Is the POV character's goal related to the story goal for every scene? Yes? Woo-hoo! Go to the next step.

No?

Revise the scenes based on the advice in the "POV Goal Internal" section.

GOAL RELATED TO PLOT

The POV character's goal must be related to the plot. You know the main story goal because it's in the blurb.

Is there a clear POV character goal that is related to the plot and story goal listed in the blurb for every scene? Yes? Woo-hoo! Go to the next step.

No?

Revise the scenes based on the advice given in the "Goal Related to Plot" section.

WHAT IF GOAL FAILS?

This doesn't mean the scene goal must fail. We're asking you to think about a what-if scenario, so the scene is tense.

Is there a consequence if the POV character fails at achieving the scene goal for every scene? Yes? Woo-hoo! Go to the next step.

No?

This most likely means the wrong goal was chosen for the scene. Revise the scenes based on the advice in the "What if Goal Fails?" section.

IMPACT ON POV CHARACTER

If it's clear there are consequences if the goal fails, this element should be easy to figure out. If the goal failed, then this is a negative impact on the POV character. If the goal succeeded, then this is a positive impact on the POV character.

Is the impact on the POV character clear for every scene? Yes? Woo-hoo! Go to the next step.

No?

We could still be looking at a scene where the wrong goal was chosen. Revise the scenes with an issue based on the advice given in the "Impact on POV Character" section.

IMPACT ON PROTAGONIST

This is the impact on the protagonist if the protagonist is not the POV character.

Is the impact on the protagonist clear in every scene? Yes? Woo-hoo! Go to the next step.

No?

We could still be looking at a scene where the wrong goal was chosen. Every scene must impact the protagonist whether the protagonist is in the scene or not, and whether they know they've been impacted or not. Revise the scenes based on the advice in the "Impact on Protagonist" section.

POV KNOWLEDGE GAINED

This is a story element that you edit at the story level. You've captured the information you need, and when we get to the manuscript level edits, this is going to come in handy.

For now, just make sure you've kept track of the POV knowledge gained for every scene. Yes? Woo-hoo! Go to the next step.

No?

Revise the scenes based on the advice in the "POV Knowledge Gained" section.

CHARACTER IN MOTION

The characters must move in every scene. This helps keep the pace fast.

Are the characters in motion in every scene?

Revise the scenes based on the advice in the "Characters in Motion" section.

Where to Next?

Onward with this scene-by-scene edit. It's time to edit for the best location, location, location.

Chapter Twelve:
Learn the Setting Story Elements

> "When a setting is well done, you feel like you've entered the world of the characters —you see what they see, and you live their story with them." —Michele Orwin, Fictionary Certified StoryCoach Editor

Fictionary Setting Story Elements

The setting is where readers immerse into the story world.

The powerhouses behind all stories are characters, plot, and settings. Now we are going to look at the Fictionary Setting story elements and how they work together with characters and plot.

A creative story editor carefully evaluates the Setting story elements that should be used in each scene. These elements show what is meaningful to the story.

These delicious details are what get the reader coming back for more.

Everything a character senses will have a particular meaning to that character. That meaning can be used to increase reader emotion.

With Fictionary Setting story elements, the creative story editor is checking if the reader will be immersed in the story world.

FICTIONARY SETTING STORY ELEMENTS:

- Location
- Date/Time
- Object
- Sights
- Smells
- Sounds
- Emotional Impact
- Location Split
- Weather
- Touch
- Tastes

The Setting story elements for each scene will be looked at with care. A creative story editor ensures the setting is described with details that relate to the plot and characters. It is that simple.

Perfecting the Fictionary Setting Elements

When chosen and described well, a setting can do the following:

1. Intensify the reader's emotional experience.

2. Deepen the relationship a reader has with the characters.

3. Increase tension.

4. Share backstory in a way the reader finds engaging.

And we will explore many more functions of setting in this chapter.

By having the POV character describe other characters in the context of the setting and how they interact with the setting, you'll give the reader a few insights:

- How the POV characters think of other characters.

- The relationship between the two characters.
- Important backstory.
- The mood of the scene.

Ensure the characters interact with the setting instead of just describing the setting.

What does the character think, do, react, and feel?

Check that the description means something to the POV character or gives insight into another character.

Does the POV character's personality affect the choice of setting?

A creative story editor can make recommendations based on the character. Is she shy and does the writer want her to be uncomfortable? Have her enter a crowded room where everyone stops talking the moment she enters.

The style of the description of the setting depends on which character is giving the description.

You know the POV character for each scene, so make sure the description is consistent with what that character would see, hear, smell, taste, touch, or think. And if it's not, let the writer know.

You'll see as we go through the Setting elements that there are scene-level and story-level implications.

We'll cover these for each Setting story element.

Suggestions from an Editor

EDITOR 12

Sensory details keep the "stage" and characters interesting. Without them, both the setting and the characters will seem flat. Using the POV character's senses to describe the action will bring your reader closer to the character. However, be careful how you do this. If the character touches something hot, don't tell the reader it's hot. Show them. The character "put her hand on a surface, whipped her hand away, and ran cold water over it" is much more effective than "she touched the surface, and it was hot."

All five senses are important. I've put a check in the Story Map for scenes where you've done an excellent job of presenting the reader with sensory detail. For others, I've left a one-word descriptor of the detail you've invoked. As you'll see, many scenes were left blank, and I would recommend looking through these scenes and seeing where you can add a sensory detail or two to flesh out the scene.

TEA with Kristina

So, truth time: I like to skim the setting description. The only time I don't is when the writer has woven the description into the story using action, dialogue, thought, and description.

The editor's suggestions showed me the good and the bad and told me how to find the related information in the Fictionary edit. I have enough information to revise accordingly.

One thing I like to recommend to a creative story editor is to check whether the setting chosen for a scene has meaning to the POV character for that scene.

For example, let's say a teenager, the POV character in a scene, was humiliated by a boy she trusted.

He asked her to the prom in front of the popular kids and then laughed at her when she said yes. Now in her mid twenties, her boyfriend chooses that same place to propose to her, and it's in front of his friends. That's a great choice for a setting to give extra meaning to the scene.

For editors, looking at all the Setting story elements in the context of where the scene takes place will help you give specific, actionable advice to the writer.

Where to Next?

We are going to start by looking at where the scene is set. To make a setting strong, the location must be chosen with care.

Fictionary Story Element: Location

A scene must be in a location; otherwise, the reader feels uneasy that they cannot settle into the story, as if they are left hanging in midair with no way to go up or down. They just know they don't want to be where they are. Meaning... they want to put the book down and do something else.

When a scene is anchored, then it is very easy to tell where the scene takes place.

> **And when a writer uses location well, then the location resonates with the POV character for the scene.**

The POV character interacts with the scene, and the reader reads the scene and knows this location is story critical. When a book's locations are well chosen, then the reader enters the story's world. The readers jump right in and are whisked away.

Readers read for entertainment and escape, and the locations where each scene takes place are one of many places in a novel that entertains, and they are an escape for the reader.

Location in this case is not the story world as a whole, although that's important; it's where each scene takes place.

Definition

The Fictionary Story Element Location is simply where the action of the scene happens.

Scene and Story Level

At the scene level, all we're looking for is where the scene takes place.

It's important to anchor the reader as quickly as possible for each scene. We are also looking for transitions from one location to the next, because we want to make sure these happen smoothly.

We'll use the other story elements along with this one to help with location consistency.

We want to check for the following:

1. Character continuity presence. Remember that character list per scene you made earlier? It's going to help now.

2. Description that the POV character, or narrator, would use.

3. Description that is plot relevant.

You'll need the other story elements to determine if the level of description is appropriate to the importance the location has in the story.

Perfecting the Location Story Element

Your fun editing task is to list the location of every scene in the story. You can think of this list as an after-draft location outline.

Early in the novel, more description of the location is important. The depth of the description depends on the genre and on the author's writing style, and how important the location is to the plot. Genres impact how much location description is required. In a sci-fi or fantasy novel, whole worlds are created from a writer's imagination. This means those worlds must be described in enough detail that the reader can see, smell, hear, taste, and feel the world.

More time should be spent describing key locations. For locations that a reader is familiar with, like a movie theater, less time can be spent.

Ensure enough detail is used the first time a location is described. Then check there are reminders throughout the story without repeat details. Just in the way a new character is introduced to a story, the location should be introduced to the reader in a story-relevant way.

When this location is being described, look at who is describing the location. Is what is being noticed relevant and appropriate?

Check scenes that occur in the same location. See if the description is consistent throughout the story and not repeated.

The style of the description depends on which character is giving the description. You know the POV character for each scene, so make sure the description is consistent with what that character would see, hear, smell, taste, and touch, or what they would think.

There can be nice characterization happening with scene location too. In Stieg Larsson's The Girl Who Played with Fire, Lisbeth Salander made a lot of money and got a new flat. When Lisbeth describes it, she mentions only a few of the rooms; when Mikael Blomkvist visits, he is amazed at the number of rooms.

This is another case of the story elements interweaving with each other.

Troubleshooting

With every location, check whether the description was done well.

At the story level, look for locations that are repeated. Does the story need more variety in these locations?

You'll notice that by using the other Setting story elements, you'll find any issues that occur with the location.

HERE ARE SOME ISSUES THAT MIGHT ARISE:

- Slow pacing: location can affect pacing. If you're finding the pacing is slow because a scene is too long, check whether the scene occurs in more than one location. An easy fix might be to split the scene into two scenes right at the point where the location changes.

- Cliché: a clichéd location might bore the reader. For example, a relationship breakup in a coffee shop.

- Not anchored: it's unclear to the reader where the scene takes place, making the reader feel disconnected from the story from lack of details.

- Too much / too little description: when editing the location, ask yourself: Is the location important to the plot, characters, or theme? If no, recommend fewer details. If yes, recommend being more generous with the details.

- POV issue: Would the location be described like that by the POV character?

- Repetitive: if the scene has the same features repeated ad nauseam, it will disconnect the reader.
- Rough transition: if there are two locations in a scene and the transition is jolted, then that might jar the reader out of the story.
- Plot: Is the location relevant to plot?
- Inconsistent: if the location details are inconsistent with how they were described previously in the story, the reader will flip back to see if they had missed something or question whether the book is worth their time.

Suggestions from an Editor

EDITOR 3:

I felt that the location setting sometimes lacked detail in the story...

For instance, Vicky describes Jaz's area as either pretty or beautiful, but the reader has no geographical reference to what makes it so.

The dog parks could be by the lake, with a backdrop of mountains, and perhaps it's so cold their breath freezes in the air, but we don't really know (there are also some excellent descriptions as well).

I don't live by Lake Ontario so I have no idea what it's like, and I don't feel I gained a lot of understanding about it through reading this story.

Another example of lack of little details would be the scene set in the doctor's room. This scene seems clinical and bare as a result, which may be reflective of what is happening in Jaz's life, but given this is where she finds out she's pregnant, it seems too barren.

> TEA with Kristina
>
> **Readers expect to be entertained and delighted by characters, plots, and settings. Some drafts will be strong in one or two of the three Fictionary supergroups, but nearly all writers have a weakness. And the location description can be one of them. As it is in my draft.**

It can be a lack of specifics, that the draft is vague, and this is something the creative story editor has to figure out.

You'll have noticed one of the editors mentioned the scene where Jaz finds out she's pregnant. An earlier comment was that she didn't react to the news. Now this editor is telling me the location lacks description in that same scene. Clearly, I need to make some revisions on the scene.

Where to Next?

Now that you have edited the location, we need to check that the location is the most powerful place for the character to be. Let's start with when the scene happens.

Everyone likes to know what time it is.

Fictionary Story Element: Date/Time

The quicker the reader catches on to the timing, the quicker they will be drawn into the scene.

Exactly what the reader needs to understand about the time depends on the scene. The reader may need to know only if the scene happens during the day or at night. However, if several years or several seconds have passed in a character's life, the reader must understand that as well. The same is true if the story jumps around in time, as we discussed when writing flashbacks.

This element is not about pacing in the scene.

Timing is about when the scene happens, not how fast paced it is.

Definition

The Fictionary Story Element Date/Time can mean the following:

1.   Time of day.

2.   Time passed since the previous scene.

3.   A particular date.

Scene and Story Level

At the scene level, Date/Time needs to help anchor the reader so the reader is comfortable and comfortable quickly. We're listing when the scene takes place in the context of the previous scene.

At the story level, a creative story editor will make sure the story timeline works.

Perfecting the Date/Time Story Element

Your fun editing task is to list the time that every scene takes place. The aim is to get a story line for the whole story and check if it makes sense to the reader.

Another way of looking at time is to think about when every scene takes place in the context of the story. When working on the timing of a scene, ask yourself, "Why does this scene have to happen now in the story?" When you ask that question of the scene, it has to make sense in the story.

Troubleshooting

Look for places where you're confused by the timing of the scene. If you can't list the timing of a scene, you know there is a problem.

Timing can also be used to increase pacing. Let's say a character has just discovered a major clue that is time sensitive. This happens on a Friday in the previous scene. In this scene, it's Monday, and the character hasn't acted on the clue. This takes the urgency out of the story. It makes the story drag. So when a story drags, look at Date/Time.

Suggestions from an Editor

EDITOR 8:

Consider providing information about how long it's been since Nick died. The last two scenes in chapter 3 have provided a reference in terms of the days passing, but you don't want readers to get confused about the timeline.

This is the first time we learn what happened to Nick, or that it is assumed he died in a car accident. This is important information, but it is just dropped there without much else. This would be an opportune time to provide more details and backstory about what happened to Nick. Keep in mind that this doesn't mean that you need to reveal everything, but readers can learn a little more information. For example, was it a rainy night, a sunny day, etc.? Was Nick driving? There are ways to give readers more information.

All that said, you only withhold information for the sake of suspense or drama if (and only if) it is relevant in the bigger picture.

TEA with Kristina

A story should be about the characters, and the plot, and the setting, not having the reader on edge because they have no idea "when" they are in the story.

Let's look at what the editor had to say. They gave a specific example stating it's not clear how long it's been since Nick died. This has huge implications to Jaz's actions and motivations. If not much time has passed, she'll still be raw. Everything she does will be influenced by the rawness of her emotions. The scene mentioned needs revision, so that Jaz is acting in a way that works with the amount of time since Nick's death.

Where to Next?

We know where the scene took place. We know when the scene took place, and one way time can be measured is by a watch. In the next Fictionary Story Element, we are going to evaluate if all the objects in the scene are needed and are used to maximum effect.

Fictionary Story Element: Object

Readers are much more engaged in a story if they can imagine the setting that stirs their emotions. It's hard to imagine a setting if there are no objects in that setting.

Watch a film without props or a backdrop, and you'd probably get confused or bored. You'd just be watching actors on an empty stage, which would make it even harder to believe the reality they're trying to portray.

Objects should not appear out of the blue; it would be like a deus ex machina but for objects. A god appears on some apparatus from above and drops the required object to the character right when they need it, which, would not be good for a novel.

Definition

An object is any item or detail to which the narrator draws the reader's attention. An object should perform a function: it could be a clue, remind a character of something, or cause conflict between characters. If the author can give the object more than one function, it will add depth to the story.

Scene and Story Level

At the scene level, do the objects spark the imagination of readers? Do you feel fully immersed in the world? Do you feel tense by an object sitting in the scene?

As a creative story editor, you must find all the objects and then make a decision. This comes back to your artistry. Are there enough well-placed objects, or are there too many? Only by looking at each scene and noting each object can you make this decision.

At the story level, objects must be story critical and be woven through the story. An object that is used for the plot—foreshadowing—should be on the page in act I.

Perfecting the Object Story Element

Your fun editing task is to note the objects for every scene; then, when an object is used in the plot, you can see when it was first mentioned and whether it is described for the effect that the story needs.

The first time an object appears in a novel, if the object means something profound to a character or is important to the plot, it should be described in detail. Alternately, the description can be minimal but memorable if the intent is to let the readers know it's there but that the author doesn't want the reader to focus on it yet.

If there is an object that plays a key role in the story, then mention it in act 1.

Key objects mentioned after act 1 could cause a problem. If a gun goes off in the final scene, you should ideally introduce it in the first act. Otherwise, the object could appear convenient to the reader, and they lose trust in the book.

When the scene has the right level of objects, we are swept up with the story. Every scene is different, but if you stumble over the number of objects in the scene, then you need to note that. If the scene is too sparse and does not feel real, then look around the scene and ask how many tangible objects have been described and how many you would have expected.

Troubleshooting

If objects appear in lists within a scene, readers find the information in the list too much to remember. They start to switch off, as they go from living the story with the protagonist to having to be cerebral. Lists gets skimmed.

Describing too many objects can make the descriptions seem vague and unimportant, or if the description is detailed, too many objects can slow the pacing.

The best way to describe an object is to have a character interact with it. If you find you're skimming objects, recommend the writer revises how the objects are used in the scene.

If you're unsure of what objects should be in a scene, ask yourself what needs to be in the scene for the reader to "see" the setting.

WHEN YOU NOTICE YOUR CLIENT IS NOT TAKING ADVANTAGE OF OBJECTS, USE THIS ELEMENT AND NOTE ONE OF THE FOLLOWING:

1. "None" when there are no objects in the scene. In the revision, perhaps plot-relevant objects should be added to the scene.

2. "Too Few" when there are not enough objects in a scene. In the revision, perhaps more plot-relevant

objects should be added to the scene.

3. "Too Many" when there are too many objects in a scene. In the revision, perhaps some of the objects should be cut and only plot-relevant objects kept.

4. "Needs Closure" when an object is not closed off ("smoking gun").

5. "Magic" for an object that magically appears. This might not be an issue in a story that involves magic but is an issue otherwise.

6. "Solves Problem" if an object appears that solves a problem too quickly and reduces the tension in a scene.

Suggestions from an Editor

We have an amazing example from one other editor, showing how an object can cause a plot hole.

These paragraphs come from scene 2 of Evolution:

Fatigue wrapped its heavy blanket around my shoulders. The ticking of the grandfather clock intermixed with sleet tapping the windows made me want to lie on the kitchen floor and never get up.

The clock had belonged to my parents and before them my grandparents. Somehow I'd ended up with it. My guess was my dad didn't want the noisy contraption in his house, so when Nick and I moved into our home on Loughborough Lake, he'd "gifted" it to me, Jaz Cooper.

EDITOR 10 COMMENTED:

The father is caring enough to give a family heirloom to his daughter but is not seen again up to scene 8?

> **TEA with Kristina**
>
> The problem the editor is highlighting is a plot hole. In this scene, the reader leaves with the impression Jaz has a close relationship with her dad. Not only does her dad not show up again until scene 8, but he also has a minor role in the story. This ends up not working because Jaz is going through extreme stress, and if she were close to her dad, he would be there to help her.
>
> This is a lovely example of how keeping track of objects together with characters can help tighten the plot.

Where to Next?

So far we've learned where and when a scene takes place, and what objects are in a scene. This is just the start of creating a world readers get immersed in.

Objects help a reader visualize a location. And, as usual, there is more. The senses are another way for the story to come to life for the reader. They can feel the story from every sense the writer uses. Let's look at the group of senses, and then we'll take a deeper dive into each one.

Fictionary Story Elements: The Senses

Editing for the senses is the ultimate show-not-tell checker.

The POV character is reacting to the world around them. They sense the world, and that filtering shows the reader the world but also shows the reader a level of characterization, too. When used well, senses will set off a story-relevant memory for the POV character. The reader can share in this, and the memory contributes to the believability of the story world.

The senses help world build the story but should not overwhelm the story.

Definition

This list will come as a big surprise.

Not!

THE FOLLOWING ARE THE FIVE SENSES:

1. Sights

2. Smells

3. Sounds

4. Tastes

5. Touch

The senses are a way for readers to experience the story world.

There is a level of inherent intimacy with the use of the senses.

Scene and Story Level

At the scene level, the edits focus on making sure that the senses are evoked.

As the POV character experiences a feeling, does everything look gray and dull because the character is dealing with a broken heart?

Check at least three senses are in each scene. That will make a three-dimensional experience for the reader.

At the story level, a creative story editor should examine the amount of time spent on each sense. Is the draft favoring one or ignoring one? Are all the senses used well?

With different POV characters, check if they have their own ways of sensing the world. Each character must have a unique way of sensing the world that is related to their past experiences, their present state of mind, and future hopes.

A draft can have intermittent usage of the senses—overuse in one scene and barely any in another. The editor will find this and point it out to the writer.

We won't repeat this section for each of the senses, as the advice is the same for all five senses.

Perfecting the Senses Story Element

A creative story editor asks a lot of questions about the story. And in this section, the questions are all about making sure that the senses are used and are story relevant.

When reading the scene, look for places that contain descriptions.

What senses are being used to describe the location?

Do these descriptions need to have the POV character's personality stamped into them?

Are these descriptions useful to the plot?

Troubleshooting

A scene without the senses is a flat scene the reader won't connect with.

The descriptions need to be full of the senses, and those descriptions need to be both plot relevant and characterize the POV character.

We'll cover troubleshooting for each of the Setting elements. They each have their own requirements.

Suggestions from an Editor

The mention of an unknown man in the first scene of Evolution prompted a helpful response from editor 6.

EDITOR 6:

Also, consider providing more details and development regarding 'the man.' Jaz has a very visceral reaction to his presence and his stare. What does he look like? What is he dressed like? This detail seems important, as if it will play a bigger factor later in the story, so heighten the tension here and provide more details. Allow readers to visualize what is happening.

HERE'S THE ORIGINAL TEXT:

"Who's that man over there?"

Katie checked him out and shook her head. "I don't recognize him."

"It's odd how intensely he's staring at us." I turned my back to him.

HERE IS THE UPDATED VERSION:

A man stared at me from across the parking lot. Eyes of charcoal held eye contact a second too long, a second that sent a shiver down my spine. Cropped hair, a rigid posture, and a muscled neck made me think military. "Who's that man over there?"

Katie checked him out and shook her head. "I don't recognize him."

"It's odd how intensely he's staring at me." I turned my back to him.

The editor has given a way to link this description to the character later in the story. When he comes into Jaz's life, there can be a reference to the description that will link the meeting to this opening scene of the story.

TEA with Kristina

About fifteen years ago, I lost my sense of smell from a head injury. What I didn't realize at the time was that this would hurt my ability to write well.

One day, not long ago, I gave a Fictionary demo and was teaching how to use the senses. I opened the Fictionary app and displayed the senses in the Story Map.

I saw one blank cell after another beside the Smell story element. To my own shock, I hadn't used smell in any scene.

Not a single one.

I was a tad embarrassed that I was teaching how to use senses, because my example was really how not to use senses.

The editor above suggested I use the senses to make the scene come to life. They give a specific example in a scene. This gave me a place to focus and to practice.

Where to Next?

Let's meet the senses. There is the old saying, "Love at first sight." So let's look at sight first.

Fictionary Story Element: Sight

Scientists believe most people process over 80 percent of the outside world using our sight, so we must make sure sight is seriously edited in a draft.

Remember that when a POV character is chosen, the writer has made a promise to their readers that they will experience the scene from that character's perspective.

Any visual description must be filtered through the eyes of the POV character. If the character can't see something, that thing can't be described by sight.

Descriptions should not only inform the reader what the POV character sees but also characterize the POV character: how they describe the sights, what they notice about what they see, and also what they think is worth mentioning.

Definition

When sight is used in a draft, it describes what the POV character sees.

Perfecting the Sight Story Element

Your fun editing task is to list everything the POV character sees in every scene.

Looking at the senses being used is looking at how closely the writer is using POV.

WHEN EDITING FOR THIS SENSE, REMEMBER SOME OF THE WAYS THAT SIGHT CAN ADD TO THE STORY:

1. Sight can be used to describe a character when they are first introduced by having another character describe the incomer.

2. Sight can be used when an object is important to the story, to the protagonist, or to the POV character.

3. Sight helps world build and shows the POV character's attitude about the world by showing what

they notice in the environment.

4.　　　Sight can be used as a flashback trigger.

A creative story editor will recommend that if something the character sees is important to the story, the writer can describe the object indirectly rather than directly.

When an editor reads the sentence, "The dog was large, over 120 pounds at least," it's clear the POV character doesn't have a strong interest in dogs. And maybe that's okay.

But what if the character has a strong interest in dogs and the dog's size is relevant to the plot? When listing the objects, the editor would take note of how the object is described and would suggest a more vivid scene.

The editor shouldn't suggest what to write but should note the description is lacking. It's up to the writer to come up with a new sentence.

Just for fun, our version of the new sentence is, "The dog jumped on the couch. Its head rested on one end, and its tail wagged against the other. The springs squeaked, and the couch sagged in the middle as the dog wiggled itself into a comfortable position."

The second description takes more words, but if the size of the dog is important, then it's worth it.

Troubleshooting

Sight is important, but sometimes it can drown out the other senses.

If the POV character reacts with no other senses, the reader will feel the scene is flat despite the descriptions.

To troubleshoot sight, it will help if you're editing all the senses at the same time.

When you look at the list of objects, people, and places in a scene, you'll know if the author got carried away with the use of sight.

Suggestions from an Editor

EDITOR 5:

[Evolution, scene 27]

This is great you have five people present and not one of them was lost sight of. The way that Jaz would be scanning everyone, that makes sense that she notices every frown, brilliant stuff!

> **TEA with Kristina**
>
> You can see in the feedback from the editor above that I have used the sight story element successfully in this scene in Evolution. This is a big positive because I can always return to this scene to see how I can repeat this success in other scenes where I might be lacking.
>
> When you're evaluating the use of sight, consider where the scene is located in the story as well as what the sight should be accomplishing.

Where to Next?

That's sight, which should be a huge part of the description, but not the only part of the senses. Let's get our noses stuck into smell.

Fictionary Story Element: Smell

The brain's anatomy means smell and memory and emotions are closely connected, which is why this Fictionary Story Element is so powerful.

By evoking a smell in the reader's mind, they are transported emotionally to their own memories.

Any odor described must be smelled through the POV character's nose.

Remember that when a POV character is chosen, the writer has made a promise to their readers that they will experience the scene from that character's perspective. The character's sense of smell and how they would smell things need to be edited.

Descriptions should not only inform the reader what the POV character smells, but also characterize that character by how they describe the smell, what they notice about the smell, and what they think is worth mentioning.

If the character can't smell something, it can't be described by the POV character.

Definition

When smell is used, it will be described by what the POV character smells in a scene.

Perfecting the Smell Story Element

Your fun editing task is to list everything the POV character smells in every scene.

When editing for smell, remember some of the ways that smell can add to the story:

1. Smell can be used by the POV character to describe a character when they are first introduced, or by having another character describe the incomer.

2. Smell can be used to trigger a memory.

3. Smell helps the world building and shows how the POV character smells the world and what they notice in the environment.

4. Smell can trigger a flashback.

Troubleshooting

Smells sometimes are used to show only repulsion, but the positive aspects of smell should not be overlooked.

A house smelling of home-baked bread can show a family that is nurturing.

To troubleshoot smell, it will help if you're editing all the senses at the same time.

Suggestions from an Editor

EDITOR 11:

[Evolution, scene 49]

I think you could add some smells to this scene. I live in the Rocky Mountains in Colorado, and I can picture where this place is, what it looks like, what it smells like (the scent of fire and burning wood and pine), what the road looks like leading up to it, the cold air at four o'clock just before the sun sets . . .

> **TEA with Kristina**
>
> **The editor is showing me how I could use the sense of smell to improve a scene. They even point out what they imagine the scene smells like, which is nothing how I imagined it smelled.**
>
> **When reviewing the senses, think about what the reader might sense from the scene. If the editor hadn't given me an example, I might not have taken the advice as seriously.**

Where to Next?

That covers smells, so let's hear all about sounds.

Fictionary Story Element: Sounds

Loud unexpected noise can make you jump, and it can make a reader jump too.

Any Fictionary Story Element that can be used to shock, foreshadow, lull, and add energy to a scene is something we creative story editors should get a handle on.

Any noise that is described must be heard through the POV character's ears.

Remember that the POV character makes a promise to the readers that they will hear what the POV character hears. The character's sense of hearing and how they would hear things need to be edited.

Descriptions should not only inform the reader what the POV character hears but also characterize the POV character by how they describe the noise, what they notice about the sound, and also what they think is worth mentioning.

This means that if the character can't hear something, it can't be described by sound.

Definition

When sounds are used, they describe what the POV character hears in a scene.

Perfecting the Sound Story Element

Your editing task is to list everything the POV character hears in every scene.

WHEN EDITING FOR THIS SENSE, REMEMBER SOME OF THE WAYS THAT SOUNDS CAN ADD TO THE STORY:

I. Sounds can be used to describe a character when they are first introduced by having another character describe the incomer. Does the character have a loud walk, a loud voice, and a loud eating style, or are they so quiet when they enter a room that they can hardly be heard, and they barely make any sound?

These are two very different people that the reader will conjure up, and readers will have different expectations.

As an editor, make sure these are all working well

to build up a sense of the character from the noise they create.

2. Sounds can be used to indicate an object is important to the story, the POV character, or the protagonist.

3. Sounds help to world build and show how the POV character hears the world and what they notice in the environment.

4. Sounds characterize the POV character, and in dialogue sounds can characterize the minor characters too. A character's reaction to noise—or lack thereof—their associations with the noise, and what they notice should inform the story and be plot relevant too. Remember Clarice talking about the "silence of the lambs" in the Tom Harris book with that name? Clarice relives the sounds of lambs being sent to slaughter and how that was also an analogy of being a recruit sent to speak with Hannibal Lecter, the most dangerous serial killer behind bars. A double purpose.

5. Sounds can trigger a flashback.

Troubleshooting

> **Noise can affect different readers in different ways. And this is true of characters too.**

A veteran suffering from PTSD might not react to a loud fireworks display as a teen would. Remember the senses can characterize, but when used incorrectly, they can strike a wrong chord.

When editing, looking at the senses can show how closely the writer uses POV.

Suggestions from an Editor

EDITOR 9:

[Evolution, scene 12]

Consider adding more details of the setting and location. This is the first time Jaz is somewhere other than at Courteous Canines. What does the room look like? What are the sounds in the room: laughter, talking, clinking of glasses, etc.? Add more sensory details.

TEA with Kristina

The scene the editor is referring to shows Jaz going to a party. It's a big moment because Jaz is afraid of crowds, and she's going to a house filled with people she doesn't know. It's a celebration of life for her husband, so she must go. I've missed another opportunity to use the senses to deepen the scene. Parties are noisy. Celebrations of life can be happy, sad, or somewhere in between. Using sounds would have been a great way to show what the mood of the party was and how that mood and those noises affected Jaz.

The more senses are used, the more they add to the mood of a scene. This is just one example to

| show how important sounds can be.

Where to Next?

We're starting to get an in-depth look at the senses, and we'll keep going. To give you a break from the senses, and to match the order of the story elements in Fictionary, we're going to have a look at the emotional impact of the location next.

> **Choosing a location for a scene must be done wisely, because it can make or break a scene.**

Fictionary Story Element: Emotional Impact

Choosing where a scene happens has a massive impact on how the reader experiences that scene.

The location of every scene in the draft needs to be edited carefully. When looking at the location, ask if it is important to the plot, the POV character, the protagonist, or the theme.

The emotional impact of the location should heighten the POV character and the readers' emotions.

> **Cliché locations dissolve the power of the emotional impact.**

Definition

The emotional impact of the location for each scene is the impact the location has on the POV character and the reader.

Perfecting the Emotional Impact Story Element

Your fun editing task is to review each location for every scene and ask if the location is the most emotionally charged place for the action of the scene to play out.

If the answer is yes, let the writer know. Keep track of this for every scene.

If the answer is no, this means revisions are required.

Does the chosen location do the following?

- Increase or decrease conflict? What choice of location could increase the level of conflict for the scene and make the conflict inevitable?
- Increase or decrease tension?
- Set the mood?
- Highlight emotion?
- Show characterization?
- Slow down or speed up pacing?

Troubleshooting

When looking at the location, the creative story editor checks that the scene is not in a location that is predictable, is meaningless, or has an easy escape.

Predictable: if a location is predictable, the reader will start to think that the story is predictable. For example, where would a character go to have a talk? If they choose a coffee house, that is predictable, but if they go to a library, where they will get shushed, it's not predictable, and it makes the conversation harder to have. And there we've just introduced conflict in the scene by changing the location.

Meaningless: when a location is meaningless, the story is missing an opportunity for the reader to feel the emotion on another level.

Easy escape: when there is an easy escape, and the POV character is not "cornered" by the location, there is a lack of tension and therefore emotion. If there is an intense discussion and a character can walk in the opposite direction, then why would they not walk away? Whereas if they are stuck in a ski lift, there is nowhere to go, and the intensity of the scene is felt. The characters must stay and face the conflict.

Suggestions from an Editor

EDITOR 13:

[Evolution, scene 16]

The start of this scene doesn't need to immediately take place after the last scene. The location of this scene can be stronger as well, which is why I've written No emotion in the Emotional Impact element. Is Jaz standing on her porch and calling Alyssa from her cell phone? There is no mention that Jaz has a cell phone. Look at ways to strengthen this scene, either with sensory details, weather, or location.

TEA with Kristina

The editor is referencing a scene where Jaz is calling her friend Alyssa to make amends for her poor behavior the last time she saw her.

In this scene, Jaz is on her front porch. The editor is correct. I took the lazy route and let Jaz connect with Alyssa from the safety of her home, where she could hang up at any moment. This location does not create an emotional impact on Jaz.

The better way would be to find a place where Jaz is uncomfortable. Make her meet Alyssa on Alyssa's home ground. Somewhere Jaz can't walk away if the conversation gets uncomfortable.

Note the editor has also mentioned an object appearing out of the sky. Where did Jaz's phone come from? Always keep in mind that the 38 Fictionary Story Elements work together. A good use of only one story element does not make a strong story.

Where to Next?

Now that we understand the power the location can have on the story, we'll look at how a location split can dilute that power and at how it can also increase pacing.

There is some editor artistry coming. Let's learn about location split.

Fictionary Story Element: Location Split

> **Pacing of a story is an artistic skill.**

It takes strong knowledge of story structure to get it right. This is where a creative story editor gives the writer actionable advice that helps the writer improve pacing.

If slower pacing was not the author's intent, it may be because a scene is too long. A shorter scene can speed up pacing. When the location changes mid scene, it's an opportunity to split the scene into two scenes and speed up the pacing.

If a scene is too long in balance with the rest of the scenes in the story, then a new location is the perfect place to break the scene into two scenes.

Location split is not about having to split a scene into more than one scene when more than one location is used in the scene. It's about finding an easy way to split a scene if needed.

Definition

This story element is used to mark the scenes that have more than one location.

Scene and Story Level

This location split element is edited at both the scene level and the story level.

At the scene level, all you're doing is marking whether a scene takes place in more than one location.

At the story level, look at the word count per scene and check for any outliers. If the outliers are one of the five Fictionary Story Arc scenes, then the extra word count might be okay. If not, check whether the scene takes place in more than one location. Then put a scene break at the new location.

Perfecting the Location Split Story Element

The fun editing task for the Location Split story element is to mark any scene that takes place in more than one location. You can do this on the first read-through.

Location Split is an advanced Fictionary Story Element. But once we have explained how easy it is to use, then the power to change a draft's pacing is at your fingertips.

Readers have genre expectations for pacing.

In literary fiction, if the pacing is too fast, then the reader can never catch their breath to get the deeper meaning of the story.

In a thriller, a murder mystery, or an adventure story, if the reader finds the pacing too slow, then they will put the book down. They are expecting to get swept up in the whirlwind of energy that these books have.

First, look at the word count per scene and see if there are any scenes that are too long or too short. For the longer scenes, all you have to do is check the Location Split story element. If there is more than one location in a scene, you know there is an easy opportunity for the writer to fix this issue.

Troubleshooting

If a scene takes place in more than one location, note this for the scene.

You'll use this when you are looking at pacing and word count per scene. You can also use this to check if the draft transitions effectively from one location to the next within the same scene.

When a location changes within a scene, more words are required to describe the transition from one location to the next.

If this slows the story. it's a great opportunity to show the writer how they can split the scene. Using a scene break character to show a change in location is much faster than describing the location change.

Look for scenes where the location changes and the POV character's goal changes.

Two goals in one scene can dilute both goals.

This is another easy fix for the writer. The editor can recommend adding a scene break character at the location change, and the goals become stronger.

Look for scenes where the location changes and the POV character changes. When the POV character changes, the goal most likely changes too. So we're back to keeping the goals strong.

Suggestions from an Editor

EDITOR 2:

[Evolution, scene 24: the scene starts with Jaz at home and transitions to Jaz meeting Alyssa at a restaurant.]

The split in locations with two quite different goals in both creates multiple POV goals which may be confusing for readers. This might be a scene worth dividing in two as a result, as both have different impacts on the character. In the first, it seems having Rose in the house brings her some peace and comfort. In the second, she is again conflicted about her role and what she should do in regard to telling Alyssa about Dan's affair.

> ## TEA with Kristina
>
> The feedback from the editor shows me why the location split within the scene doesn't work and why this scene should be two scenes.
>
> In the first half of the scene, while at home, Jaz's goal is to clean out some of Nick's clothes from the closet. This is a big moment for Jaz, as she's starting to accept that Nick is dead. Jaz's external goal is to make room for her things in her closet and make it smell less like Nick.
>
> In the second half of the scene, Jaz's external goal is to meet Alyssa for lunch despite the panic attacks she's prone to in public and to tell Alyssa her husband, Dan, is having an affair.
>
> The two goals are completely different. By having them in the same scene, you can see how the other elements get muddled. How do I answer the What if Goal Fails story element or determine the impact on Jaz if the goals aren't

aligned.

And if I can't answer that, neither can the reader.

Where to Next?

Now that we know where the scene takes place, when it takes place, which of the first three senses were used, whether the scene takes place in one location, and whether that location is the best place to create strong emotional impact, we'll look at the weather and see how it adds to the story.

Fictionary Story Element: Weather

Weather is a force of nature, and that force adds depth to a story.

We are all part of the natural world, and characters in a novel are no different. The weather can create tension or conflict. How a character reacts to the weather or how the weather enhances the character's mood deepens characterization.

In a draft, the weather should not read like a weather forecast. The power of weather comes from how it affects the characters, how it affects the plot, and how it affects the other Setting elements.

Definition

We all know what weather is. In a story, weather must enhance or contrast the emotions of the characters in the scene.

Scene and Story Level

At the scene level, look at the weather and how the emotions in the scene are enhanced or detracted from the characters' state of mind. The weather in a scene can also be thematic.

At the story level, check how weather is used throughout the story. Does the use of weather fit with the story the writer is telling? Look for places where the use of weather is repetitive. If the weather is important to the story and the conflict in the story, the tension caused by weather must increase as the story develops.

Perfecting the Weather Story Element

Your fun editing task is to list the weather for every scene.

The weather affects our moods. These weather-related feelings are the extremes, but much like the Emotional Impact story element, we need to look at the weather and ask, "Does the weather make the scene stronger?"

Check whether weather is used in an active way. This is a show-not-tell story element, and when the character is running through a rainstorm without an overcoat, it might be different from how they would joyfully splash if they are wearing the correct clothes for a rainstorm.

The characters can be characterized by their reactions to the weather.

Some people cannot stand the sun and prefer the drizzle, and others love to play in the snow.

When you have a list of weather per scene, you can ensure the draft is consistent with the weather from one scene to the next.

When the weather plays an important role in the story, it can be a character versus nature story.

If the weather changes the course of the story, then this is plot-related weather (the tornado in The Wizard of Oz, for instance).

WHEN LISTING WEATHER, USE THE FOLLOWING:

1. None: weather is not used at all in a scene. This may be okay if the scene takes place indoors.

2. Inconsistent: the weather is inconsistent from one scene to the next.

3. Weak: the weather doesn't strengthen the mood of the scene.

4. Not plot: the weather is not related to the plot.

5. Not character: the weather is not related to characterization.

And don't forget the all important √. The writer needs to be encouraged, and to do that, they need to know when they've used an element well.

Troubleshooting

There might be issues in the draft where plot holes occur. If, for instance, there is a storm in a chapter in the first act and that knocks the radar out on the boat, and this causes the inciting incident to occur, great. But if later there is another storm and the radar is knocked out again, then the reader will see a repetition, and the character did not learn from the first mistake.

If every time there is a storm at sea, the radar gets knocked out, then the reader will find this boring and repetitive.

Suggestions from an Editor

In the scene being commented on below, Jaz and Katie are in a car, taking a long drive to a wolf center. There are two dogs in the back seat.

EDITOR 9:

There is still weather in this scene with the heater blasting warm air, the dogs' breath fogging up the windows, and Katie rubbing her hands together. However, the weather doesn't seem to add any tension to the scene. In fact, the scene lacks a little tension altogether. There's no real mention of Jaz's emotional state beyond the discussion about Tom and Nick. Given she's just visited the site her husband died at, the reader may expect a little more.

> ## TEA with Kristina
>
> **The editor has shown me that I use weather a bit in Evolution but not as much as I should. The specific advice shows that I missed an opportunity to make life hard for Jaz.**
>
> **The advice has shown me I've set the scene up to use weather but didn't follow through. So I have options. Perhaps the windows getting fogged cause Jaz to nearly have a car accident. Perhaps her cold hands make it hard to steer. I'm going to revise the scene and use weather to add tension.**

Where to Next?

We're on to the final two Setting story elements. Next up is the Taste story element. And then we'll finish with Touch. Doesn't it feel great to almost be done?

Fictionary Story Element: Tastes

We crave food. It is our source of fuel, and the reader gets a visceral delight from reading about food. The goal is to get readers to react to the book by licking their lips. When readers react physically to the writing, they are deep inside the story world.

Remember the POV character makes a promise to the readers that they will taste what the POV character tastes. Let's make the tastes vivid and alive for the reader.

Descriptions should not only inform the reader what the POV character tastes, but also characterize the POV character by how they describe the taste, what they notice about the taste, and what they think is worth mentioning.

If the character can't taste something, it can't be described from the POV of the character.

Definition

Taste is what the POV character tastes during a scene.

Perfecting the Taste Story Element

Your fun editing task is to list everything the POV character tastes in every scene.

When editing for this sense, remember some of the ways that taste can add to the story.

I.   Taste can be used to describe a feeling the POV character has about another character. If the POV character is in love, they will think the food is wonderful, but if they are scared, they might find the food bitter.

2.   Taste can be used when a meal is important to the story or to the protagonist.

3.   Taste helps to world build, shows how the POV character is nourished in the world, and demonstrates what they notice in the environment.

4.   Taste can trigger a flashback.

Troubleshooting

If taste is not used anywhere in the story, this must be noted.

Look for scenes where taste is overused. Writers can get carried away when describing a meal. Not every scene has to have a meal, but the sense of taste can be used in many ways. Look for this sense in metaphors and similes.

Look for scenes where taste doesn't have a purpose. For example, taste can be used to foreshadow an event. Bitter is a flavor in the natural world that is poisonous. We inherently know this, and it can be used in a thriller if someone is slowly poisoning another.

Look for places where taste is used too often. This can be distracting to a reader.

Suggestions from an Editor

EDITOR 13:

> Notes from scene 5
> Only two senses are in the scene: sight and touch.

TEA with Kristina

The editor tells me that my setting story elements are being underused. In this scene wine is being drunk, so there is the perfect space for the taste to be mentioned. With this insight I can go back and add a sentence about the wine, to bring the experience to life for the reader.

> **"The taste sense in your prose quite literally means creating descriptions that are rich in flavor. When you do this, you bring your reader into the story and they experience it with the character."** — **Sacha Black**

Where to Next?

On to the final Fictionary Story Element: Touch. Let's get a feel for this element.

Fictionary Story Element: Touch

Touch is about physical connections with other people and the world around them. It is an intimate sense.

Descriptions should not only inform the reader what the POV character feels but also characterize the POV character by how they describe the texture, what they notice, and what they think is worth mentioning.

If the character can't feel something, it can't be described by their sense of touch.

Definition

Touch is anything the POV character feels via their skin.

Perfecting the Touch Story Element

Your fun editing task is to list everything the POV character touches in every scene.

WHEN EDITING FOR THIS SENSE, REMEMBER SOME OF THE WAYS THAT TOUCH CAN ADD TO THE STORY.

1. Touch can be used to describe a feeling the POV character has about another character. It can also foreshadow when a minor character reacts badly to the antagonist's touch. If the POV character is uncomfortable around another character, then they might shudder at their touch.

2. Touch, by its nature, is about proximity. If the POV character is close enough to touch something, that helps build an atmosphere of fear or of safety or of intimacy or of anywhere on that spectrum. The reader will react to the object, and those reactions show the reader the inner feelings of the POV character.

3. Touch helps to world build and shows how the POV character reacts in the world and what they

notice as they feel their way through the environment.

4. Touch can trigger a flashback.

Troubleshooting

Touch can show a level of intimacy that needs to be acknowledged in the story.

If a character is touched by another character and they don't flinch, then they must be close both physically and emotionally.

If the POV character does not react to a stranger's hand on them, then the reader will stumble over the passage, as it will not feel right.

A child reaches out to touch things when they are interested, and so, too, should a POV character. Readers will notice when the characters don't touch anything in a whole story. Fictionary Story Editors should determine whether the writer uses the character's whole body properly—unless there is a plot reason not to, of course.

To help the writer, edit for the following:

1. A group of scenes in a row where touch hasn't been used.

2. Types of touch that repeat too often.

3. Touch that doesn't have a purpose in the story.

Suggestions from an Editor

THE FOLLOWING CAME FROM THE EDITOR SUMMARY LETTER BY HEATHER WOOD, FICTIONARY CERTIFIED STORYCOACH EDITOR:

The tea pot has been stored there because she drank tea with Nick. She is pulling it out of a place of storage in her kitchen to resume this act of drinking tea with Tom, the new man.

> **TEA with Kristina**
>
> **The editor has shown me that I have the teapot as an important object, but more important is Jaz pulls out the teapot, touches it, then she is in a stable relationship. This use of touch, and noticing its significance, is a powerful way to show deeper meaning in the story. It shows the senses that are not just world building, they can be used in theme building, and in foreshadowing. By showing me how she saw this, it has taught me how I can see my own story, and the depth that is in there.**

Where to Next?

That's the end of the 38 Fictionary Story Elements. Now on to the actionable insights and how they can transform the edit.

But first let's go to a summary of the Setting story element.

Setting Elements Summarized

In chapters 9 and 10, where you learned the plot elements, you learned to ensure you start the story edit from a place of strength, and we suggested using the first eight story elements to edit a scene for the scene name, its purpose in the story, what type of opening and closing type is used, whether the reader is anchored, whether the reader is hooked at the beginning of the scene, and whether they are driven to read the next scene.

After that, you learned tension keeps the reader worried, conflict keeps the reader engaged, and a character's history, whether told through a revelation, a backstory, or a flashback, connects the reader to the character.

Remember, you learned how to structure scenes using the Scene Middle, Scene Climax, and Action/Sequel story elements. We ended the Plot story elements by understanding what a reader learns compared with the protagonist.

In Chapter 11: Learn the Character Story Elements, we started with a character list. Knowing who every character is and why they are important to the story, provides a solid foundation for editing characters.

Choosing the right POV character for every scene is a must for writers, and an editor's job is to ensure that was done.

Goals drive the story forward, but only if they are related to the story and have an impact on the characters. We checked for plot holes and ended with making sure characters are in motion to keep the pacing fast.

IN THIS CHAPTER, YOU LEARNED THE FOLLOWING:

- The importance of choosing the location to create a strong emotional impact on the reader and the characters.
- Why time is important.
- How objects and the senses bring the location to life.
- How weather can be used to enhance the mood of a scene.

We've covered all the Setting elements. Are you wondering what comes next?

For the editor working on someone else's book—woo-hoo! You have finished your scene-by-scene edit and can now move on to the actionable insights.

For the writer editing their own novel, you have a choice. Some writers like to revise the scenes now based on the Setting elements, and some like to keep going, working their way through all the story insights. Please remember, you are the artist, and the choice is yours.

If you want to revise now, here are some tips.

LOCATION

Have you reviewed the section "Location" and found there were no areas to troubleshoot? Yes? Woo-hoo! Go to the next step.

No?

Revise the location issues and fix any areas you discovered in the troubleshooting section of "Location."

TIMING

This is a story element that is the ticking clock. When the reader knows the time, then they are drawn into the scene. Is there a clear timing at the start of every scene? Yes? Woo-hoo! Go to the next step.

No?

Go to each scene without the timing and revise and add the timing to each scene.

OBJECT

The reader needs to have concrete objects that are story critical. When the reader feels that the setting is well described and every object has been placed for a reason, they trust the writer.

Are there clear objects for every scene? Yes? Woo-hoo! Go to the next step.

No?

Revise the scenes, add any objects that are needed later in the story, and cut any objects that are not used in the story.

SIGHT

Sight is an enormous sense for readers to connect with. Not only do they get oriented by sight, but they see the world through the POV character or the narrator. If there is no issue with the POV character's sight, then ask, "Does every scene use the sight sense?"

Yes? Woo-hoo! Go to the next step.

No?

Go back to every scene and revise how the POV character would view the world, what they would notice, how they would notice it, and how what they notice is plot relevant.

SMELL

Smell and memory are closely related. Has smell been used effectively throughout the story?

Yes? Woo-hoo! Go to the next element.

No?

Revise and add the senses into the scene in a plot- and character-relevant way.

SOUNDS

Noise is powerful. It can be used to wake the reader up, or to lull them into a false sense of security. The sounds that the POV character notices help the reader connect with the story world.

Does the reader have the opportunity to hear the world the way the POV character or the narrator does? Yes? Woo-hoo! Go to the next step.

No?

Revise the scenes and add in the sense of hearing to show the reader what the POV character or the narrator notices.

EMOTIONAL IMPACT

Where every scene is located must have emotional resonance for the POV character. Has every scene been chosen with this heightened meaning?

Yes? Woo-hoo! Go to the next step.

No?

Go back to every scene and look at the location. Ask how the location can make the POV character's emotional state heightened.

LOCATION SPLIT

The reader has a huge amount of information they must take in when reading every scene and moving to a whole new scene can overwhelm the reader. Is the scene in one location?

Yes? Woo-hoo! Go to the next step.

No?

Look at the scene and use the Location Split advice to see how you can revise the locations for the best clarity.

WEATHER

Is weather used to perfection in every scene?

Yes? Woo-hoo! Go to the next step.

No?

Look at the scenes you've marked for revision and see how the POV character reacts to the weather. Do they mention it, or do they wrap up to go out and meet it? Revise the scene so the reader knows what kind of day it is.

TASTES

All the senses help make the scenes memorable. Does the scene have the POV character experiencing taste?

Yes? Woo-hoo! Go to the next step.

No?

Revise the scenes with an issue based on the advice given in the taste section.

TOUCH

The sense of touch and how the POV character reacts to it are brilliant for combining with the Setting elements to make the character pop out. Does every scene evoke the sense of touch?

Yes? Woo-hoo! Go on to the Fictionary Actionable Insights.

No?

Revise the scenes based on the advice given in the touch section.

Where to Next?

Woo-hoo central! We are off to the Fictionary Visual Insights. An actionable insight is an image that enables you to see the story in a new way. You're going to love how they will turn you into one of the world's best editor.

Meet   Learn   Action

Chapter Thirteen:
Action Visual Insights

"The Story Map, a customizable view of your story elements, helps you expand or narrow your revision focus with ease." — Pamela Hines, Fictionary Certified StoryCoach Editor

Answers, Answers, Answers!

Up to this point, we've treated the writer who is editing their own book and the professional editor editing someone else's book mostly the same. We are all editors.

But when it comes to revisions, that's the writer's job. The editor's job is to make suggestions to the writer but not do the revisions.

Throughout this chapter, we'll highlight the differences between the writer's job and the editor's job.

At the start of this book, we showed you the three stages that make up the creative Fictionary story-editing process. Early on, you checked the story promise and that a story exists.

As an editor, whether you got a yes or a no to the question "Is there a story?" you went on to scene-by-scene editing.

As a writer, we hope you revised your story until you got a yes to the question "Is there a story?" and then went on to scene-by-scene editing.

When you edited at the scene level, you checked how each story element worked for each scene. Then you looked at the pattern that these elements made. At the scene level, you have used all the 38 Fictionary Story Elements.

You are so close to the end of your editing journey. You will now find how to make all the hard work you have done actionable.

> **This section is about how to take the brilliant work you've done and finish creating actionable advice, so the draft can be revised.**

These next steps answer the question at the beginning of this book:

How can we take a draft and turn it into a novel that has an opportunity to become a bestseller?

Editing versus Revision Recap

Remember the difference between editing and revision is that editing is an evaluation tool. When editing a book, you are looking at finding out if the story works. The creative story-editing process is all about giving actionable advice that can be used in the revision process.

> **When the author revises their work, they are going into the story using MARCS: Move, Add, Revise, Cut, Split.**

The author reads the editing advice and revises the book.

The Next and Final Editing Stage

Editing using the 38 Fictionary Story Elements was a thorough process, but it's not quite the whole edit. We are here to cheer you on through the next stage to get the final editing advice to go along with what you've done already.

This next step involves visually editing the manuscript. We'll show you how to see the story and make suggestions. We'll start with ways to see the story at the manuscript level and then cover how to see the story structure using the supergroups: Plot, Character, and Setting.

We're going to review the story arc last. You edited using the story arc at the beginning of the edit. If you're the writer, you performed any revisions necessary to make sure there is a story.

After that, you edited using the story elements.

> **For the writer, the next step is to use the revision plan you put together using the story elements to revise each scene. Once that's done, it's time to go back and look at the overall structure again. This is important because revisions cause structural changes, and you want to make sure the story arc works and that there is still a story.**
>
> **For the editor, the next step is to summarize the revision plan so the writer can understand and act on the detailed revisions being suggested. Seeing the manuscript visually helps you be one of the world's best story editors.**

SPECIFICS TURN EDITING INSIGHTS INTO ACTIONABLE ADVICE.

If you're using Fictionary to edit, after you have filled in the story elements, you are going to love the manuscript insights. If you're not using Fictionary, hopefully you've at least created a spreadsheet where you have data you can turn into insights. This is where technology helps artists.

You will look at everything you have edited so far and make decisions based on your findings.

When nearing the end of the edit, the creative story editor promises the writer there will be actionable revision advice.

Actionable advice is the magic of a creative story edit.

Let's get into it!

Meet the Fictionary Insights

We'll take you through the journey of reviewing insights that help you edit the manuscript structure.

Then we'll look at each of the supergroup insights for plot, character, and setting and update the revision plan.

And finally, we'll come back to the story arc.

Note that the process is a little different between an editor who is editing someone else's story and an editor performing a self-edit.

The former won't perform any revisions, and the latter will.

The insights are what make Fictionary Story Editors the best story editors. Not every piece of revision advice must be written into the final draft, but the reasons behind every piece of revision advice are supported by empirical editorial evidence.

MANUSCRIPT INSIGHTS

- Story Arc
- Word Count per Scene
- Scenes per Chapter
- Story Map

PLOT INSIGHTS

- Purpose of Scenes
- Scene Opening Types
- Scene Closing Types

CHARACTER INSIGHTS

- Characters per Scene
- Scenes per Character
- POV Characters
- Character Arc

SETTING INSIGHTS

- Setting Elements per Scene

Empirical Editorial Evidence

When you edited each scene against the 38 Fictionary Story Elements, you kept track of what was done well and what needed improvement. Hopefully you also kept notes for these suggestions on a per-scene basis.

If you're the author, it's time to start revisions. What fun!

If you're the editor, it's time to create a summary letter to give to the writer. Super fun!

The Fictionary Story Editor observes and notes the patterns in the draft. The Fictionary Story Editor uses their story knowledge to interpret it, and then the interpretation is the specifics that make up the actionable advice. And those interpretations are on the next pages.

Remember the tools that you will be using to turn the evaluation into actionable advice.

The Actionable Fictionary MARCS

Move or Add or Revise or Cut or Split

Actionable editing advice is action editing. Look to move, add, revise, cut, or split.

Edit the draft and ask, "Does this need Moving, Adding, Revising, Cutting, or Splitting when considering the whole manuscript or to make a scene more powerful?"

We'll explain each insight and how to find your MARCS in the remainder of this chapter.

The Manuscript Insights

Editors are treasure hunters. We look for the dazzling, the gorgeous, and the delightful. And yet the less-spoken-about side of treasure hunting is the ability to recognize what is not treasure.

At least not a treasure in the draft we are editing. Anything that does not add to the story needs to be given MARCS—an actionable suggestion.

At the manuscript level, we're going to start with the word count per scene, then move on to the scenes per chapter.

Word Count per Scene

Scenes are the building blocks of a story, and the word count per scene affects the pacing and balance of a story.

Word count per scene shows readers, sometimes without them noticing, that a scene is important, because it's given a higher word count. A very short scene shows readers the action is being highlighted and the reader should remember it.

Scene length is chosen by the writer. It doesn't happen by accident. The editor needs to check if it works.

PACING

Pacing comes from many places, and at the story level the word count per scene is important to control so the pacing is controlled. A long scene compared to those around them is a slower scene, and a shorter scene feels faster.

Remember the modern reader now often uses a smaller screen to read via e-readers or smartphones, and so scene length should be taken into account. Smaller page sizes due to technology would make longer scenes seem to go on and on. Therefore, reading devices must be considered when editing for pacing at the word-count-per-scene level.

BALANCE

Balance is about having a book where the reader trusts that the story has been well crafted. If the scenes are different lengths and that has not been planned to create that pacing effect, then the balance should be reviewed.

A longer scene says a scene is important and tells the reader to pay attention to it. This means the five Fictionary Story Arc scenes should be longer than those around them.

The following is the first action to check for word count balance:

Look for scenes that have a word count longer than the five story arc scenes. Scenes with a longer word count than the inciting incident, plot point 1, middle plot point, plot point 2, and climax must be edited.

FIRST

Reread those scenes and ask the following questions:

- Can the scene be split into two or more scenes? If yes, then go for it.

- Can the scene be revised to shorten it? If yes, then go for it. This is a good time to see if there is too much backstory in a scene, if an entry hook occurs too late, or if an exit hook occurs too early. Text before and after hooks are great places to look for cutting.

SECOND

The second action is to look for short outlier scenes and make sure the length is intended. Reread the outlier scene and ask the following questions:

- Should the actionable advice be to add more plot-relevant details to the scene, more setting details, or more character details?

- Or should two short scenes that are in the same location be merged?

THIRD

The third action is to look for longer outliers locally to that scene:

- Are there any scenes that are two or more times longer than the other scenes? Yes?
- Does it make sense for the story? Perhaps it's the climax scene, so it's okay. If not, look for ways to recommend shortening the scene as mentioned in the first action above.

If you're the writer, make the revisions before going on to the next step.

If you're the editor, summarize your suggestions for word count per scene and give per-scene notes on how the writer might address the issues.

Scenes per Chapter

Chapters are made up of one or more scenes. This is the next level of foundation for a story and should be carefully organized, because the number of scenes in a chapter will impact the pacing and flow of the story.

> **Chapters can be organized on a theme basis, on a POV basis, on a time basis, and so on.**

There are many choices for a writer, and the editor must comment on whether the chapter structure works.

If the story has more than one scene in a chapter, then look at why the story groups certain scenes together. What are these scenes saying thematically? Are all from one POV? Or does each chapter have a scene from each of the dual POVs from the story? These questions will help you edit the scenes-per-chapter structure.

The first quick check: look for chapters with a large number of scenes compared to other chapters. If all the chapters have three or fewer scenes and one has ten scenes, that will feel off to readers.

The quick solution is to find the best place to split the chapter into two chapters. A new chapter can be started when the POV character, the timing of the scene, or the location changes. Look for scenes within the chapter that do one of these and suggest starting a new chapter.

You can also look to see if every scene in the chapter is needed. If you edited the scene while editing using the story elements, did all the scenes have a purpose? If not, perhaps the scenes with no purpose could be cut. That reduces the number of scenes in a chapter by one.

Is there a scene in the chapter whose purpose is to reveal backstory? Check if the backstory is needed at that time or if the scene could be moved to a later chapter.

The next step is to look for a pattern in the chapters.

As the editor, can you tell if the writer planned how the chapters would be organized?

Chapter grouping

CHAPTERS CAN BE GROUPED AS FOLLOWS:

1. By theme.

2. By POV.

3. By time. Books that jump back and forth in time often use this technique.

4. By having a consistent number of scenes in every chapter.

If you're the writer, make the revisions before going on to the next step.

If you're the editor, summarize your suggestions for scenes per chapter and give per-scene notes on how the writer might address the issues.

Where to Next?

For both Word Count per Scene and Scenes per Chapter, the action is based on Move or Add or Revise or Cut or Split.

If you're the writer, you've made the revisions and you're happy with the word count per scene and the scenes per chapter. You'll come back and review this again after you've completed the revisions. For now, congratulations on getting your draft to a solid structure.

If you're an editor, then keep working on your summary letter.

It's time to delve deeper into the structure. We'll look at the manuscript using the Plot Insights.

The Plot Insights

Plot is what happens in the story despite the order in which the story is told. Structure is about the readers emotions; it is the ordering of the events in the story that elicits the highest level of emotion.

Plot and structure together influence how readers experience the story.

At the manuscript level, the following are the Plot Insights:

1.   Purpose of Scenes

2.   Scene Opening Types

3.   Scene Closing Types

Each of the above was edited at the scene level during the scene-by-scene edit. You kept track of all three for every scene.

Now we're going to look at the elements at the structural level, and this is why insights are needed for these elements.

The Actionable Fictionary MARCS

Move or Add or Revise or Cut or Split

We'll keep MARCS in mind as we look at the Plot Insights.

Purpose of a Scene

Every scene—and we mean every scene—must have a reason for being in the story.

During the scene-by-scene edit, you kept track of the purpose of each scene. You also kept track of scenes where you weren't sure of the purpose. With all this information, you can now take an objective look at each scene and determine if each one deserves a place in the story.

If you're using Fictionary, it's time to look at the Purpose of Scenes insight.

The first action to edit the Purpose of Scenes is to reread all scenes where you noted that you didn't know the purpose of a scene on the first editing pass.

- Do you understand the purpose now? Yes? That's good, but it still might mean there are problems with the scene. Is there a way the writer could revise the scene to make the purpose more clear to the reader.

- Is the purpose still unclear? The actions are revise or cut. When you decide to revise, then look at the surrounding scenes and where the scene is in the story. Does a red herring need to be added? A character introduction? Should this be an establishing-the-setting scene?

There is normally a small hint of what the scene could be, in a word or a sentence, that needs to be expanded upon. When the decision is to cut, explain why that scene does not work. Relate it to the skeleton blurb from Chapter 3: Meet the Story Promise.

A lack of movement of the protagonist toward or away from the goal and the stakes is a common reason to cut a scene.

Remember the protagonist does not have to be in a scene to have the action in that scene move them closer to or further from the story goal. This cutting advice can be reenforced by looking at the Character Arc insight, but first we will look at advanced editing using the Purpose of Scenes insight.

The second action is to look for repetitive scene purposes. If there are too many similar purpose types in a row, the pacing could be slow. For example, if the scene purpose is character introduction for three or more scenes in a row, this might get boring to the reader. Anywhere you see three or more of the same purpose types in a row, check that it works for the story.

Scene Opening and Closing Types

Unintended repetition is boring. It's great if you're trying to memorize something but not great for keeping readers engaged in a story. When you're at the copyediting phase, repetition can be used in prose for effect. At the structural level, it's a problem.

> **TEA with Kristina**
>
> I created the Scene Opening and Closing Types insights because of a conversation I had with my husband. He'd just read the draft of the first novel I'd ever written.
>
> After he told me all the things he loved about the story, he asked, "Do you know you start most scenes in a doorway?"
>
> I didn't believe him. But when I checked, guess what I found. I started too many scenes in a doorway. That was when I started thinking about repetition, which led to the story elements for Opening and Closing Types and Entry and Exit Hooks.

Now you get the payoff for keeping track of opening and closing types throughout the draft.

There are four types:

1. Dialogue

2. Thought

3. Description

4. Action

Again, we're looking for patterns. Too many scenes in a row that start with the same type or end with the same type will bore the reader.

THE FOLLOWING ARE THE ACTIONS TO TAKE:

1. Look for areas in the story that have three or more of one type in a row. Then review those scenes and suggest revising the opening or closing type.

2. Look for types that are not used or are used infrequently. Look for areas in the story where one type was used for more than three scenes in a row.

    These are areas to suggest adding the unused type.

Where to Next?

For the purpose of a scene, the opening types, and the closing types, the action is based on Move or Add or Revise or Cut or Split.

If you're the writer, you've made the revisions, and you're happy with these three insights, move on to the next set of insights.

If you're an editor, use the information learned here and keep working on your summary letter.

Next we get to explore the manuscript structure based on the characters. Yes, you read that right.

Characters and structure must work together to create a bestseller.

Let's see what we can learn.

The Character Insights

Readers must connect with the characters, or the writer has work to do.

Readers want to have someone to follow through with the story.

They want to love and hate characters. The importance of getting the characters right in a draft cannot be overstated.

AT THE MANUSCRIPT LEVEL, THE FOLLOWING ARE THE CHARACTER INSIGHTS:

1. Cast of Characters

2. Characters per Scene

3. Scenes per Character

4. POV Characters

5. Character Arc. This one is not what you think it is. It's a little secret we're going to share, so get ready. It's going to knock your socks off.

We're going to test whether all characters are needed in the story, then whether all characters are needed in the scene. Then we're going to test whether characters appear in too few or too many scenes. After that, we'll test the POV structure. And finally we'll review the protagonist's character arc.

The Fictionary Story Editor's actionable advice for the Character elements uses all the same Fictionary MARCS.

The Actionable Fictionary MARCS

Move or Add or Revise or Cut or Split

We'll keep this in mind as we look at the Character insights.

Cast of Characters

Fictionary has listed all characters in the draft in one place. If you're not using Fictionary, this is the time to make a list of characters including first and last names.

Now you've got a list. Why do you care?

THE FIRST ACTION:

Check whether any of the names are too similar to each other. Do this by comparing first names, then last names, then first against last. For example, if one character's first name is Thomas and another character's last name is Thomson, this is too close.

The reader will get confused.

Suggest to the writer to change one of the names.

THE SECOND ACTION:

Check how many characters are in the story. While reading the story, did you get confused on who a character was?

This could be because the description was unclear, or it could be because there are too many characters in the story.

The Scenes per Character insight is going to help you fix this.

Characters per Scene

While we're on the topic of too many characters, let's look at how many characters are in each scene.

Check how many characters are in each scene.

THIS INFORMATION IS CRITICAL TO EVALUATING A SCENE.

- Are there scenes with more than seven characters? Yes? Reread the scenes and check whether this works. Many characters per scene can work. A scene where a team is being introduced or awards given could have a lot of character names.

- If there were scenes where you had trouble remembering who a character was, check whether it's one of the scenes with a lot of characters. The advice to the writer is to revise the scene and look for characters who can be cut from the scene.

- Look for the outliers. In any scenes with fewer than two characters, make sure that the tension in the scene is strong enough. Conflict is easier if there are at least two characters in a scene, if there is only one, then this needs to be reviewed. Add or revise is the action here.

- Look at any scenes with large numbers of characters. In any scenes that are at the opposite end, have a look to see whether any of the characters are doing the same job.

- The more characters in a scene, the more a reader can get lost. In scenes that lie at the upper end of word count, read them and then advise to cut, or revise, or move characters from the scene. Ask if each named character is story critical. If they do not add to the plot in that scene, cut them. Move them out of the scene if they are not part of the scene goal.

- Do the extra characters all come into conflict with or cause tension to the POV character?

If you're the writer, revise the scenes now, and then we'll move on to how many scenes each character is in. There's no sense editing Scenes per Character until you've finalized what scenes each character is in. The writer is actively editing, revising, and editing again during this phase of the process.

For the editor, update your summary letter with your suggestions about the number of characters per scene.

Scenes per Character

Important characters should be in more scenes than minor characters. Sounds simple, right? It is, when you have a structured way to edit this.

During the scene-by-scene edit, you kept track of who was in each scene. Now you're going to use that information to edit the characters at a structural level.

This insight shows you how many scenes a character is in.

IT WILL HELP YOU DO THE FOLLOWING:

1. Get to know the characters in the book. You got to know them when you listed each character in a scene.

2. Determine the importance of each character.

3. Edit whether a character's page time is plot relevant.

4. Edit if a character's introduction is correct for their story importance.

When characters are on the page, we need to gauge if they are well weighted. How critical are they to the plot? Should a minor character who has no plot relevancy be named?

YOUR ACTIONS ARE THE FOLLOWING:

1. Check that the protagonist is in the greatest number of scenes compared to other characters. If not, either the wrong protagonist was chosen or there are scenes that need to be revised to include the protagonist. The POV insight is going to help more with this.

2. Check that the protagonist enters the story early. If the protagonist is not in the first scene, there must be a strong reason. If there isn't, the opening of the story needs to be revised.

3. Check that all major characters are introduced before the middle plot point. Often the protagonist's support team is built between plot point 1 and the middle plot point. You can see that up to now it's all about the protagonist. And since the protagonist is the most important character, this is how it should be.

4. Did you notice there were too many characters in the story when you reviewed the cast of characters or the characters per scene? Yes? Then look for characters who appear in only one scene. When a

character is named, the reader will assume they are important. If they are not, suggest revising the scene so the character is not named. Or maybe the character can be cut from the story.

If you're the writer, make revisions now based on the edit you just did.

If you're the editor, add your comments regarding scenes per character to the summary letter. By now the summary letter is growing into strong, actionable advice for the writer. But there's still more to add.

POV Characters

In terms of POV, there are two types of novels. Ones that are written from a single POV and others that are written from multiple POVs.

When editing the draft at a structural level, and there are multiple POV characters in the story, it's important to track the POV each scene is written in, so you can look at the balance of the POVs over the whole story.

A multiple POV story means the reader experiences the story from the senses of more than one character. The feelings, actions, and senses of the scene are all derived from the POV character's experiences.

If the novel you're editing is written from a single POV, you can move on to the protagonist's character arc.

LET'S GET STARTED. THE FOLLOWING ARE YOUR ACTIONS:

1. Is the protagonist the POV character for the greatest number of scenes. Yes? Then awesome. No? Then revisions are needed.

2. Check the order of the POV scenes. Is the protagonist the POV character for the first scene or for a scene early in the story? No? Then revisions are needed

3. Check the first time a character is the POV. Are they introduced properly? No? Then revisions are

needed

4. Check how many POV characters exist? More than seven? Yes? Then check if all are needed. For the characters who have only one or two scenes in their POV, see if the story works better if any of the scenes were written from a major POV character.

> **If you're the writer, revise the scene based on the edit you just did.**
> **If you're the editor, update the summary letter with actionable advice.**

Protagonist's Character Arc

Let's start with a quick review of what the character arc is, because as you will remember we have a different way of looking at a character arc. We are using the protagonist and the story goal to determine whether the protagonist is closer or further away from the story goal by the end of a scene.

During the scene-by-scene edit, you kept track of whether a scene brought the protagonist closer to their story goal, further away from their story goal, or neither.

> **Fictionary draws the character arc for you. You can quickly see if this is a major problem for the writer or a minor problem.**

Flat lines on the character arc are places in the story where the protagonist gets no closer or further away from the main story goal. Remember the main story goal is found in the blurb.

YOUR ACTION:

1. Check for scenes where the character arc is neutral. This means the scene doesn't drive the story forward to a conclusion. Here the edit is to recommend revising or cutting the scene. Ask why this scene is in this story. Would this story be better with this scene cut? Or would it be better if it were revised? A scene where the protagonist is not getting closer to or further from the story goal is one form of overwriting. Making an informed decision, look to see if cutting or revising would be the best option. Remember that even if the protagonist is not in the scene, the actions of the scene can still move the protagonist closer to or further from that story goal.

2. Check for too many scenes in a row where the protagonist is closer to achieving the story goal by the end of the scene. The reader will feel the tension decreasing because the protagonist is too successful. Anything more than three scenes in a row should be checked. In this case, the story can get

dull for the reader.

3.   Check for too many scenes in a row where the protagonist is further away from their goal. This one
is a little trickier than the second point above.
Here the placement of the scenes is important. For
example, plot point 2 should be the lowest point
for the protagonist in the story, so the scenes leading up to it should take the protagonist further
away from the goal.

Where to Next?

**For the Character insights, the action is based on Move
or Add or Revise or Cut or Split.**

If you're the writer, you've made the revisions and you're happy with these
five insights. Except for the character arc, changes made because of these insights won't impact the structure of the story, so you don't have to come back
and review them again.

If you're an editor, keep working on your summary letter.

Next we're looking at the final supergroup.

The Setting insight.

Let's see what we can learn.

The Setting Insights

We are evolved to problem solve and survive in the environment around
us. Readers want to know where they are throughout the story. The setting can
influence how the reader reacts to the story. There are two sides to the setting
that you are looking at. Is there any setting in the scene? Yes? Woo-hoo! Go to
the next action.

If no, ask why not. Does the scene come to life without it? Where are the characters located? Where is the plot happening? Is the setting not being used to its fullest?

Now we are going to look at the location in even greater detail.

The Actionable Fictionary MARCS

Move or Add or Revise or Cut or Split

We'll keep this in mind as we look at the Setting insights.

Location Names

1. Check whether any of the names are too similar to each other. Do this by comparing the location names. Are there any location names that are too similar and that might confuse the reader, such as two towns called Talke and Taulke Pits? In fiction, make sure the names of the locations are distinct.

2. Check how descriptions of locations are in the story. While reading the story, did you get confused about where a character was? This could be because the description was unclear. Use the Setting insight to find the first time a scene is in a location. Read the description from the first scene.

3. Were there any locations that you had trouble remembering where the character was? The advice to improve the story is to revise the scene to look at the location description and how the POV character moves through, and interacts with, the loca-

tion, and ask, "Has this been described fully?"

Purpose of Location

Locations should add to the story. As a Fictionary Story Editor, you should ask whether you can name the purpose of each location.

The action is to list the location of each scene and list the purpose of that location. Is its purpose working with the purpose of the scene? Do they work in harmony with each other, or are they in opposition to show the character in even greater relief? The Emotional Impact of Scene and Purpose of Scenes will help define this.

Locations per Scene

The action is to check how many locations are in each scene.

THIS INFORMATION IS ALSO CRITICAL TO EVALUATING A SCENE.

- If there are two or more locations, look at how the draft describes each new location.

- To orient a reader, when you are in a new location, even if the draft has been taken there before, the location must be described. Poor anchoring takes from the pacing, and if the descriptions of a new location are in the second half of the scene, look to see if they slow down the scene's pacing. Could these scenes with multiple locations be split into two scenes? Cross-check with scene word count.

Check word count for short scenes with their neighboring short scenes and then look at the location. Are these two scenes in the same location? Could they be added together?

Scenes per Location

Look at the Setting insight and look at the number of scenes at a particular location.

YOUR ACTION:

Read all the scenes at one location: the initial one and all the subsequent ones. Does the initial description and how the POV character moves through and interacts with a location create enough of an image for the reader, or is it too much and slows down the pacing? In subsequent locations, does the information repeat, or is it described in a new way that will add to the emotional impact of the location?

NEXT LOOK AT THE LOCATIONS IN ALL THE STORY ARC SCENES.

1.   How does the location work in each of these locations to help increase the impact of the Story Arc scene?

2.   If the location has been visited before, have some of the initial location landscapes now come into use?

3.   If the location was described, why was it described? Was it to show character or was it to be used in the plot later? If for character development, then how do they see it differently? If for plot, how is it used in the climax scene?

4.   If this is the first time a location is visited, is the description enough that the pacing has not been slowed down? Is there a scene location that could mirror this new location so the description could be referred to and only plot critical differences could be looked at?

The Timeline

Once the time and date are laid out in this Fictionary Story Element across the whole story, this forms the timeline so you can see how the story works. Does it all go in one direction? Does it time hop? Are those time hops well anchored?

This timeline is used to see if there is a pattern to the time hops or if they are ad hoc.

When you see a clear pattern that the reader will be able to get on board with, then you can give actionable advice. Sometimes it might be every even chapter is in one timeline, and every odd is in another. Or there should be two scenes in every chapter, one from each timeline. If the past has less weight than the present in the story, perhaps it should be every two scenes in the present and one from the past. Repeatedly make sense from the artistic part of your editing but also from the story's needs.

Where to Next?

The Story Arc is one of the most powerful editing tools that a creative story editor can use. The Story Arc gives you insight into the deepest structure of the draft. In the next section, we will show you how to harness this, and you can take your story to the next level.

The Story Arc Insight

Earlier in this book, we used the story arc to check if a story existed in the manuscript.

Determining whether there is a story is a major editing task. By this point in the book, you know how to figure this out.

Reviewing the story arc is an early task in the creative story-editing process. It's also the task that closes out the edit.

Now we're looking at the story arc after the edit is complete. This is to make sure all the edits you've made, and all the revisions that will be made, will turn the manuscript into a full story.

This is the final creative story-editing check.

If you're an editor who is self-editing their own story, you'll review the story arc after every major revision or structural change. The goal is to ensure you stay on track with the story and stay on track with the five Fictionary Story

Arc scenes. You'll review the story arc again once you're finished with your revisions. You'll keep revising until your story is perfect.

For the editor—who has not written the draft—you'll deliver a story arc to your client that shows what scenes you believe are the five Fictionary Story Arc scenes. You'll show them if the scenes are in the right place doing the right things. This is incredibly useful to the writer.

Congratulations!

You've made it through a creative story edit. Well done!

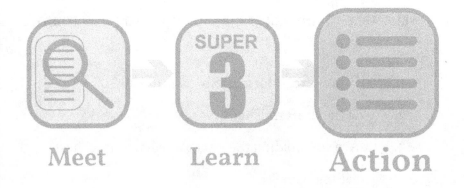

Meet   Learn   Action

Chapter Fourteen:
Action your Editing Success

"Great stories are formed by characters who keep their eyes on the prize: the story goal" —Polly Watt, Fictionary Certified StoryCoach Editor

You Are an Editor

Editing, especially creative story editing, is fun. It is empowering to have the tools to finesse a draft into a strong story.

After reading this book and using the advice, you are a powerful creative story editor. And a brilliant one too.

"I am a brilliant editor." You should repeat that every time you edit.

First, you built the skeleton blurb from the client's original blurb. Then you wrote the working synopsis and tested the manuscript to determine whether a story exists. This is a powerful step in the editing journey.

Then you used the 38 Fictionary Story Elements to edit the manuscript, first looking at the story as a whole, then on a scene-by-scene basis. Then you looked at the story-level edit again.

Now you've joined the world's best editors: you are a creative story editor.

YOU WERE ABLE TO ANSWER THESE QUESTIONS YOU HAD FOR THE DRAFT:

1.   Was there a story in this manuscript?

2.   Is the draft finished?

3.   Are you holding the next award-winning, best-selling book?

A Yes, a Yes, and a Yes

It works because you found a story in the manuscript. It works because you make revision recommendations to make it shine. It can win awards and become a bestseller.

Now you know the secrets to perform a creative edit—secrets that now that you know them make you wonder why every editor hasn't read this book. Why every creative story editor does not give this level of editing feedback is beyond us, too. The secrets in this book are a method, a recognition of hard work, and actionable advice.

Nothing held you back.

You were able to perform a full edit. You had a process and a method that is comprehensive, objective, and actionable.

A Repeatable Editing Process

You found out how to structurally edit a manuscript, starting by standing back and admiring the story structure, then reviewing right down to the scene level. We hope you have found the process to be versatile and that you can use it repeatedly. This process will make the next book easier to edit because you will know what makes a good story.

You are a creative story editor, and you have an editing plan. You have the blueprints, the building plans, to turn the rough draft into a book with built-in beauty.

That Extra Editing Advice

In this book, we used examples from professional editors.

That was a huge boost.

Having those extra editors, you could see how the method works for many editors. It worked for them, and now it has worked for you. By using the Fictionary software and process, your final edit is comprehensive, objective, and actionable.

Throughout this book, we showed you examples of real-life edits. You saw what thirteen different editors said about the draft novel Evolution. And you also got to see Kristina Stanley's response to the feedback.

You also got practical advice on how to edit a novel. That theory is important, and now you know how to use it.

The theory is a backdrop to the main event—a process you can now use again and again.

Story Editors Are Artists

You are an artist. You were before you read this book, and with this method, you are still. Now you are a story editor who edits the structure of a story. You'll make artistic choices throughout every edit you make from now on using this process.

You are in control of your future edits.

What Happens after a Creative Story Edit?

The art of beautiful prose comes after creative story editing. Beautiful prose contains the artist's voice plus the style that fits the genre of the story.

Because you started with the story edit first, you did not waste time on copyediting text that might have been cut or revised.

Copyediting is the time for beautiful prose.

Then after the copyedit and formatting, proofreading needs to happen. You'll have noticed that we don't call proofreading editing. It's the final check after formatting that there are no typos, mismatched heading, or similar issues. The books should be as close to perfect as possible before proofreading.

And then the book is ready to go out to the world!

How to Use This Book Again and Again and Again

Every time you have a manuscript ready to edit, get this book out.

Go to Chapter 3: Meet the Story Promise and start the edit with the blurb.

Then it's time to import your manuscript into Fictionary and get started editing. After you've imported your manuscript, go to Chapter 4: Meet the Fictionary Story Test and perform the Fictionary Story Test. When you know there is a story, start the scene-by-scene edit. Using this book can make all the stories you edit the best they can be.

If you are using this book together with Fictionary software, you will be editing more quickly and more thoroughly with every edit. Fictionary has given you a structured method to keep track of the vast amount of information involved in a story edit and to see the story in a visual manner. It saved you time with the visual insights that show you where a story is or isn't working.

That's the secret behind Fictionary.

Your Future

Your future is full of great story edits because you are a creative story editor.

We cannot wait to read about your edits.

Editing to Success is not about revealing a magic formula. It is to empower your editing skills and give you the tools so you can perform a successful edit. The world needs great stories, and for that to happen, the world needs you.

Go and story edit the world!

Appendix

Editing Process Overview: Action the Process

"Without character movement, your story comes to a standstill. Words easily express talk and thought, but motion needs showing. Add motion to your scene and your characters come alive." — Casper Pieters, Fictionary Certified StoryCoach Editor

Editing Process Overview

This section is an overview of the process. You can keep coming back to this page to get a feel for where your edit is.

Perfecting the Scene Name

Your fun editing task is to read each scene in the story and name it.

There is a three-words-or-fewer rule to naming a scene. If you can name the scene in three or fewer words, brilliant. Try to name the scene by what is shown in the scene. Not what you think it shows. Not what you want it to show. But by what is there in the scene.

Perfecting the Story Arc

Your editing task is to find the five Fictionary plot point scenes, ensure they are located in the best place in the story, and ensure that they are doing everything they must do.

Perfecting the Purpose of a Scene

Your editing task is to list the purpose of each scene in three words or fewer.

Perfecting the Scene Opening Type

Your editing task is to list the opening type for every scene. Then evaluate the list for the number of each type and the order they are used. Go through each scene of the novel and label the scenes with one of the four types. Then check to ensure that they aren't repetitive and that all four types have been used.

Perfecting the Scene Closing Type

Your editing task is to list the closing type for every scene. Then evaluate the list for the number of each type and the order they are used. Go through each scene of the novel and label the scenes with one of the four types. Then check they aren't repetitive and that all four types have been used.

Perfecting the Scene Anchoring

Your editing task, which you can do at the same time as the opening type and opening hook, is to note whether each scene is anchored in POV, time, and setting. You're not revising at this stage. The goal is to end up with an overview to see if the scenes are anchored.

Perfecting the Scene Entry Hook

Your editing task is to read every scene opening and look for an entry hook. To edit each scene, read the first one or two paragraphs of the scene and mark the state of the entry hook.

Perfecting the Scene Exit Hook

Your editing task is to read every scene ending and look for an exit hook. To edit each scene, read the last one or two paragraphs of the scene and mark the state of the exit hook.

Perfecting the Scene Tension

Your editing tasks are to look for tension in each scene, using the story goal found in the Fictionary Skeleton Blurb, and look for places where the POV character is at risk or where the protagonist is closer to or pushed further from the story goal, even if they are not in the story.

Perfecting the Scene Conflict

Your editing task is to find the places in the scene that stop the POV character from achieving their scene goal.

Perfecting the Scene Revelation

Your editing task is to note all the revelations and see if they are well placed for the plot to work. On the first editing pass, you can use this element to remind yourself of when in the draft information was revealed. For example, let's say too much is revealed early in the story and it's reducing the tension in a story. Note where the revelation would be better placed.

Perfecting Backstory

Your editing task is to note every instance of backstory and ask the following three questions:

Is the draft revealing the backstory in an engaging way?

Is the backstory always told to the reader instead of shown?

Is the backstory plot relevant?

Perfecting Flashback

Your editing task is to note every flashback in the story and look at how each flashback is entered into and left by the POV character.

Perfecting the Scene Middle

Your editing task is to list the scene middle in three words or fewer for every scene.

Perfecting the Scene Climax

Your editing task is to list the scene climax in three words or fewer for every scene. Does the scene climax address the scene POV goal? If it does not, then the scene notes should suggest revising the scene so the scene POV is addressed.

Perfecting the Action/Sequel

Your editing task is to decide whether the scene is mostly an action or a sequel. List this for each scene and look for patterns.

Perfecting the Reader Knowledge Gained

Your editing task is to look at the scene's beginning, middle, and end. Then note what is revealed to the reader; keep note of any information the reader gains but the protagonist doesn't. Check for scenes where the protagonist is not in the scene and list the key information the reader learned.

Perfecting the Scene Character List

Your editing task is to list every character in every scene. Also, list every character mentioned in every scene.

Perfecting the Scene POV

Your editing task is to list the POV character for each scene. This will help you see the structure of the story.

Perfecting the Scene POV Goal

Your editing task is to list the POV goal for every scene.

Perfecting the Character Arc

Your editing task is to read each scene and mark the character arc as positive, neutral, or negative.

Perfecting the Scene POV Goal Internal

You have two editing tasks for the POV Goal Internal. The first is to determine the story-level goal for the protagonist. The second is to list the internal goal (if there is one) for the POV character for every scene.

Perfecting the Scene Goal Related to Plot

Your editing task is to list if the external POV goal is related to the plot for every scene. It can be as simple as putting "Yes" and "No" for the Goal Related to Plot story element. Or you can list why it's not related to the plot.

Perfecting the Scene What if Goal Fails

You have two editing tasks for this story element. The first is to list the consequence if the goal fails, and the second is to keep track of how many times the POV character fails to achieve their goal versus achieves their goal.

Perfecting the Scene Impact on POV Character

Your editing task is to list the impact the scene has on the POV character for every scene.

Perfecting the Scene Impact on the Protagonist

Your editing task is to look at how the protagonist feels at the beginning of the scene and at the end of the scene, and mark a + or a - if they end up feeling happy or sad, respectively.

Perfecting POV Knowledge Gained

Your editing task is to list any new information the POV character learns for every scene. You'll use this information to check for plot holes.

Perfecting Character in Motion

Your editing task is to mark each scene for characters being in motion or not, then see if this is a big issue for the story or only happens once or twice.

Perfecting Location

Your editing task is to list the location of every scene in the draft. You can think of this list as an after-draft location outline.

Perfecting Timing

Your editing task is to list the time in which every scene takes place. The aim is to get a story line for the whole story to see if it makes sense to the reader.

Perfecting Object

Your editing task is to note all the objects for every scene; then when an object is used in the plot, you can see when it was first mentioned and if it is described for the effect that the story needs.

Perfecting Sights

Your editing task is to note all the visuals for every scene; then when a visual is used in the plot, you can see when it was first mentioned and if it is described for the effect that the story needs.

Perfecting Smells

Your editing task is to list everything the POV character smells in every scene.

Perfecting Sounds

Your editing task is to list everything the POV character hears in every scene.

Perfecting Emotional Impact

Your editing task is to look at the scene and decide if the location is the most emotionally charged place it could be for the POV character.

Perfecting Location Split

Your editing task is to mark any scene that takes place in more than one location.

Perfecting Weather

Your editing task is to list the weather for every scene. The Story Map is going to help you edit the weather once you have a full list.

Perfecting Taste

Your editing task is to list everything the POV character tastes in every scene.

Perfecting Touch

Your editing task is to list everything the POV character touches in every scene.

Skeleton Templates

Skeleton Blurb

Protagonist _____

Must _____(Story Goal)

Otherwise _____ (Story Stakes)

Skeleton Synopsis-
Overview

Skeleton Blurb

5 Fictionary Story Arc Scenes

Resolution

Skeleton Synopsis
Story Arc Scene breakdown

Scene name

POV Character

POV Goal

Scene Middle

Scene Climax

Impact on POV Character

Glossary

Act I

The first quarter of the novel, where the characters, the main story goal and the stakes are all shown to the reader. This is Aristotle's beginning.

Act II

From Plot Point 1 to Plot Point 2, and everything in between. This is Aristotle's middle.

Act III

Everything after plot point 2 through to the climax, and the resolution. This is Aristotle's end.

Action (Opening/Closing type)

Type of scene opening for a scene that opens with a fast pace.

Action / Sequel

The two types of scenes in a book. One is the fast paced high energy scene, the other is slower, where the character is reacting to an action scene.

Action Scene

Movement and dialogue dominate the scene.

Actionable Advice

Actionable advice is a specific recommendation the writer can use to make revisions.

Advanced Story Element

Reader Knowledge gained is an example of an advanced element.

After-Draft Outline

By filling out the scene name, scene middle, and scene climax for each scene, you will have a full after-draft outline.

Anchored

How the reader is settled into a scene by knowing the point of view character, the time of the scene, and the location.

Antagonist

The character who is in direct opposition to the protagonist and stands between the protagonist and the story goal.

Backstory

Explains character's motivation to reach the story goal.

Bestseller

A book readers love, we believe, mainly as it is structurally sound.

Blurb

Readers buy a book on its promise. This promise is the description of the story that includes who the protagonist is, what their main story goal is, and what's at stake if they don't achieve the main story goal.

Blurb Promise

The reason a reader buys the book. They want the book to be about what the blurb says. Successful books keep this promise.

Chapter

The portion of a novel made up of scenes.

Character

A person or animal or other being who is in a story.

Character Arc

The relationship the protagonist has to the external story goal. It is positive if they are closer to the story goal and negative if they are further away.

Character List

Characters in a scene and characters mentioned in a scene.

Character Story Elements

The readers connect with the character and follow them thorough the story. These elements test the characters' structural strength.

Character's Arc

Starts when a character enters the story and ends when they leave the story. And is measured how far they are to or from the story goal.

Characters in Motion

A Fictionary Story Element used to check if characters are moving in each scene.

Climax

The scene at the end of the story where the story goal is addressed. It is the scene with the biggest emotion and word count compared to those close by it.

Closing Type

The first sentence in a scene is one of these types: dialogue, thought, description, action.

Combined Protagonist

A combined protagonist is two main characters where both characters want the same thing, meaning their goal for the story is the same. In their struggle to achieve the goal, they will both suffer or benefit from the same events.

Conflict

Action that pits two or more characters against each other.

Copyediting

The editing that is done after a structural edit and after the revisions.

Creative Story Editing

Structural editing that mixes artistry with craft knowledge to create a powerful story.

Creative Story Editor

An editor who has a process to evaluate a story's structural strength using artistry and craft knowledge.

Description (Opening/Closing type)

An opening or closing type used when the first sentence of a scene is written in narrative format.

Deus Ex Machine

External forces, and not the protagonist, address the story goal in the story's climax or scene climax.

Dialogue (Opening/Closing Type)

An opening or closing type used when the first sentence of a scene is written in the format of a character's speech.

Draft (Manuscript or Novel)

An umbrella term that can cover any unpublished work in progress from the first draft through to the final draft.

Draft Blurb

Your secret weapon throughout the editing process. This is a blurb meant only for the eyes of the editor.

Editable Draft

A draft that has the 5 Story Arc scenes in it.

Editing Journey

From first draft to ready to publish.

Entry Hook

The reason a reader is drawn into a scene.

Episodic Story

A story that contains scenes that don't relate to the plot and story goal.

Event

What happens in a scene that is caused by a character(s) or causes a character(s) to react.

Exit Hook

The reason a reader is drawn into the next scene.

External Character Arc

At the end of each scene the character is closer to or further from their story goal. The external character arc connects these positives and negatives. Flat lines are major editing issues that show the scene needs reworking.

External Goal

What a character wants in the story, not what they want in life.

Fiction

Stories based on made up events.

Fictionary

The company that created StoryTeller and StoryCoach.

Fictionary Certified StoryCoach Editor

The world's best story editors, as they have passed the rigorous Fictionary certification program. The only one of its kind in the world.

Fictionary Character Arc

We use the protagonist and the story goal to determine whether the protagonist is closer or farther away from the story goal by the end of a scene.

Fictionary Story Arc

The 5 plot point scenes drawn to show where the 5 scenes are located in the story.

Fictionary Story Arc Scenes

They are the five plot point scenes drawn on the story arc.

Fictionary Story Elements

The 38 key attributes that an editor must use to edit each scene.

Fictionary Story Test

Shows the editor if there is a story in the draft.

Fictionary StoryCoach

Software for professional editors performing story edits.

Fictionary StoryTeller

Software for writers to perform a story edit on a fiction or narrative non-fiction manuscript that they have written.

Flashback

A flashback is an action scene that shares an event that happened in the past and is written in active form.

Genre

Stories that fit a similar form or style.

Goal Related to Plot

Check this to see if the scene goal is related to the plot.

Group Protagonist

The protagonist entity is a group of character, a world, or a society.

Impact on POV

How the POV character reacts to the action in the scene.

Inciting Incident

The inciting incident contains the action that changes or disrupts the protagonist's ordinary life.

Internal Goal

An internal goal is related to a major character weakness. This weakness should make it difficult for the character to reach their external goal.

Main Character

The protagonist.

Manuscript

An unpublished book.

Middle Plot Point

The middle plot point scene should have something terrible or life-changing happen to the protagonist.

Non-Fiction

Prose based on true events or facts.

Non-Story Arc Scenes

Scenes in a manuscript that are not the inciting incident, plot point 1, the middle plot point, plot point 2, or the climax.

Opening Type

A choice of four types: dialogue, thought, description, action.

Outlier Scene Word Count

A scene that has a vastly different word count than the scenes around it and this was not done intentionally.

Page-Turner

A book readers want to read in one sitting. Notice the reader is mentioned. A quiet literary book can be just as much a page-turner as a high-action thriller.

Pantser

A writer who doesn't outline their story before writing it.

Plot

What happens in the story.

Plot Hole

Something that defies logic happens in the story.

Plot Point 1

The moment in the story when the protagonist accepts the story goal.

Plot Point 2

The moment in the story when the protagonist is at their lowest emotional or physical state.

Plot Story Elements

A story is based on a series of events. These plot elements test these events' structural strength.

Point of View (POV)

The story or scene is filtered from one character's perspective. This filtering shows the reader what the character is like.

Point of View Character

The character who the reader will experience the scene through.

POV Goal

In every scene, the POV character must have a scene goal.

POV Goal Internal

The POV character weakness that makes it difficult to achieve their external goal.

POV Knowledge Gained

A way to keep track of what the POV character knows at what part of the story.

Prologue

A scene that occurs before chapter one.

Proofreading

The final review of a manuscript after formatting and before going to print.

Protagonist

The main character in a story.

Protagonist Entity

A protagonist made up of one or more characters.

Published Blurb

The blurb that is written on the back cover of a published book and used for marketing.

Purpose of Scene

The reason the scene is in the story.

Reader Engagement

The reader accepts the story's promise and is fully immersed in the story.

Reader Knowledge Gained

Where you record the story critical information that the reader has learned.

Resolution

This is everything after the climax scene and to the last word.

Revelation

Something new a reader learns in a specific scene.

Revise

Making changes to the content of a scene based on an editor's suggestions.

Revision Notes

Notes the editor keeps for themselves or for their client when they are creating a revision plan.

Revision Plan

The plan created during the first pass at evaluating the story against the story elements. This includes the story element data, notes per scene, and the Fictionary insights.

Scene

A portion of a story where characters do something. A scene will have a beginning, a middle, and an end.

Scene Anchoring

Ensuring the reader knows who the point of view character for a scene is, where the scene takes place, and when the scene takes place within the first 3 paragraphs of a scene.

Scene Climax

A portion of scene where the POV goal is addressed.

Scene Middle

A portion of scene between the opening hook and the scene climax.

Scene Name

The editor's description of a scene in 3 words or fewer.

Scene Structure

A scene is a mini story, it must have an opening hook, a POV character, a POV goal, a what if goal fails and a scene climax.

Scene Time

To go with scene anchoring and time element.

Scene-by-Scene Editing

Evaluating one scene at a time and making editing suggestions for each scene.

Scenes per Chapter

The visual insight showing the number of scenes in every chapter in the manuscript.

Self-Editors

Editors who give actionable advice on their own work.

Self-Employed Editors

Editors who give actionable advice on their others work and are free-lance.

Self-Publishers

Writers who self publish their work.

Setting

Where the story and each scene are located.

Setting Story Elements

The readers connect with the setting, and it is how they enter into the story. These elements test the settings' structural strength.

Skeleton Blurb

Shows the protagonist, their story goal, and what's at stake if they don't achieve their goal.

Skeleton Synopsis

Six paragraphs that tell the story, using the blurb in the first paragraph and the 5 story arc scenes filling the rest of the paragraphs. The ending must be revealed

Story

A narrative that has an inciting incident, a plot point 1, a middle plot point, plot point 2, a climax, and a resolution.

Story Arc

A diagram showing the location of the inciting incident, plot point 1, middle plot point, plot point 2, and climax in a story.

Story Arc Insight

Fictionary's visual insight showing the inciting incident, plot point 1, middle plot point, plot point 2, and climax in a story.

Story Editing

See Creative Story Editing.

Story Editing Journey

After-draft and before copyediting.

Story Editor

See Creative Story Editor.

Story Elements

The key aspects that must be evaluated for every scene and story to ensure the story has the potential to become a bestseller.

Story Goal

What the protagonist must achieve in the story. A reason for the reader to read.

Story Map

Where you find the 38 Fictionary Story Elements listed per scene in a table format.

Story Stakes

These are the consequences for the protagonist if they do not achieve the story goal.

Story Structure

The story's DNA.

StoryCoach

Software for professional editors performing story edits.

Story-Level Issue

An issue that occurs in the structure of the story.

StoryTeller

Software for writers to perform a story edit on a fiction or narrative non-fiction manuscript they have written.

Synopsis

A short summary of the story that the protagonist, the story goal, and the main plot points and the story's ending.

Tension

The anticipation something bad or good will happen.

Thought (opening/closing type)

An opening type used when the first sentence of a scene is written in the format of a character's thought.

Visual Insights

An image showing critical information about the story.

What if goal fails

These are the consequences that will happen to the POV character if they do not succeed at the POV scene goal.

Word Count per Scene

The number of words in a scene.

World build

The descriptions used to create the fictional world that the story inhabits.

Index

Acknowledgments

Thank you to our Copy Editor, James Gallagher. He taught us the art of detail.

The enthusiasm we received when we asked three wonderful people to beta read Secrets to Editing Success was phenomenal. Their insights into the book helped us make it better. Thank you, Celeste Keckley, Lisa Taylor, and Annette G.

Thank you for catching the errors. Any that are left all belong to us.

Thank you to Lisa Stringfellow and HarperCollins/Quill Tree Books for kind permission to use the blurb from the sensational Fictionary-edited book: A Comb of Wishes (HarperCollins/Quill Tree Books 2022)

Thank you to Sacha Black for her kind permission to use her quote.

Thank you, Heather Wood, Fictionary Certified StoryCoach Editor, for her kind permission to use a direct excerpt from her edit of Evolution.

Thank you to the Fictionary Certified StoryCoach editors who provided quotes. These are:

Shane Millar	Ryan Rivers	Polly Watt	Michele Orwin
Heather Wood	Kara Henderson	Lisa Taylor	Brigitte Lavoie
Pamela Hines	Sherry Leclerc	James Gallagher	Casper Pieters

Kristina Stanley

Co-authoring a book is an exciting and motivating experience. Working with Lucy is a dream come true, and the book would not be what it is without Lucy. My first thank you goes to her. My life-time partner and husband, Mathew deserves a lot of thanks for his continual support of my writing adventures. And thank you to everyone who reads this book. I sincerely hope it helps you tell a better story.

Lucy Cooke

Thank you Kristina Stanley for asking me to co-author this book with you. It has been an honor. My parents have always taught me to follow my dreams and my love of books. Thank you for being wonderful. Thank you to the Fictionary Community. Our collective love of editing keeps me inspired. Thank you to my writing friends. A special shout out to all the Fictionary Certified StoryCoaches. Thank you to my children, hopefully one day I will get to read the stories you write. And finally, to my husband, thank you for your patience, and your copious cups of coffee, and your ability to make computers say "yes". You are a legend.

About the authors

Kristina Stanley

Combining her degree in computer mathematics with her success as a best-selling, award-winning author and fiction editor, Kristina Stanley founded Fictionary and is the CEO. Fictionary helps writers and editors create better stories faster with software, an online community and training.

Her novels include The Stone Mountain mystery series and Look the Other Way. Her first novel Descent was nominated for the 2014 Arthur Ellis Unhanged Arthur for excellence in crime writing. Descent is also published in Germany by Luzifer-Verlag. Blaze was shortlisted for the 2014 Crime Writers' Association Debut Dagger.

The Author's Guide to Selling Books to Non-Bookstores and Your Editing Journey are her non-fiction books. Her short stories are published in The Ellery Queen Mystery Magazine, and Voices from the Valleys. She is the Story Editing Advisor to The Alliance of Independent Authors and was on the board of directors for the Story Studio Writing Society.

Lucy Cooke

Lucy Cooke is a Fictionary Certified StoryCoach Editor and Business Development manager at Fictionary.

This is her first book.